Pastor Diotrephes

PASTOR DIOTREPHES:

A STUDY OF WOLVES IN SHEEP'S CLOTHING

By

Thomas Ross

Pastor Diotrephes: A Study of Wolves in Sheep's Clothing

All Scripture quotations are taken from the King James Version (KJV) of the Bible.

Published by Virtue Paths Publishing (San Francisco, CA)
virtuepaths.com

Library of Congress Control Number: 9798992239249

ISBN **979-8-9922392-6-3** (Hardback)
ISBN **979-8-9922392-4-9** (Paperback)
ISBN **979-8-9922392-5-6** (eBook — EPUB)

Cover design by Virtue Paths Publishing
First published in the United States of America

CONTENTS

I.) DEDICATION

This book is dedicated to the Lord Jesus Christ, the Good Shepherd who lays down His life for His sheep (John 10:15) and the sole Head of the church He has purchased for Himself, "that in all *things* he might have the preeminence" (Colossians 1:18).

II.) PREFACE

Dear Sheep,

Grace and peace to you from God our Father, and the Lord Jesus Christ our Savior. You have the astonishingly great and glorious privilege of belonging to the flock of that great Shepherd of the sheep, the incarnate Son of God. Your ascended Shepherd, who died for you and then swallowed up death in victory, will soon come again and receive you to Himself. He works everything together for good for you. He will never, ever fail you. He loves you. Amazing fact! *He loves you.*

Furthermore, you have the joy of fellowship with other redeemed and holy people in the church of Christ. The communion of saints on earth is a blessed foretaste of the joys of heaven forever. As you see the image of your heavenly Father, of your Elder Brother, and of the sanctifying Spirit in your fellow saints, you find the fellowship of their kindred minds to be like that of the blessed ones above.

But are you ready for your wolf-encounter?

"What are you talking about?" you ask. Let me explain. As Christ had eleven godly apostles, so today you are surrounded by many godly pastors. There are many today who are like the godly Peter, the godly Andrew, the godly Matthew, the godly John, the godly James, and the godly Paul, and you have the privilege and joy to follow them as they follow Christ and point you to His Word.

But Christ also had one Judas. There are also men like Judas today—unconverted men, anti-Christ men. Some are domineering. Some are thieves. Some are perverts.

Some are pastoring.

Nor are they just pastoring false churches that have obviously corrupt doctrine—although they are indeed pastoring plenty of those. No, there are some modern Judases pastoring churches with great doctrinal statements; with reverent worship services; with evangelistic zeal; with preaching that sounds good. Does Satan have a better tool than such wolves for turning such good churches bad? Satan was able to inject wolves into the leadership of churches associated with the Apostle Paul (Acts 20:29-30). The Apostle John warned about Diotrephes (3 John 9-11). The church pastored by Jesus Christ Himself during His earthly ministry (Matthew 10:4) had its Judas.

If God in His good providence allows you to serve Him on earth for many years, you will almost certainly encounter one—or more—of such evil, anti-Christ men. Maybe you will hear about this wolf when he attacks a good church nearby with which yours is in fellowship. Maybe you will be shocked when you find out that a preacher who visited your church and preached to your congregation manifests himself later to be Diotrephes. Are you ready to offer Biblical counsel when you encounter wolf-torn sheep? Do you know how to bind up their wounds, giving them the solace found in Jesus Christ's fulness?

Maybe the unthinkable will happen—Judas will find a way

into the leadership of your own church.

It happened in the first church, pastored by Christ Himself on earth. It can happen in your church, too. Are you ready for a wolf-encounter—that close, that personal, that dangerous, that life-or-death?

You need to be ready. Your own pastor could turn out to be a domineering anti-Christ, usurping the Lord Jesus' preeminent position over your actions, your heart, and your conscience. Your own pastor could turn out to be a thieving Judas, robbing God and His people. Your own pastor could turn out to be a filthy pervert, devouring women—or men—or little girls or boys to slake his insatiable lust.

What will you do if you find out that someone whom you have trusted, and esteemed very highly in love because of his holy pastoral office, turns out to be a wolf set on devouring you—or your spouse—or your children? Are you ready?

What will you do if you are in the ministry yourself, and someone you trust, someone with whom you are serving the Lord, who likewise has the holy garb of a shepherd, suddenly reveals the hair, the howl, and the sharp teeth of a wolf? Are you ready?

You need to be ready. The world is filled with the bloody carcasses of sheep who were not ready for their wolf-encounter. The world is filled with other sheep—torn, mangled, wounded, deeply scarred—who were not ready for their wolf-encounter. The world is filled with other sheep who mourn daily over the loss of their own little lambs, lambs devoured by a bloodthirsty wolf who crept into the flock, secretly. *Are you ready?*

God's Word provides sufficient guidance so you can be completely equipped (2 Timothy 3:16-17) to win when you have your wolf-encounter. You can be girded with God's armor, with His shield, and with His sword, ready to defeat the wolf when he attacks (Ephesians 6:10-18). Churches that are properly forewarned and forearmed can both keep the large majority of wolves from ever getting in and quickly neutralize any that make it inside. The sheep can be successfully protected (Acts 20:29-30; Revelation 2:1). Your sole offensive weapon, the sword of the Spirit, the Word of God (Ephesians 6:17), can bring you victory over the worst of the wolves. Is your spiritual sword girded on? Can you use it skillfully? Are you ready for your wolf-encounter?

For your own spiritual welfare, you must be ready. For your family's spiritual welfare, you must be ready. For your children's spiritual welfare, you must be ready. For your church's spiritual welfare, you must be ready. For God's glory and for the advance of His kingdom, you must be ready. *Are you ready?*

You must also be ready to Biblically battle the wolves for the sake of the large majority of godly pastors who are neither Judas, nor Diotrephes, nor anti-Christ, but are Christ's godly under-shepherds. You must know how to identify and deal with the wolves so that you can recognize when godly pastors are falsely slandered by wicked men and by their spiritual father, Satan. Those who are ready for their wolf-encounter are also ready to rejoice in their many encounters with true pastors. Just as they do not make the error of assuming that there are no Apostles Judas or Pastors Diotrephes today, so they do not make the grievous and dangerous error of slandering and rejecting the holy ministry of Christ's many true servants because of the corruption of a few.

Those who are ready do not leave the churches of Jesus Christ when they encounter a lone wolf, as if the presence of such a wicked one invalidates Christianity. On the contrary, they recognize that Christ Himself had predicted the presence of such. Those who are prepared are well aware that in this fallen world there is no organization on earth that can, with 100% success, keep out all sin and all deceitful hypocrites, and this fact makes them set their affections all the more on their sinless, ascended Lord and on that holy New Jerusalem where they will dwell with their good Shepherd forever, the wolves being finally, completely, and eternally banished.

Christ had eleven true apostles and one false one—not eleven false ones and one true one, nor twelve true ones and zero false ones, nor twelve false ones and zero true ones. Both receiving the many who are true and rejecting the minority who are false is critical. Can you?

You will certainly encounter some of the many righteous, and will almost certainly at some point encounter one or more of the few wicked. *Are you ready?*

III.) WHO IS PASTOR DIOTREPHES?

Pastor Diotrephes Represents A Small But Dangerous Minority

The large majority of pastors in Biblical churches are godly men, faithfully serving their Lord, Jesus Christ.[1] They are objects of Christ's tender care and concern, lovingly caring for their spiritual flock, the congregation Christ has entrusted to their care. They are men of sincere love for Christ and for His people. While they are no more sinless than were the apostles (Matthew 16:22-23; 26:70; 1 John 1:8), like the apostles they are godly spiritual leaders whom Christ's people should cheerfully obey and follow as they follow Christ (Hebrews 13:7, 17), esteeming them very highly in love for their holy work's sake (1 Thessalonians 5:13).[2]

However, it would be unbiblical to assume that every individual with the title of "pastor" in a Biblical church[3] is godly. Among Christ's twelve apostles, there was one Judas (Matthew 10:4). The first seven deacons appointed by the Jerusalem church (Acts 6:1-7) included six godly men, of whom one became the first Christian martyr (Acts 7), but also one wolf, Nicolas, who started the corrupt Nicolaitan heresy.[4] Jerome notes:

> *Not all bishops are true bishops. You notice Peter; but mark Judas as well. You look up to Stephen; but consider also Nicolas [the deacon, Acts 6:5] whom the Lord in His Apocalypse abominates [Revelation 2:6, 15], the man*

> *whose foul and shameful teachings gave rise to the Ophite heresy. Let a man examine himself and so let him come. Ecclesiastical rank does not make a man a Christian.*[5]

The Apostle Paul warned the elders of the church at Ephesus (Acts 20:17)—whom he had likely had a role in training himself—that "grievous wolves [would] enter in among you, not sparing the flock," and "also of your own selves shall men arise, speaking perverse things, to draw away disciples after them" (Acts 20:29-30). Among the general body of sheep there would be some wolves; and among the general body of faithful elders there would be some who would be the servants of Satan. The other elders were to diligently "watch" for such perverse men in their number, follow Paul's example, and "ceas[e] not to warn every one night and day" about them. Relying on God's strength, they were to evaluate all things by the "word of his grace" (Acts 20:31-32).[6] Third John 9-11 gives the inspired record about one such false-pastor,[7] true-wolf, Diotrephes:

> *9 I wrote unto the church: but Diotrephes, who loveth to have the preeminence among them, receiveth us not. 10 Wherefore, if I come, I will remember his deeds which he doeth, prating against us with malicious words: and not content therewith, neither doth he himself receive the brethren, and forbiddeth them that would, and casteth them out of the church. 11 Beloved, follow not that which is evil, but that which is good. He that doeth good is of God: but he that doeth evil hath not seen God. (3 John 9-11)*

It would be exceedingly foolish to think that men like Judas, Nicolas, and Diotrephes would arise only in the first century. "Perils among false brethren" who do not understand gospel "liberty" but seek to bring Christ's sheep into spiritual slavery or "bondage" have not been not limited to the apostolic era.[8] In ancient Israel there were times when the godly could sorrowfully testify, "I saw under the sun the place of judgment, *that* wickedness *was* there; and the place of righteousness, *that* iniquity *was* there" (Ecclesiastes 3:16). So also in this dispensation, Satan has empowered wicked men from the first century until modern times, using such wolves to do grievous harm to Christ's congregations and people.[9]

Pastor Diotrephes Loves Preeminence

What does Diotrephes look like? What does Scripture teach about how to identify him? Diotrephes "loveth to have the preeminence among" the saints (3 John 9).[10] He has "a special interest in being in the leading position, wishes to be first, like[s] to be leader ... with [a] focus on controlling others."[11] He "like[s] or love[s] to be first in rank or position ... desire[s] to be first ... desire[s] to order others."[12] But true Christians, having become partakers of the divine nature in regeneration (2 Peter 1:4), possess sincere love and warm, friendly, filial affection for and devotion to Jesus Christ, comparable (although infinitely inferior) to the love the Father has for His Son. The Father and the Son likewise have such love for their people, and, by the Spirit sent by the first two Persons of the Trinity to indwell and unite them, Christians have the same kind of love for one another;[13] they "love as brethren" (1 Peter 3:8).[14] They have "a special interest ... intimate ... close association" with one another as true "friend[s]," seeing each other as "beloved" and "dear," and are "loving, kindly disposed, [and] devoted" to one another,[15] as they are to Jesus Christ. As Christ personally knows, calls, and leads each of His beloved sheep by name[16] (John 10:3), so true Christians have true love and personal, caring affection for one another, hospitably recognizing[17] each other by name[18] (3 John 14). Diotrephes, by contrast, has no such love—he loves himself,[19] his own life,[20] and his own preeminence,[21] not Christ and His sheep. He does not long for spiritual fellowship with and knowledge of Christ, nor for such communion with His saints. Rather, Diotrephes wills what is best for himself. His pleasure and desires are preeminent (Titus 1:7);[22] he exhibits "preoccupation with [his] own interests";[23] and, nursing grudges against those who do not sufficiently grovel before him,[24] he can easily lash out in explosive anger at anyone who dares cross him.[25]

> *[Diotrephes, as self-willed,] is properly one who pleases himself, who is so pleased with his own that nothing pleases him besides[.] ... He is one so far overvaluing any determination at which he has himself once arrived that he will not be removed from it ... obstinately maintaining his own opinion, or asserting his own rights, [he] is reckless of the rights, feelings and interests of others[.] ... [T]here are men who are ... at once soft and hard, soft to themselves, and hard to all the world besides; these two dispositions being in fact only two aspects and outcomings of the same sin ... love of self. ... [He is like] the hedgehog, which, rolling itself up in a ball, presents only sharp spines to those without, keeping at the same time all the soft and warm wool for itself within.*[26]

Like Haman, Diotrephes may wish to wreak overwhelming revenge against perceived slights to his own preeminence, even if they are, as with Mordecai, truly conscientious obedience to Scripture (Esther 3:1-6). The true pastor fundamentally loves

Christ and has friendly affection for and loving devotion to his Lord and to His flock. Diotrephes has a fundamental love, affection for, and devotion to himself.[27]

True Christians are God's spiritual kings and priests (Revelation 5:10), the beloved adopted children of God the Father (Galatians 4:6), Jesus Christ's spiritual brethren (Hebrews 2:12), and sacred temples of the indwelling Spirit (1 Corinthians 6:19). Secure in God's unchanging grace, they have a holy and humble boldness, dignity, and spiritual liberty in Christ:

> *Slavery to sin degrades humanity, but serving Christ ennobles God's children with true liberty (Gal. 5:13; 1 Pet. 2:16). Paul exhorts us, "Stand fast therefore in the liberty wherewith Christ hath made us free, and be not entangled again with the yoke of bondage," but instead devote yourself to "faith which worketh by love" (Gal. 5:1, 6). God's children are heirs of liberty (Rom. 8:21), a liberty that the Spirit already manifests among them (2 Cor. 3:17).*
>
> *A good conscience washed in Christ's blood, restored through repentance, and fortified through proven obedience makes the Christian intrepid and fearless. "The wicked flee when no man pursueth: but the righteous are bold as a lion" (Prov. 28:1). God's adopted children need not cringe and cower before their Father (Rom. 8:15), and if not before God, then not before anyone.*
>
> *Living by faith forms within us ... "a kingly spirit" or "an elevated mind" with "a free and good conscience" that is not enslaved to men or earthly things. By this kingly spirit, Paul pursued Christ wholeheartedly and counted all other things as worthless in comparison to him (Phil. 3:7–10). Faith*

lifted Moses above the visible things of this world, so that he "refused to be called the son of Pharaoh's daughter; choosing rather to suffer affliction with the people of God, than to enjoy the pleasures of sin for a season; esteeming the reproach of Christ greater riches than the treasures in Egypt ... not fearing the wrath of the king: for he endured, as seeing him who is invisible" (Heb. 11:24–27).

The wicked are easily corrupted and turned aside by influential leaders, but "the people that do know their God shall be strong, and do exploits" (Dan. 11:32). ... God's children have "a royal heart" and "an excellent spirit" that empower them to be "courageous" and to "persevere" with "great and lofty things in view," namely, the invisible, eternal kingdom of Christ. Even in this life, if you examine a true believer, you can see "the radiance of the image of God," which is his "majesty and glory."

Therefore ... "conduct yourself with a holy, but humble greatness of mind, as kings, 'who will not be brought under the power of any[thing],' as that great man [Paul] said (1 Cor. 6:12). Ye are too noble, and of too high a condition to suffer yourself to be enslaved to any sin, or to any creature, without and contrary to the will of God." ... [Christians] are not to allow anyone to control them by either favor or disfavor, or out of love or fear for them, and thus be drawn away from obedience to our sovereign King." ... [P]ress on in the battle. Remind yourself and your brethren of God's promises. Pray without ceasing. Train your conscience to follow the Word of God and not your experiences and feelings. Develop spiritual nobility by defying your fears and disciplining yourself to practice righteousness despite the opposition of earth and hell. When you follow Peter in cowardice, follow him also in tearful repentance and restoration. By God's grace, you

> *may become like [a mighty spiritual warrior] who in his life never fear[s] the face of man.*[28]

Diotrephes, as he is still enslaved to his sin, and is therefore in bondage to fear (Romans 8:15), does not comprehend the spiritual light, liberty, and joyful service of the children of God. Rather, he strives to bring the saints into bondage (2 Corinthians 11:20; Galatians 2:4), harshly demanding slavish service and engendering slavish fear in his self-exaltation. Ignorant of the free and loving service of God's sons, he fights for the dictatorial control with which Satan and the Antichrist rule their slaves.

Pastor Diotrephes Usurps Christ's Supremacy

While Jesus Christ "is the head of the body, the church … that in all *things* he might have the preeminence" (Colossians 1:18),[29] Diotrephes idolatrously usurps the preeminence of Christ by loving to have preeminence himself.[30] Diotrephes' attitude is the opposite of that of John the Baptist, who testified that Christ "is preferred before me: for he was before me … He must increase, but I must decrease" (John 1:30; 3:30). The first Baptist's humility, exaltation of Jesus Christ, and delight in Christ's voice (John 3:29) was an important aspect of his true greatness (Matthew 11:11), while Diotrephes' proud self-exaltation and despising of Christ's voice in Scripture is central to that spiritual wolf's true despicableness. Diotrephes' self-exalting self-love manifests itself in his arrogating to himself the prerogatives and honor Christ alone must receive in His church, in a manner comparable to the way the Antichrist exalts himself against Christ (2 Thessalonians 2:4). As Jesus is the *Christ,* the *Messiah*, the Lord's Anointed One, so modern sons of Diotrephes frequently claim to be the Lord's Anointed,[31] exalted above the common people. In a unified theme that covers the Johannine letters,[32] John's first epistle warned of "many antichrists" who, coming before the ultimate eschatological Antichrist (1 John 2:18), would manifest both doctrinal and practical aberrations. These antichrists would be led by the spirits of devils to both doctrinally and practically deny both the Father and Son, "refus[ing] to pay any attention to, disregard[ing], [and] renounce[ing]"[33] them and so denying in practice that Jesus is the Christ—the saving and sovereign Lord—and denying the sovereign authority of the Father and the Son.[34] Second John similarly warns of such deceivers and antichrists (2 John 7), while Third John provides an enfleshed example of such in Diotrephes.[35] Like the Antichrist, Diotrephes is willing to "change ... [God's] laws" and to lash out against any saint who refuses to go along (Daniel 7:25). Diotrephes may, like the Antichrist and like Judas (John 13:27), be demon-possessed. Judas, as the prototypical wolf in sheep's clothing in leadership in the church, did not manifest Satan's indwelling through outwardly strange behavior such as residing in a graveyard or casting off all his clothing (Luke 8:27); rather, Judas' Satanic indwelling manifested itself in a cold and calculating willingness to betray and oppose Christ, in deceit, and in a suppression of conscience for the purpose of advancing what he perceived as his own interest.[36]

Diotrephes may usurp the church polity Christ has established in Matthew 18:15-17 to instead himself cast people out of the church on his own authority (3 John 11), corrupting

Biblical congregational church government for some form of hierarchy, whether of independent elder-rule, elder and deacon rule, or of a form of Presbyterianism or Episcopalianism. Christ, the Good Shepherd, left His deserved preeminence with the Father to become Man and then willingly laid down His life to gather the sheep into His fold (John 10:11). Godly under-shepherds manifest the same sort of humble self-sacrifice for their sheep. But Diotrephes casts sheep out of the church in order to preserve or increase his undeserved preeminence. Christ washed the feet of His disciples in loving, self-sacrificial service (John 13) and was "much displeased" at any who would keep even the lowliest and youngest children from Him and His blessing—but Diotrephes is "much displeased" if others question or take from him his idolatrous preeminence and personal power.[37] Often, Diotrephes does not limit himself to usurping the ecclesiastical order Christ the Head gave to His church. Throughout Scripture, idolatry is associated with all kinds of other sin, including rampant sexual immorality.[38] A congregation that allows Diotrephes to usurp Christ's place is in fearful danger of a man with a reprobate mind bearing rule over them who uses his position of power to fulfill his lusts (Romans 1:18-32).[39] Those who turn men into idols may find that their new gods act very immorally.

Pastor Diotrephes Will Be Cast Down into Hell

Striving for preeminence, Diotrephes instead reaped infamy and everlasting shame, as will his modern successors. Other than what 3 John records, history has preserved very little about Diotrephes. He cast out God's saints to establish his own preeminence for a very little while, then died and went to hell forever with the rest of those who have never known God (3 John 11). He took none of his preeminence with him—only his judgment—while his preeminence and this-worldly glory quickly faded away. Only his eternal shame remains known. "Diotrephes barely makes a ripple in history,"[40] but the record of His sin remains, both in God's mind and in His revealed Word. "What a guy. Nice going Diotrephes. [You] didn't think [you would] get into the Bible so everybody throughout the rest of history would know what you were did you? But you did."[41] In like manner, the deeds of every modern Diotrephes will be revealed to all the world at the Great White Throne judgment of Jesus Christ (Revelation 20:11-15).

Third John 11[42] indicates that Diotrephes is unconverted, one of those who is not a doer of good who is from God, but is not "of God," who "doeth evil," and who "hath not seen God" (3 John 11). The Lord Jesus had clearly taught, and the Holy Spirit led the Apostle John to record in his Gospel, that those who are born again and are thus "of God" will become people who are doers of good.[43] The man who is "born again" is one who does truth[44] in the light and has deeds wrought in God (John 3:3, 21). While those who are Christ's beloved friends do what He commands (15:14),[45] everyone who practices or is doing sin is sin's slave (8:34), doing what he has seen from his father, the devil (8:38, 41, 44). Thus, it is "they that that have done good" who enter into "the resurrection of life," while "they that have done evil" suffer "the resurrection of damnation" (John 5:29),[46] because those truly regenerated, having been justified by repentant faith alone in Christ alone, not by works, become God's work, created in Christ Jesus unto good works (Ephesians 2:8-10).[47] Those who are doing or practicing sin are of the devil, while those born of God cannot be doing or practicing sin, because of the new nature they have received (1 John 3:8-9). "In this the children of God are manifest, and the children of the devil: whosoever doeth not righteousness is not of God, neither he that loveth not his brother" (1 John 3:10). It is "every one that doeth righteousness" who "is born of [God]" and therefore "abides for ever" (1 John 2:17, 29). Those who, having been transformed inwardly in the new birth, are doing Christ's commandments, will enter the heavenly city—while those who are practicing abominations and lies cannot (Revelation 21:27; 22:14-15).[48] Diotrephes is among those who do evil, not good (3 John 11); he manifests a lifestyle of proud striving for preeminence, refusing to receive those identified with Christ's apostles, doing evil, speaking slanderous nonsense-speech against God's people, fighting against those who do love and receive the sheep, and casting the righteous out of Christ's flock.[49] He will, therefore, be in the lake of fire with all other evildoers.

Furthermore, being "of God"[50] is Johannine language for the new birth. Those who receive Christ are "born ... of God" (John 1:13) and therefore hear God's words, unlike those not born of God (8:47). They are "born of God" as the "children of God" (1 John 3:9-10), and are delivered from the devil, having through true faith been "born of God" (5:1, 4, 18-19), while false prophets like Diotrephes are not "of God"—that is, are not "born of God" (4:1-4, 6-7), and therefore have never "seen God" (3 John 11), as the righteous have already and will in a greater way in the future kingdom.[51] While the first-century dictator Diotrephes was not born again, it is possible for even a regenerate man to act like a Diotrephes in certain ways because of his indwelling sin, often combined with poor training, spiritual immaturity,[52] bad influences, and Satanic deception. John warns even "beloved" saints to refrain from imitating evil men like Diotrephes and their evil practices. Instead they must follow Christ the Good Shepherd, godly men, and their practices (3 John 11).[53] The righteous must beware that they not "use as a model, imitate, emulate, [or] follow" Diotrephes.[54] A true Diotrephes is unregenerate, but the regenerate can be negatively influenced by him and his ways. This ought not to be. Thus, God provides godly pastors, and all other spiritual leaders, many important spiritual principles from the negative example of Diotrephes.

Pastor Diotrephes Violates Matthew 18:15-17

Out of reverence for Christ's Word and love for erring saints, the godly pastor will, when necessary, model and encourage others in the church to approach privately fellow congregants who have sinned against them. If the sinning individual clearly refuses to listen, then the Christian sinned against will take two or three additional witnesses, being careful to maintain scrupulous accuracy that "every word," every specific detail of an accusation, is tabulated accurately, as it would be done in a court of law (Deuteronomy 17:6; 19:15). If the sinning person refuses to listen to the group, then he must receive a fair trial before the entire church. If he is clearly guilty, but refuses to listen to the entire congregation, the church must sorrowfully remove him from church communion and membership (Matthew 18:15-17).

Historically, Baptists have conformed to Christ's mandate that the power of excommunication pertains not to a pastor alone, or to a small group within the church, but to the whole congregation,[55] after the accused person has received a fair trial. In non-Baptist religious "societies ... a few select individuals, met in secret session, are allowed the right to excommunicate members; but ... in Baptist churches, members are tried and acquitted or excluded by the whole church, met in public conference, as they were in the days of Christ and the apostles."[56] In the words of the 1644 *London Baptist Confession of Faith:*

> *Christ has likewise given power to his whole [Acts 2:47] Church to receive in and cast out, [Romans 16:2] by way of Excommunication, any member; [Matthew 18:17] and this power is given to every particular Congregation, [1 Corinthians 15:4] and not one particular person, [2 Corinthians 2:6-8] either member or Officer, but the whole.*[57]

Baptists have historically, and correctly, seen that Matthew 18:15-17 teaches that the final step of excommunication involves a trial before the whole church:

> *[T]he "one or two" are represented as "witnesses." Who are witnesses? Persons, who bear testimony in a case, pending between contending parties, in order that the truth of every word of a charge preferred, may be established. If, then, [Matthew 18:15-17 involves] an interview for receiving the testimony of witnesses, with a view to present conviction, how clearly it is a trial. ...*

> *[T]here must be a trial—a proceeding which shall bring out the complaint; and the admission, or proof of its justice. … No language can sufficiently express the importance of the idea of a trial … in all steps of discipline.*[58]

Someone who does not listen to the two or three must be brought before the whole "church," and if he is found guilty, "the church must withdraw its fellowship from him, and put him away from them … but not without a trial." The person accused "should be allowed to hear the evidence against him, know the witnesses, and be permitted to answer for himself. If the accused disproves the charges, or if he confesses the wrong, makes suitable acknowledgment, and, so far as possible, reparation, with promise of amendment, in all ordinary cases, this should be deemed satisfactory, and the case be dismissed."[59] Pendleton notes:

> *[If two or three fail to resolve an issue,] the case must be brought before the church. The facts connected with it must be stated. The arraigned member must have ample opportunity to defend himself. If his defense is satisfactory to the church the matter goes no farther. Or if the brother, while the investigation is going on, becomes convinced of his guilt and makes confession, the church must forgive him. If, however, the offence is established by conclusive proof, and there is no penitence leading to confession, the act of exclusion must take place. The church must withdraw its fellowship.*[60]

Baker comments:

> *[T]o exclude a public offender without giving him a hearing and affording him an opportunity to defend himself … is at variance with the rules of God's word, for, 1st. The word of God teaches, that an individual is not to be condemned except upon the testimony of "two or three witnesses."*

See Deut. xvii. 6 and xix. 15, for the original law on this subject. In the latter passage, it is said, "One witness shall not rise up against a man for any iniquity, or for any sin, in any sin that he sinneth; at the mouth of two witnesses, or at the mouth of three witnesses, shall the matter be established." For evidence of the incorporation of this law in the Christian code, see Matt. xviii. 16; 2 Cor. xiii. 1; 1st Tim. v. 19. … 2d. From the word of God, it further appears, that witnesses were required to give in their testimony in the presence of the accused. This is evident from all the reports of trials recorded in Sacred Writ. In that most iniquitous trial, the most unparallel for injustice of any recorded to the annals of criminal jurisprudence—in the trial of the Prince of Peace—the right to confront his witnesses was not withheld. That the witnesses gave in their testimony in his presence, is apparent from the whole narrative as well as from the interrogatory of Pilate; Matt. xxvii. 13. "Hearest thou not how many things they witness against thee?" Reason and observation concur in teaching the importance of respecting this rule of right. … 3d. The same authority teaches us, that the accused should be allowed to answer for himself. This privilege was conceded to the Saviour, by the high priest, when the false witnesses gave in their testimony, "and the high priest arose, and said unto him, Answerest thou nothing? what is it which these witness against thee?" Matt. xxvi, 52. The same right was conceded to the apostle Paul, on the occasion on which he delivered his eloquent and ever memorable address before Agrippa. "Then Agrippa said unto Paul, thou are permitted to speak for thyself. Then Paul stretched forth the hand and answered for himself," &c. Acts xxvi. 1, &c. When the Pharisees, on one occasion, manifested a disposition to condemn the Saviour, unheard, Nicodemus appealed to them, John vii. 51. "Doth our law judge any man before it hear him, and know what he doeth?" He evidently considered their conduct, in this instance, as of a most unjustifiable character; abhorrent alike to the principles of natural equity, and the spirit and letter of their judicial code. …

To try and condemn an individual, either in the church or out of it, without giving him a hearing, and allowing him

> *to face his accusers, is to establish a precedent that is dangerous in the extreme. ... To withhold from an offender any of his just rights, is [also] to preclude the likelihood of effecting the ends for which we resort to the exercise of church discipline. To inflict a wanton injury upon an individual, is certainly not the most effectual way of bringing him to acknowledge the injuries he has done, either to the church or to the cause of Christ. The slightest deviation from the rule of right, on the part of the church, will tend rather to confirm the offender in his offences. It will excite prejudice against us, close the doors of his head and heart against our appeals and remonstrances; and, like a coat of mail, render him invulnerable to the most pointed reproofs. Such a course of conduct, moreover, instead of shielding the church from reproach, will expose her but the more. While she is attempting to stop up the breach which the offender has made in her walls, she pulls down a whole broadside. ... Learn, then, to respect the rights of offenders, if you would have them brought back to the exercise of a godly sorrow for their sins, and would shield yourselves, and the cause of Christ, from reproach.*[61]

The Bible teaches the following Baptist practice:

> *The Church is to pass the final sentence, after a full and fair hearing of the whole case. ... [This is] prescribed by Christ as a positive law for His churches, always and everywhere; and that it abides invested with all the sanctions of divine authority; that it cannot be abrogated, nor departed from with impunity. ... [E]very Church [must] require a strict and invariable compliance with its requirements[.] ... [Someone who, like Diotrephes,] attempts to bring before the Church, or in any other way make public, any matter of private grief or offense, before he has fully pursued the above course, according to the Gospel rule, he makes himself an offender thereby – subject to ... discipline. ... Any one tried by a Church should be allowed every opportunity, both as to time, place and circumstance, to vindicate himself. The very justice of Christ's house should incline to mercy. It should be made manifest that the object is not to punish, but to reclaim. ... Every person so*

> *tried has a right to demand and receive copies of all charges against him, the names of the accusers and witnesses, both of whom he shall have the privilege of meeting face to face, hearing their statements, bringing witness on his side, and answering for himself before the Church itself as the ultimate and authoritative tribunal. ... All persons on trial, or having been excluded, have a right to receive authenticated copies of the records of all proceedings held by the Church in their cases[.] ... [T]he entire body [must not] be so swayed from right and justice as not to give any member under accusation a reasonable hearing and an equitable treatment. ... In every case of exclusion the charges against the member, and the reasons for his exclusion, should be carefully and accurately written out, and entered on the records of the Church, the excluded member [being entitled] to receive an authentic copy if he desires it. ... [Those who] take any other than the scriptural course, they become themselves offenders against the Church, and subject to its discipline.*[62]

Wills notes:

> *[C]hurches ... demonstrate[d] a concern for fairness and justice. ... The clerks left ample evidence that churches called witnesses and evaluated evidence[.] ... Although they may have sometimes decided [obvious] cases in summary fashion, they could look as carefully into evidence and testimony as any secular court. ... The most frequent issue of due process ... had ... to do ... with scripture. ... [I]f the accusers had neglected the "gospel steps," the triple warning formula of Matthew 18 ... the charge was ruled out of order. ...*
>
> *Church power, moreover, inhered in all the members of a church, and it could be delegated to no other individual or group. Baptists eschewed monarchial and aristocratic models for local church government because Jesus commanded the entire church to expel the sinner (Matt. 18:17) and the church at Corinth expelled an immoral man by vote of the majority (2 Cor. 2:6). They established pure democracies ... in regard to their ecclesiastical polity. ... If*

> *then any [other] body attempts to use this right [to discipline,] he so far makes himself an Anti-Christ.*[63]

Baptists rightly took the steps of Matthew 18:15-17 very seriously. Any attempt by Diotrephes to cast persons out without private rebuke, attempts at reconciliation before two or three, and then a fair trial before the entire congregation, were viewed as a usurpation of the commands of the preeminent Lord, Jesus Christ, and thus as a doctrine of Antichrist.

Diotrephes, however, usurps Christ's order. He may unilaterally expel members from Christ's church (3 John 11), may omit steps Christ ordained in Matthew 18, casting Christians out after a hearing before a panel but without a trial before the congregation, or may bias or prohibit the steps of Matthew 18 from being properly followed, so that "every word" and thing[64] that pertains to the matter cannot be established fairly, as it would be in a law-court (Matthew 18:16; Deuteronomy 17:6; 19:15), but only evaluated with Pastor Diotrephes' thumb pressing heavily on the scale, so that the pre-determined outcome he wishes can be reached. The Apostle John wrote to the entire church, but Diotrephes sought to cut off information to the congregation not filtered through himself (3 John 9). A hungry beast eager to devour, he is unlikely to stop his depredations with one sheep, but will cast out and destroy, over and over again.[65] Diotrephes naturally uses the substantial power he wields in his pastoral office to hide truth that would undercut his grasp on power from the congregation he tyrannizes.[66] He uses his position to hide facts that would cause sincere Christians in the church to question the validity of his judgments about those whom he wishes to cast out. Rather than acting like a loving pastor seeking to help his straying sheep, Diotrephes may, like an ambushing wolf springing suddenly upon its unsuspecting prey,[67] suddenly spring accusations on an unsuspecting sheep without giving the sheep the time or ability to defend itself, so that he may cast the sheep out of the church. Diotrephes will set a variety of traps and snares (Psalm 140:5; 141:9), using tools such as cunning, crafty deceit (Ephesians 4:14) and fear (Proverbs 29:25), to destroy those he views as threats to his power, both personally and through his servants (1 Samuel 18:21). "A snare conceals its deadly danger in order to take its victim by surprise and destroy him before he can deliver himself."[68] Hating any righteous reproof or questioning, Diotrephes will speak destruction and threats,[69] using treachery, deceit and fraud[70] to ensnare and condemn (Psalm 38:12) others as sinners[71] based on the smallest alleged infraction (Isaiah 29:21); he differs greatly from righteous leaders, who do not ensnare others to trap and control them (1 Corinthians 7:35). Violating the Biblical pattern for church discipline is a clear mark of Diotrephes (3 John 11).

Pervert Pastors Diotrephes Ensnare Victims

Perverted sons of Diotrephes also employ snares[72] to devour the objects of their lust. Nor are perverted Pastors Diotrephes any more likely than simple power-hungry Pastors Diotrephes to stop with just one victim; lust for pleasure, as for power, is insatiable. They ensnare the unwary with flattering words (Proverbs 7:21-23) as well as commanding their subordinates from a position of power (Genesis 39:7, 12). Once victims are seduced into crossing a line, they are trapped:

> *[A pervert Pastor Diotrephes is a] powerful, persuasive man [who] seduced, groomed, and broke down a woman until she was in so far she could not see a way out. Once they have crossed a certain line, whether it be an inappropriate text message, an intimate voicemail, a subtle caress, an unexpected kiss or something else, the trap is sprung. The leverage then turns to blackmail. For that woman to leave that situation and confide in her husband, or for that teenager to go tell his or her parents, would require an enormous amount of courage. Only eternity will reveal how [often] this has occurred.*[73]

The devil uses many snares[74] to suddenly and unexpectedly bring victims under his control.[75] So does his son, Diotrephes.

Pastor Diotrephes Attacks the Christian's Conscience

Diotrephes may usurp other rights Christ alone has over His flock. "The Lord Jesus Christ ... is only Lord of conscience; having a peculiar right so to be"[76] (1 Corinthians 10:29); but Diotrephes, since his conscience is seared with a hot iron (1 Timothy 4:2), impure, and defiled (Titus 1:15), does not understand the work of Christ's Spirit in leading the Christian to hear the voice of Christ his Shepherd in Scripture (John 10:3, 16, 27), so that the Christian obeys the Lord Jesus out of a "good conscience," a "pure conscience,"[77] and is "fully persuaded" in his own mind (Romans 14:5). One has a "good conscience" when he wishes to live rightly and commendably "in all things."[78] Godly elders persuade the sheep to obey Christ and themselves as they lead and model obedience to Christ (Hebrews 13:17), highly valuing a good conscience for themselves and respecting the consciences of other saints (Hebrews 13:18). But Diotrephes, weaponizing his personal authority, either carelessly tramples the consciences of the sheep or deliberately breaks their consciences down as he seeks to compel obedience to ideas neither stated in Scripture nor by good and necessary consequence drawn from Scripture, demanding for himself and his own ideas the sort of unconditional obedience and trust that Jesus Christ rightly demands from His flock. Diotrephes "bind[s] the consciences of men, in the manner of antichrist's disciples."[79]

A crucial part of "receiving" other Christians is showing great respect for their consciences. Righteous overseers value the conscience—Diotrephes views it as an obstacle to his preeminence. The inspired command "receive ye" (Romans 14:1)—given because "God hath received" (14:3) one's fellow Christian—begins Paul's extended discussion of the extreme importance of respecting other Christian's consciences (Romans 14:1-15:7). His discussion ends with another imperative, "receive": "Wherefore receive ye one another, as Christ also received us to the glory of God" (15:7). Respecting the Christian conscience is a crucial aspect of receiving one's brethren. Thus, Diotrephes' refusal to "receive the brethren" (3 John 10) fits perfectly with cavalier carelessness about their consciences.[80] Rather than supporting the consciences of Christians, and by manifestation of the truth commending himself and his commands to every man's conscience in the sight of God, Pastor Diotrephes handles the Word of God deceitfully to claim for himself the conscience-rights that pertain to Christ alone (2 Corinthians 4:2). A dictatorial Diotrephes tramples the Christian consciences of those whom he casts out and deliberately breaks down the consciences of those who remain in the congregation, so that they follow him blindly; a pervert Diotrephes deliberately breaks down the consciences of others in order to prepare them to become objects of his lust. When Diotrephes seeks to violate a Christian's conscience, the Christian must continue to obey Christ's Word and his own conscience, for "the end of the commandment is charity out of a pure heart, and *of* a good conscience, and *of* faith unfeigned ... holding faith, and a good conscience; which some having put away concerning faith have made shipwreck" (1 Timothy 1:3, 19). Violating his conscience is the way to be "destroy[ed]" (Romans 14:15).[81] Christ's godly shepherds recognize the extreme importance Scripture places upon a pure conscience. Diotrephes does not.

Pastor Diotrephes Does Not Receive the Brethren

In the first century, Diotrephes did not "receive"[82] the apostles or apostolic teaching, nor the brethren (3 John 9-10). A modern Diotrephes does not "receive" the brethren "into [his] presence in a friendly manner" or "welcome"[83] them with the attitude of an elder who is "given to hospitality" (1 Timothy 3:2), one who is a "lover of hospitality" and a "lover of good men" (Titus 1:8). Rather, Diotrephes forbids others from receiving brethren and casts them out (3 John 10). He is suspicious of newcomers,[84] especially if he thinks they may in any way challenge his desire for "preeminence" with the gifts and abilities they have received from Christ for the church. They are valuable to whatever extent they help Diotrephes be preeminent, not to whatever extent they may glorify Jesus Christ and advance His kingdom. Their money and their menial service may be accepted, but their persons and the gifts the Spirit has given them are not, for Diotrephes sets them at naught (Romans 14:10), showing by his attitude or manner of treatment that they have no value or worth in his eyes. They are beneath his consideration, to be rejected disdainfully, regarded as of no significance, and therefore worthy of maltreatment.[85] Godly Jonathan rejoiced when David slew "ten thousands" of the enemies of God, although Saul his father was only ascribed "thousands";[86] but "Saul was very wroth, and the saying displeased him," because the ungodly king thought his prestige and position were threatened by David's work for God's kingdom (1 Samuel 18:1-9). Rather than the attitude of Peter, who called himself a "servant" first and an "apostle" second (2 Peter 1:1), Diotrephes has the attitude Christ warned about concerning the Pharisees, who loved "greetings in the markets, and to be called of men, Rabbi, Rabbi. But be not ye called Rabbi: for one is your Master, *even* Christ; and all ye are brethren" (Matthew 23:7-8).

Diotrephes believes he must maintain a "mystique" of being on a higher plane, of "walk[ing] where no other can walk ... a gap that cannot be and ought not to be bridged ... touched by God's hand as no other man, called to stand where no other has a right to stand," causing the mere lowly church member to have a "dread in" his heart of the pastor, who is "God's anointed."[87] He may refuse to invite those not in his special circle to his home. He may be quick to think the worst (cf. 1 Corinthians 13:5), projecting his own unclean ways of acting and thinking upon the pure minds and motives of the righteous.[88] His judgment clouded by his pride,[89] he acts based on "evil surmisings" (1 Timothy 6:4), groundless "opinion[s] or conjecture[s] based on slight evidence ... evil conjectures, false suspicions"[90] that form his basis for condemning others on the flimsiest grounds.

Pastor Diotrephes Demands Blind Obedience

Scripture indicates that there is an appropriate place for questioning if preaching and teaching is accurate (1 Corinthians 14:29) and a place for free and open discussion among church members (Acts 15:7). The Bible is clear that that the obedience to which pastors can properly call their sheep is based on persuasion from Scripture, not a blind, slave-like subjection.[91] But Diotrephes, because he does not have a tender, New Covenant heart that wants most of all to obey the sweet voice of Christ in Scripture, is less concerned with whether what he is preaching and teaching is what God's Word actually means than with his personal authority and preeminence. Having no zeal for the honor of God, his desire is that others excuse his "si[n]" but give him "honour ... before the ... people" (1 Samuel 15:30).[92] He may easily get defensive or lash out if asked, respectfully, about the content of his messages—he accepts lavish adulation, but Berean searching of the Scriptures to verify whether what he is saying is true is unacceptable (Acts 17:11). Unable to rest confidently in the Lord whom he does not personally know, out of Saul-like insecurity (1 Samuel 28:5)[93] Diotrephes may, rather than training others to search the Scriptures for themselves, order them to just to trust and follow him blindly,[94] improperly equating implicit, unquestioning trust in his person with the implicit, unquestioning trust properly due to Jehovah alone.[95] The Lord Jesus, resting securely in His Father's smile as His eternal Son and sharing fully in His Father's everlasting love for His sheep (John 13:1-3), humbled Himself to take the position of a servant of servants (1 Samuel 25:41) by washing His disciples feet, as a pattern for the apostles and all Christian leaders to follow (John 13:4-14; Philippians 2:5-11); Diotrephes, insecure and fearful in his usurped position and with a heart full of self-love, fighting to obtain and maintain preeminence, demands submission to his own person and harshly casts out any who stand in his way or fail to idolatrously grovel before him. Diotrephes perverts the Biblically warranted honor due to a godly pastor into a sacrilegious usurpation of the unhesitating and absolute submission that befits Jesus Christ alone, teaching things which he ought not for the sake of his own shameful gain.[96] Individual Christians are no longer God's priests with a genuine relationship with Christ, people whom the Spirit can guide directly through the Word—rather, Diotrephes makes himself the intermediary between the congregation and God. All Christians are no longer God's Spirit-anointed people (1 John 2:27) underneath the great Anointed One, Jesus Christ—rather, Diotrephes himself, and he alone, is God's Anointed.

Since Diotrephes' heart has not been captivated by the glorious, gracious love of the Father in Christ by the Spirit,[97] he views God as a "hard"[98] Master (Matthew 25:24), one who is "hard, strict, harsh, cruel, [or] merciless"[99] in His dealings with men and with himself. He therefore requires from others the slavish obedience (Matthew 18:28) that, in his spiritual blindness, he assumes is demanded by the God he does not really know (Luke 15:29),[100] taking Christian liberty away from the Father's adopted sons and bringing them into bondage (Galatians 2:4). While "God hath not given [his people] the spirit of fear; but of power, and of love, and of a sound mind" (2 Timothy 1:7), Diotrephes' harsh rule drives God's flock, in fear, to cast aside a sound mind to blindly follow his decrees, even if they violate Scripture and their consciences. Jehovah's words through Ezekiel describe Diotrephes exactly: "The diseased have ye not strengthened, neither have ye healed that which was sick, neither have ye bound up *that which was* broken, neither have ye brought again that which was driven away, neither have ye sought that which was lost; but with force and with cruelty have ye ruled them" (Ezekiel 34:4). In order to generate "evidence" to cast out sheep or to protect his preeminence, he will gladly use intimidation (John 9:20-23) or lengthy and repeated sessions of bullying (John 9:13-34). He is happy to divide family members against one other (John 9:18-23). The issue is not obedience or disobedience to Scripture, but submission to Pastor Diotrephes' person and edicts.[101] He understands the slavish service of Hagar but not the freedom of the sons of God, whose faith works by love (Galatians 4:21-5:6). Diotrephes, therefore, seeks to have "dominion over"[102] the "faith" of the saints (2 Corinthians 1:24), to exercise lordship over them the way the heathen did their servants (Luke 22:25), bringing them into bondage and devouring them that he might exalt himself (2 Corinthians 11:20; Galatians 2:4),[103] reducing God's freeborn children to spiritual slavery. In order to maintain his position, he will happily cast out whatever and whomever is necessary, whether the apostolic teachings of the New Testament or those who know the voice of the good Shepherd in Scripture (John 10:4-5) and are constrained by the love of Christ to follow Him first.

Pastor Diotrephes Prates

Diotrephes also engages in "prating" with "malicious words" (3 John 10).[104] He "indulge[s] in utterance that makes no sense" and "talk[s] nonsense,"[105] often out of "ignorance of what is involved."[106] He "utter[s] foolishness."[107] When he gives pastoral counsel, as he is not a wise man, he frequently rushes to judgment without being careful to ascertain all the necessary facts and without wisely evaluating them. Pastor Diotrephes' tendency to rush to harsh, inaccurate, and often simply false judgments are connected to his proud over-estimation of his own wisdom.[108] Like the unclear vision of someone who attempts to see through billowing clouds of thick smoke, his pride clouds his judgment.[109] As a "proud"[110] man, his spiritual sickness and mental ailment[111] confuse his judgment so that he condemns others based on his "evil surmisings," lightly-evidenced conjectures (1 Timothy 6:4). He is sloppy with Scripture and other truth, but extremely careful with his own reputation. Following his advice is spiritually destructive; because he is himself inwardly twisted (Matthew 17:17), his words are "perverse,"[112] spiritually twisted, ones that mislead and turn others away from the right ways of the Lord (Acts 20:30; 13:10). His counsel perverts the mind and heart[113] when taken seriously—the more seriously his advice is taken, the more inward spiritual devastation his words cause. He is a "vain talker"[114] (Titus 1:10), a "vain jangle[r]" (1 Timothy 1:6);[115] as such, his words must be rejected as empty nonsense, not received as the wise, Biblical wisdom of a godly pastor: "the godly teaching and the faith according to Christ brands [his] foolish language as godlessness."[116] Diotrephes is inwardly "unstable" (2 Peter 3:16; 2:14),[117] a troubled sea that has no rest (Isaiah 57:20), so his unstable counsel troubles[118] the sheep (Galatians 5:10), causing them "inward turmoil, stir[ring] [them] up, disturb[ing], unsettle[ing], [and] throw[ing] [them] into ... mental and spiritual agitation and confusion,"[119] with the result that they are not strengthened and established spiritually,[120] but spiritually weakened, falling from steadfastness (2 Peter 3:17),[121] from their firm commitments to Biblical convictions and beliefs,[122] the more seriously they take his counsel. What he says does not agree with Scripture, but he wants others to follow him without understanding, without questioning, and even if it requires them to violate their consciences[123]—and failure to do so is, in his mind, rebellion upon which he will crack down harshly with "malicious words" (3 John 10)—evil speech that cuts, tears, crushes, and wounds. His words and deeds tear into the sheep like the claws and teeth of hungry wolves. If one of God's sheep refuses to follow him and his words instead of the Good Shepherd and His inspired words, Diotrephes' "prating ... with malicious words" manifests itself in "bring[ing] forward idle accusations" and "mak[ing] empty charges,"[124] "spreading nonsense ... with evil words" and "bring[ing] unjustified charges against"[125] that saint, so that he can cast God's sheep out of Christ's church (3 John 10) and maintain dictatorial, cultic control. Diotrephes is a "deceiver"[126] (Titus 1:10), a "deceitful worker"[127] (2 Corinthians 11:13). He is a liar, willing to speak "perverse things" (Acts 20:30), twisting truth to maintain his grip on power, hide his sins, and do whatever is necessary to maintain his grasp on preeminence. In order to protect himself and his reputation, he may, like Ahab and Jezebel, use cut-outs and subordinates[128] who blindly follow him as his emissaries to effect his unrighteous actions and accomplish his purposes (1 Kings 21:8-15).[129] In the way that Christ's enemies used deceit to accuse Him,[130] so Diotrephes is willing to "tak[e] advantage through craft and underhanded methods,"[131] falsely accusing God's sheep and casting them out, abusing the trust and power he has by virtue of his pastoral office to lead unsuspecting Christians to simply trust his lies and slanders without verification, as well as deceitfully misusing Scripture (2 Corinthians 4:2) to support his agenda.

Pastor Diotrephes Deceives

However, Pastor Diotrephes does not only use nonsense-speech. King Saul made ridiculous false accusations (1 Samuel 20:30-31; 22:8, 13), but he could also say nice words that sounded humble, righteous, and repentant (1 Samuel 15:25, 30; 16:21, 25) when he thought that they would help him gain or continue to grasp preeminence. To fulfill his desires and get what he wants,[132] Diotrephes can use "good words and fair speeches"[133]; that is, "smooth, plausible speech," as "a bad person who makes a fine speech."[134] Pastor Diotrephes can make "argument[s] that soun[d] good but [are] false" and use "words that are well chosen but untrue"[135] in order to "deceive the hearts of the simple" (Romans 16:18), those who believe, without verification, his every word (Proverbs 14:15). He can sound like the kindest and gentlest person when it helps him achieve or maintain preeminence. Furthermore, Diotrephes is both "deceiving, and being deceived" (2 Timothy 3:13). He not only deceives others with his lies, but he also deceives himself (Galatians 6:3; Titus 3:3)—through the frightful blinding power of sin, Diotrephes frequently convinces himself that his slanders and deceit represent reality.[136] In the alternate universe within his darkened mind, inconvenient realities where he is a wicked sinner disappear, replaced by illusory (but much more flattering) non-history where he is a righteous hero. He then leads others to wander in darkness as he provides them counsel that makes sense in the fairy-tale world in his head, but has devastating consequences in the real world where Jesus Christ is the truly preeminent and sovereign One. Diotrephes' dissimulation can be convincing enough to "carry away" not only himself but even godly spiritual leaders, sons of consolation like Barnabas (Galatians 2:13; Acts 4:36), when those godly men sinfully fail to verify Pastor Diotrephes' assertions. When one hears only his side of a matter, his persuasive speech[137] may be very convincing (Colossians 2:4)—but his assertions crumble when they are carefully examined from Scripture and when not only his accusations, but those whom he accuses, receive a fair hearing (Proverbs 18:17).[138]

Diotrephes can justify his underhanded tactics to establish and maintain his preeminence because, deceiving and being deceived (2 Timothy 3:13), he has conveniently convinced himself that his "gain is godliness" (1 Timothy 6:5). It may be convenient for his bank account to enter or remain in a position as a head pastor. Alternatively, as a "proud" man (1 Timothy 6:4),

Diotrephes may have an eye to his preeminence as "gain"[139] (1 Timothy 6:5) in other ways that are not strictly financial. The pastor is the Lord's Anointed, and he is the pastor, so what contributes to his "gain" in prestige, power, and other non-strictly financial forms of "gain" must be "godliness"—no? One who threatens his preeminence, by derogating from his personal prestige, insufficiently covering up his sins, refusing his amorous advances, or failing to render to him the unconditional surrender due to Jesus Christ, is not just opposing Pastor Diotrephes—no—he is actually against God Himself. For Diotrephes' "gain" is "godliness," and thus anything that undermines the authority of Diotrephes must be undermining the authority of the Most High. When Diotrephes casts out righteous sheep or corrupts Biblical church government, he is not just looking out for his own personal welfare, he reasons—no, he is defending pastoral authority, and, indeed, God's own authority. If he has to be a little "destitute of ... truth"[140] to bring about that good end (1 Timothy 6:5), if he has to "to cause another to suffer loss ... through illicit means"[141] and "cheat"[142] a bit, use just a little "deception or trickery"[143] to bring about that worthy end, what is that? A Pastor Diotrephes who lords over a large, influential congregation may convince himself that God's kingdom could not advance properly without him,[144] and his merits outweigh his demerits;[145] a little underhanded dirty-business to protect his preeminence is therefore justified for the greater good. A Pastor Diotrephes who holds a smaller work in his iron fist may convince himself of something similar, just on a smaller scale. Who could take over if he had to step down? Pastor Diotrephes may also believe that his own reputation is more important than not only the flourishing but even the survival of the congregation he rules;[146] certainly his preeminence must be preserved, even if a few saints must be cast out or in other ways ruined along the way. A few good eggs must be broken to make the omelet Diotrephes can deliciously devour. Furthermore, Diotrephes may project his dishonest plotting and scheming into his "evil surmisings" (1 Timothy 6:4) about others—they are acting underhandedly against him (he surmises), so he can play dirty, too. In any case, however sound or invalid the arguments used may be, the conclusion is clear—a little dirty-work to maintain his preeminence is justifiable. Indeed, Pastor Diotrephes may have covered up sin so many times that, having completely seared his conscience, he does not even have any twinges of conscience left when he, once again, employs deceit to maintain or increase his preeminence. Lying may have become completely natural to him.

While Pastor Diotrephes deceives others—and himself—because he says in his heart, "The LORD shall not see, neither shall the God of Jacob regard *it*" (Psalm 94:7), in the real world—God's world—Pastor Diotrephes' deception and evil is bounded and controlled by the Almighty God who "worketh all things after the counsel of his own will" (Ephesians 1:11), to His ultimate glory, and for His people's good (Romans 8:28-39). Sovereign over all things, "with him *is* strength and wisdom: the deceived and the deceiver *are* his" (Job 12:16):

> *[T]he simplest men that are deceived are not below his notice; the subtlest men that deceive cannot with all their subtlety escape his cognizance. The world is full of deceit; the one half of mankind cheats the other, and God suffers it to be so, and from both will at last bring glory to himself. The deceivers make tools of the deceived, but the great*

> *God makes tools of them both, wherewith he works, and none can hinder him. He has wisdom and might enough to manage all the fools and knaves in the world, and knows how to serve his own purposes by them, notwithstanding the weakness of the one and the wickedness of the other. When Jacob by a fraud got the blessing the design of God's grace was served; when Ahab was drawn by a false prophecy into an expedition that was his ruin the design of God's justice was served; and in both the deceived and the deceiver were at his disposal. ... God would not suffer the sin of the deceiver, nor the misery of the deceived, if he knew not how to set bounds to both and bring glory to himself out of both.*[147]

Jehovah sees, knows, and even (without in any way being the author of the sin) foreordains the deceit of both Diotrephes and Diotrephes' master the devil—father of lies and liars—for His glory and for the good of His beloved people. Diotrephes, lusting for preeminence, rages, wars, destroys, and deceives for power, but what he means for evil, God—His throne unshaken, serene, and undisturbed—means for good, and overrules for His all-wise and perfectly holy purposes (Genesis 50:20).

Pastor Diotrephes Demands Partiality

In the context of righteous and sinning elders, Paul strongly stresses the importance of impartial judgment: "I charge *thee* before God, and the Lord Jesus Christ, and the elect angels, that thou observe these things without preferring one before another, doing nothing by partiality" (1 Timothy 5:21).[148] The only command in the pastoral epistles with a preface longer than 1 Timothy 5:21's "I charge thee before God, and the Lord Jesus Christ, and the elect angels ..." is the command to preach the Word in 2 Timothy 4:2: "I charge *thee* therefore before God, and the Lord Jesus Christ, who shall judge the quick and the dead at his appearing and his kingdom; Preach the word ..." (2 Timothy 4:1-2). Impartial judgment of both the strong majority of righteous elders and the minority of ungodly ones (1 Timothy 5:17-25) is critically important for a healthy church. However, Pastor Diotrephes teaches, and too many Christians with a blind spot for Diotrephes agree, that it "is of the utmost importance" for assistant pastors, deacons, and everyone else to "ALWAYS exal[t] the pastor, deferring to him in all things" in "absolut[e] subordinat[ion]."[149] However, the Holy Spirit did not make of utmost importance always backing the pastor, but made of utmost importance the necessity of impartial judgment of elders, especially in the context of accusations. Rather than blind obedience, absolute subordination, and always exalting and deferring to a head pastor, an elder must, as with all others, be judged "without preferring" him before any other, so that absolutely "nothing" is done by "partiality." Both a sheep in the church and a pastor overseeing the sheep must receive "a judgment that" does not "involve[e] taking a side beforehand, prejudgment, discrimination."[150] There can be no "prefer[ring] beforehand" or "decid[ing] beforehand"[151] that a pastor is either guilty or innocent, nor can the scales be weighted either in favor of or against the pastor. One must not "make a decision based upon unjustified preference"[152] beforehand or "for[m] ... an opinion ... before the facts are known."[153]

> *[The command to judge "without preferring one before another" in 1 Timothy 5:21] is attested as a legal technical term in papyri. It corresponds to the Latin praeiudicium, a prejudgment in the sense of a preceding sentence, "a prior,*

> *anticipatory decision which can or must serve as a norm for a later decision in another or the same case." In 1 Tm. 5:21 ... [the] meaning ... is a prejudgment or preconceived opinion in favour of the accused or accuser which would hinder judges from exercising the justice required in church discipline[.]*[154]

Not only must judgment be made "without preferring one before another," but absolutely "nothing" must be decided out of "partiality." One cannot be biased in favor of someone who accuses a pastor of something, even if that person is a family member or friend. Nor can one have a "strong preference" and "inclination"[155] in favor of or against a pastor, except in the sense in which all people should be presumed innocent until proven guilty (1 Corinthians 13:5-7). Not only can one not always back (or oppose) the pastor, one cannot have "a decided ... preference for"[156] or against, "an inclination or proclivity of mind"[157] for or against his side, or make a judgment based on "personal attachment, partiality, [or] favour."[158] The righteous pastor, confident in Christ and aware that he is "blameless" (1 Timothy 3:1), will not fear being improperly adjudged guilty by godly sheep if he is extended the common presumption of innocence rightly ascribed to all while the standards mandated in 1 Timothy 5 and Matthew 18 are practiced. He is humbled to be esteemed "very highly in love" for his work's sake and therefore presumed to be innocent of unfounded charges (1 Thessalonians 5:13; 1 Corinthians 13:5, 7). He has a holy confidence in the face of unbiased judgment, knowing that by God's grace he is qualified for his position. He therefore welcomes impartial judgment, knowing his clean conscience and aware that he has no need to place a thumb from his holy hands on the scale of justice. Pastor Diotrephes, on the other hand, insecure in his unrighteous preeminence, will use the weight of his power and position to require that he be treated with great partiality and preferred before all others. He is not just innocent until proven guilty, but is innocent, period; questioning his innocence is like questioning God. On the other hand, those whom he accuses are guilty until proven innocent, or, indeed, guilty based on his bare word and worthy of being cast out. While Scripture makes impartiality of the utmost importance, Pastor Diotrephes makes partiality in his favor of the utmost importance, both so that his miserable failures to be blameless remain hidden to the eyes of other men and so that he can cast out the innocent on false pretenses.

Christ Commands Impartiality

Impartial judgment is the proper application of the second greatest commandment, "Thou shalt love thy neighbour as thyself" (Matthew 22:39). It is best because it honors God's great command requiring it (1 Timothy 5:21), and it is also best for the righteous pastor, for the sinning pastor, for the righteous church member, for the sinning church member, and for the church of Christ and His kingdom. Impartial judgment protects righteous pastors from slander and false accusations. They receive the presumption of innocence due to all Christians but especially emphasized for the elder (1 Timothy 5:19-21). Gainsayers cannot say that the only reason an overseer has not been found guilty of something is because he had his thumb on the scale and manipulated events to reach his predetermined result. The knowledge that he is not above the discipline of the church also provides him an extra motive, underneath the overarching one of love for God, to resist his indwelling sin (1 John 1:8-10) and to continue walking on the narrow way of holiness. Impartial judgment is also best for both a born-again pastor who disqualifies himself by sin and even for Pastor Diotrephes. While Pastor Diotrephes does not care about the judgment of God and so willingly covers up his wrongdoing through orchestrating partial judgments to preserve his preeminence, he will nevertheless face a fearful reckoning when he stands before Christ's great white throne (Revelation 20:11-15). Impartial judgment, which justifies removing him from his position, makes it more likely that he will not be hardened in pride, but will come to repentance and not face the eternal condemnation of the devil and his angels (1 Timothy 3:6; Matthew 25:41). Similarly, a born-again pastor who has disqualified himself by sin will face terrible chastening if he gives in to the temptation to retain his position by coercing prejudiced judgment. He would be far better off, to all eternity to come, if he allowed impartial judgment to uncover the truth and served Christ lawfully (2 Timothy 2:5) as a faithful church member who was no longer in the pastorate, at least until he again meets the qualifications (1 Timothy 3).

Impartial judgment is best for the righteous church member. It protects him from being unlawfully cast out from that holy place of God's worship that he prizes above all earthly joys. It assures him that things are being done fairly with an eye to God's honor in His congregation. Impartial judgment is also best for the sinning member who deserves discipline. Someone who deserves to be placed under discipline, but is excommunicated in an improper way, is hindered from seeing his need to come to repentance. The unbiblical manner in which he was removed from the church body is a stumbling block that keeps him from seeing his own sin. Furthermore, he can use the wrong methods by which he was removed as a justification to pull others out of the church who can themselves see that the way matters were handled was not right. When the steps of Matthew 18 are scrupulously and impartially followed, the whole congregation knows God's Word was rightfully obeyed and the person excommunicated deserved it, protecting the congregation from his negative influence and contributing to the sinning person's repentance.

Impartial judgment is best for the congregation as a whole. Every member knows things are being run by the Book. They know there is no shady funny-business going on somewhere that is being hidden to protect the guilty. Impartial judgment is best for Christ's worldwide kingdom. It keeps saints in the church and in the pulpit and keeps wolves out, encouraging the flourishing of individual congregations and protecting them from the reproach that arises when the world sees wicked men in positions in God's house where they ought not be. Truly, the infinite wisdom of the Holy Spirit is seen in His dictating the command: "I charge *thee* before God, and the Lord Jesus Christ, and the elect angels, that thou observe these things without preferring one before another, doing nothing by partiality" (1 Timothy 5:21)!

Pastor Diotrephes Must Be Exposed

Scripture teaches that Diotrephes must be exposed. A church led by a preeminent Pastor Diotrephes is in grave danger of ceasing to be Christ's church, becoming instead Diotrephes' own "church."[159] The Apostle John declared that he would "remember"[160] the "deeds which" this wolf in sheep's clothing "doeth" (3 John 10), "putting" others "in mind"[161] (Titus 3:1), "call[ing] to mind," "bring[ing] up"[162] the corrupt words and deeds of Diotrephes. Diotrephes' name was specifically mentioned by the Apostle John in the public letter of 3 John, intended for all Christ's churches in every place, and part of the infallible New Testament canon. Furthermore, John did not wish for Diotrephes to continue devouring and casting the sheep out for long periods of time—rather, he intended to come "at once, immediately"[163] and expose this false pastor. While those who agree with the aberrant theology of Diotrephes insist that pastoral sin must remain covered,[164] Scripture commands concerning the sinning elder: "Them that sin rebuke before all, that others also may fear" (1 Timothy 5:20,[165] cf. 5:17-25). "It becomes a sad duty sometimes to expose the wicked ambition of a man with the rule or ruin policy."[166] Historically, Baptists would publicly expose those excommunicated for serious sin. Indeed, they were especially conscientious to so publicly expose sinning pastors, so that these wolves could not go on to harm others elsewhere:

> *Baptists ... [would] announc[e] in print the crime and excommunication, either in secular and religious newspapers or in ... printed minutes of association meetings. Churches published excommunicants, especially excommunicated clergy, when they refused to submit to*

> *discipline, lest they attempt to escape the stigma that their crimes deserved and to palm themselves off as blameless. ... In the case of excommunicated preachers, they also demanded the return of their license or ordination papers ... churches generally published refusals. ... Associations assisted in publishing the excommunicants.*[167]

Godly pastors do not engage in coverups. They follow Scripture. Their "exhortation[s] ... [are not] in guile" (1 Thessalonians 2:3); they do not "tak[e] advantage through craft and underhanded methods," utilizing "deceit, cunning, [and] treachery,"[168] because they are not deceitful people (John 1:47). They know that Proverbs 28:13 is true for both individuals and for entire congregations: "He that covereth his sins shall not prosper: but whoso confesseth and forsaketh *them* shall have mercy." They "have renounced the hidden things of dishonesty, not walking in craftiness, nor handling the word of God deceitfully; but by manifestation of the truth commending [themselves] to every man's conscience in the sight of God" (2 Corinthians 4:2).

Christ's Sheep Must Be Received

Not only must Diotrephes be exposed, but those unjustly cast out by Diotrephes must be received. The Apostle John's strong commendation of Demetrius suggests that he was one who was slandered and opposed by Diotrephes, either as a traveling evangelist or missionary whom Diotrephes refused to receive (3 John 9), or as a faithful member of the congregation over which Diotrephes had assumed dictatorial control and who was cast out by Diotrephes, or both.[169] "It seems ... likely that

Demetrius may be a person in the church who has felt the wrath of Diotrephes ... punished by this powerful leader in the church."[170]

> *Diotrephes ... rejected Demetrius, and, in rejecting him he was rejecting the apostle who endorsed him. ... Diotrephes was the sample ecclesiastic to whom church order meant more than love to Christ's sheep. ... Unhappily, the spiritual descendants of Diotrephes are many ... self-seeking, self-important ... lording it over their brethren and arrogating to themselves the right to say who may or may not be recognized. And woe unto any who opposes their pretentious ipse dixit! John himself ... had no fear of the anathema of Diotrephes, but many a humbler worker has been utterly discouraged and turned aside by the presumptuousness of men of similar spirit. To such the message comes: "Beloved, follow not that which is evil, but that which is good. He that doeth good is of God (whether approved by Diotrephes or not), and he that doeth evil (whatsoever his ecclesiastical standing) hath not seen God" (ver. 11). It is evident that the servant who had been so ruthlessly barred out by this self-elected leader is the man named in verse 12. "Demetrius hath good report of all men, and of the truth itself: yea, and we also bear witness, and ye know that our witness is true." But it matters nothing to the rigid advocates of a pseudo-church-order that a man is honored of God, that he proclaims the truth, that his walk is blameless, that many can testify to his devotedness and his piety, as also to the spirituality and helpfulness of his ministry ... he must be treated as a publican and a sinner, or rejected as though he were a blasphemer. How shocking it all is, and what an insult to the Head of the Church and to the Holy Spirit of God!*[171]

Whether a member of Diotrephes' congregation, a traveling preacher, or both, it is very likely that Demetrius was not received by Diotrephes. Diotrephes either cast out Demetrius, or he would have done so were it in his power.

The Apostle John, who had personally heard Christ teach on church discipline and would have taken Christ's commands very seriously (Matthew 18:15-20), not only refused to receive Diotrephes' *faux* excommunication, nor only privately and silently set it aside, but publicly and strongly opposed it. He identified Diotrephes as one who "hath not seen God" and who followed "that which is evil," while Demetrius was "of God" and both was and did "good" (3 John 11). John not only bore personal record to the fidelity of Demetrius, but joined with his testimony that of others: "we ... bear record" (3 John 12).[172] John the Elder and many others knew that "Demetrius hath good report of all *men*, and of the truth itself" (3 John 12).[173] While Pastor Diotrephes talked nonsense against Demetrius, slandering and spewing accusations against the godly man with "malicious words" (3 John 10), the consistent, abiding witness[174] of the Christian community who knew Demetrius was good. He had proven himself faithful over time in the eyes of a multitude of righteous witnesses. More importantly, "the truth itself" bore witness to Demetrius: unlike Diotrephes (John 8:44), Demetrius' actions were consistent with the teaching of Scripture and were born witness to by that Spirit who inspired the Word.[175] It was good that many saints bore witness to Demetrius' integrity—it was essential that God Himself knew and testified of it. People did not think well of Demetrius because of ignorance or because of a successful cover-up of his sins, but because the inward and outward orientation of that godly man was within the way of righteousness. History testifies that Demetrius became the pastor of the church at Philadelphia, being commended by the Apostle John.[176] The Apostle did not allow Diotrephes' condemnation to ruin Demetrius' ministry or in the least reduce that saint's opportunities for Christian service—rather, Diotrophes' condemnation was an occasion to offer Demetrius full-throated support and praise. "John emphasizes … Demetriu[s'] … good standing, in order that Gaius may receive him with confidence, and that others may be favorably influenced."[177] John and many others continued to bear public witness to Demetrius' integrity, not only within the narrow confines of the congregation over which Diotrephes tyrannized, but in the larger Christian community. Gaius, the original audience of 3 John, who served Christ at a different church from the one where John ministered as an elder (3 John 1; Romans 16:23),[178] along with a host of other godly men, "knew"[179] that the testimony of many to Demetrius' godliness and integrity was true (3 John 12). The inspired epistle of 3 John was to be read in all churches. Neither the Apostle John, nor Gaius' church, nor the churches where 3 John was publicly read, provided cover for Diotrephes' evil deeds, nor looked askance at Demetrius because of Diotrephes' malicious prating. The lovers of light would have nothing to do with Diotrephes' unrighteous actions, his coverups and lies to maintain preeminence, his condemnation of the godly, and his secret deeds of darkness:

> *And this is the condemnation, that light is come into the world, and men loved darkness rather than light, because their deeds were evil. For every one that doeth evil hateth the light, neither cometh to the light, lest his deeds should be reproved. But he that doeth truth cometh to the light, that his deeds may be made manifest, that they are wrought in God. (John 3:19-21)*

Sheep cast out by Diotrephes, and sheep not received by Diotrephes, must be the more heartily loved and received by all God's saints.

IV.) HOW CAN I MAKE SURE I AM NOT PASTOR DIOTREPHES?

The True Pastor: Horrified by Diotrephes

Godly and regenerate men, sincere under-shepherds who love Christ and have the Spirit of Christ in them, find Diotrephes horrifying. Through God's grace to them, they are willing to follow the example of their Master, the Lord Jesus, and to lay down their lives for the well-being of the flock entrusted to them (John 10:11). They are utterly unwilling to do the work of Satan in scattering their flock. How can a sincere pastor both make sure he is not Diotrephes and also avoid Diotrephes-like tendencies from arising in his ministry through the temptations of the world, the flesh, and the devil?

True Pastor—True Conversion

First, every pastor must be truly converted himself and have a solidly grounded, Scriptural assurance of his own regeneration. The Apostle Paul was right to warn about unconverted pastors (Acts 20:30); Gilbert Tennent was likewise right to warn about the danger of an unconverted ministry during the Great Awakening;[180] and it would be foolish to assume that everyone who finds his way into the pastorate of a

Biblical church today is truly converted. The most fundamental problem with Diotrephes is that he has never been born again. Therefore, his unregenerate heart follows what is evil, and he does evil, having never spiritually seen God (3 John 11) through the supernatural work of the Father, Son, and Spirit (Matthew 11:27-28; 2 Corinthians 3:14-4:6). If you have never genuinely repented and believed on the Lord Jesus Christ (Mark 1:15), but instead have substituted the repetition of a "sinner's prayer,"[181] or some other merely human decision, for true conversion[182]—which produces the holy life of love and fellowship with God and His saints described in 1 John[183]—you have absolutely no business being in the Christian ministry. If you struggle with doubts about your conversion, or if you are controlled by habitual sin that indicates that you either do not have true spiritual life or that your spiritual life, if present, is very weak, or if you do not have a well-grounded assurance of salvation,[184] you have no business being in the pastorate until those struggles are decisively and definitively resolved. Agreeing with orthodox Biblical doctrine does not mean you are converted—Satan also knows orthodox doctrine (James 2:19). Diotrephes could have lisped many doctrinally sound words and could easily have omitted from his doctrinal statement his love for preeminence and lack of love for the saints. His professed faith could have looked quite good—but many will be in the lake of fire with doctrinal statements as accurate as the orthodox doctrine their father the devil knows and hates. Unconverted pastors will probably have congregations full of unconverted people,[185] while spiritual novices (1 Timothy 3:6) and other spiritually immature true Christians can also do tremendous harm when inappropriately placed in the pastorate in violation of the command to "lay hands suddenly on no man" (1 Timothy 5:22).

True Pastor—Christ-Consecrated Separation

Second, you should recognize that the Diotrephes-pastor is someone from whom to practice clear ecclesiastical separation. The influential "Baptist" leader Jack Hyles, and other carnal men, have filled many Baptist churches with corrupt teaching on the pastoral role that would justify a vast army of Pastors Diotrephes.[186] Do not lead your church to fellowship, nor engage in Christian fellowship personally, with those who follow such unbiblical, pro-Diotrephes doctrines. It may make your flesh feel good to preach at a church or a conference where you are not only (properly) esteemed highly in love for your holy work's sake (1 Thessalonians 5:13) but are also (idolatrously) exalted to a place of preeminence that should be reserved for Christ alone. However, you must recognize that, as a pastor, you are in special danger of "being lifted up with pride" and so "fall[ing] into the condemnation of the devil" (1 Timothy 3:6). It is far too easy to ascribe glory to ourselves when God is saving souls and transforming lives through the Word that we preach, and when people look up to us, trust us, and show us great honor.

True Pastor—True Lowliness

Do not call yourself the Lord's Anointed, nor allow other people to give you that title—reserve it, in this dispensation, for the Messiah alone, the One to whom all the anointed priests and prophets in the Old Testament pointed. Befriend humble, godly, Christ-like men and avoid those who make it too easy for you to think of yourself more highly than you ought to think. Preachers and churches with a soft-spot for Diotrephes will be bad influences upon both you and upon your flock. Furthermore, the idolatry of Diotrephes is too often associated with shameful immorality that could both defile your church and give it a bad name. In addition, even if you never rule like a Diotrephes, fellowship with others that are open to Pastor Diotrephes may lead to him replacing you and bringing to nothing the work you labored for before the Lord. In a difficult situation, those with an affection for Diotrephes will give you Diotrephes-like advice.[187] Rather than reminding you of the inspired requirement to "try" professing Christian leaders (1 John 4:1-3), "to make a critical examination ... to determine genuineness, put to the test, examine" them,[188] they will give you the Diotrephes-type counsel that you should blindly and unconditionally trust and cover for another sinner if he happens to be a head pastor. If we are fools when we trust our hearts (Proverbs 28:26), we are fools to have Christian fellowship with those who teach that, rather than evaluating everything with Scripture (Acts 17:11), Christians should unquestioningly follow whatever their pastor says. Even if one's pastor is among the saintliest of men—and a vast host of pastors are among the excellent of the earth—he still has indwelling and deceiving sin in his heart (Romans 7:14-25). Indeed, the more godly a pastor is, the more he will see and grieve over his own remaining sin, and the more he will detest this kind of blind loyalty. The New Testament records clear acts of sin, bad advice, and poor examples by the apostles themselves.[189] If you are born again, you cannot really be Diotrephes. However, in the same way that Judas led the other apostles to unjustly condemn an astonishing act of love by a very godly person,[190] so fellowship with Diotrephes-type people gives occasion for the devil, your sinful flesh, and worldly ideas of leadership (Mathew 20:25-27) to impact your philosophy of ministry, creating situations where you can hurt, instead of help, the sheep. Diotrephes can hurt your sheep; he can hurt your family; and he can hurt you. Someone who has good standards of dress or music, or who uses the right Bible version, but supports the ministry philosophy of Diotrephes, is someone to reprove, rebuke, exhort, and separate from if he remains unrepentant. Such a person is not someone to unify with, engage in Christian fellowship with, or receive advice or counsel from. In the Johannine epistles, Diotrephes is an antichrist. Should you maintain ecclesiastical fellowship with antichrist, as long as he comes to you in nice clothes with the right Bible version under his arm? Should you have a tender spot in your heart for the doctrines of antichrist?

Godly pastors must also recognize the broadness of Paul's warning in 2 Timothy 4:3: "For the time will come when they will not endure sound doctrine; but after their own lusts shall they heap to themselves teachers, having itching ears" (2 Timothy 4:3). Can people turn aside from the right way because of an ear that itches to hear about worldliness in heart or appearance, or compromise in a variety of Biblical standards? Certainly. But can a pastor also fall into very unwise courses of action by surrounding himself with those who will tickle his ears, telling him that he is always right (1 Kings 12:1-16), pandering to the pride and self-confidence in his flesh, flattering him, telling him that he is the Lord's Anointed, that he has a unique relationship with God by virtue of his office above all mere Christians, and that he deserves and should demand from the sheep the kind of unquestioning leadership that Christ Himself rightly commands? Yes. Righteous church leaders should instruct their flock on the respect due to godly pastors, while also refusing to allow anyone to put them in Christ's place. They must hate—not encourage—flattery, blind obsequiousness, and boot-licking groveling. The flock must know they ought to take their pastor's Biblical counsel very seriously, for he is very often exactly right. They must also know that he is not a secondary god whom they must follow blindly, for no pastor other than Jesus Christ is always right. The church must know both "Remember them which have the rule over you, who have spoken unto you the word of God: whose faith follow, considering the end of *their* conversation" and "Stand up; I myself also am a man" (Hebrews 13:7; Acts 10:26).

You must never, ever distort the interpretation or application of Scripture one jot or tittle for your personal advantage, or for any other reason whatsoever, teaching what you ought not for shameful gain (Titus 1:11). What the Bible actually teaches, in its context, must be proclaimed without adulteration, no matter what the cost (2 Timothy 4:1-2). Furthermore, Christ, true God and true Man, Himself leads, supports, strengthens, and sanctifies His body the church, and all His saints individually, by His Word and Spirit in ways that a righteous pastor, as he is not incarnate God but is mere dust and ashes, simply cannot replicate. By God's grace and for His glory, you can fulfill your holy calling—but if you (even unintentionally) usurp Christ's role out of a weakness for

Diotrephes-style leadership and seek to play God for every member of your flock, in your finiteness you will fail to help them the way Christ, in His infinite fulness, can, and you will sink under a burden that is too heavy for you to bear: "Thou wilt surely wear away, both thou, and this people that *is* with thee: for this thing *is* too heavy for thee; thou art not able to perform it thyself alone" (Exodus 18:18; Numbers 11:14). Remember, Diotrephes seeks preeminence—you must seek lowliness. O man of God, flee from pride and follow after meekness (1 Timothy 6:3-11)!

True Pastor—True Procedure

Proper procedure is critical when godly pastors, in sincere sorrow for a sinning person and out of sincere and selfless love for Christ, His church, and for sinners, lead their congregation to righteously practice church discipline. A detailed church constitution can protect righteous church leaders and the entire body of saints from sinfully acting, in the heat of a moment, too much like Diotrephes by not allowing accused members, not only the falsely accused innocent but even those clearly guilty, Biblically warranted rights. Procedures recommended in historic Baptist church manuals should be followed, such as providing accused persons the charges against them in writing, giving them the opportunity to cross-examine accusers, and allowing sufficient time between the steps of Matthew 18:15-17 so that a congregation is not acting in precipitate haste and in the heat of passion, but deliberately, in love and with a sound mind (2 Timothy 1:20).[191] Congregations and their pastors must not "si[n]" in improper "hast[e],"[192] and so follow the negative example set in the hasty trial and condemnation of the Lord Jesus Christ (Matthew 26:65-66). Bridges notes:

> *Also, that the soul be without knowledge, it is not good; and he that hasteth with his feet sinneth [Proverbs 19:2]. ... His soul is without knowledge. Ignorance gives perpetuity to folly. ... [I]t is not, because the people know much, that they ever become the willing subjects of any factious or unprincipled demagogue. ... [T]he man without knowledge, instead of "pondering his path," hasteth with his feet—misseth his aim—sinneth. ... As opposed to consideration, acting hastily is sin. Not taking time to enquire, he is without knowledge. This impatience is a ruling evil—the genuine exercise of self-will—"not waiting for the counsel of the Lord." Godly Joshua offended here. Saul's impatience cost him his kingdom. David's haste was the occasion of gross injustice. Jehoshaphat's precipitancy—asking counsel after, instead of before, his course—was sharply rebuked. Rash experiments—the result of haste—often threaten serious evils in the state. The same spirit rends the Church with schism. ... [H]ow much sin has been the fruit of a few rash words or hasty lines! A sudden impulse has taken the place of considerate principle. Let us ever remember, that without self-discipline, there can be no Christian consistency or stability; that in a thousand cases haste may plunge our feet into sin, if not into ruin; and that out strength is to stand or sit still, and see how God will appear on our side, to make a way for us through many a deep water of perplexity. "He that believeth shall not make haste."*[193]

Those who are unrepentant and guilty must be removed, while those who are innocent must be protected. Not only the result, but also the procedures that lead to the result, are important as a church performs her solemn duty to maintain a membership of visible saints. Godly pastors must resist the temptation to modify Biblical procedures even when it is very clear that an accused person is guilty, bitter, and hostile to the church and her leadership. If even the obviously guilty are given their day in court in the world, how much more must the church follow Christ's mandates in her solemn duty of guarding a regenerate and holy membership?

True Pastor—True Christian Walk

Furthermore, even a righteous man has enough indwelling sin within him to act too much like Pastor Diotrephes if he fails to stay close to Jesus Christ. An immature true Christian who manifests too much of the spirit of Diotrephes should not be in Christ's holy ministry until he better understands Christ's true heart for His sheep. A spiritually mature pastor must also keep constant watch over his own heart, lest his flesh seduce him into sinfully manifesting far too much of the spirit of Diotrephes. Jehovah required that Israel's king have God's Word "with him, and he shall read therein all the days of his life: that he may learn to fear the LORD his God, to keep all the words of this law and these statutes, to do them: that his heart be not lifted up above his brethren, and that he turn not aside from the commandment, *to* the right hand, or *to* the left" (Deuteronomy 17:19-20). Daily reading of Scripture was essential for a king who would humbly fear God, keep his commandments, and not have his heart lifted up above his brethren on account of his exalted position. While the New Testament never calls pastors "kings" except in the sense that all Christians are kings and priests

(Revelation 1:6), the principle for spiritual leadership remains. If you allow yourself to get so busy—even with good and important things—that serious time in God's Word and prayer (Acts 6:4) is neglected, your yet-sinful heart can far too easily become filled with pride. Do you wish to avoid Diotrephes-like tendencies in your ministry? Be sure that you are hearing the sweet voice of the Good Shepherd every day, and with reverent love and fear, submitting to that sweet speech of the living Word in the written Word (John 1:1; 17:17). In the midst of many things demanding your time, remember that God "hath shewed thee, O man, what *is* good; and what doth the LORD require of thee, but to do justly, and to love mercy, and to walk humbly with thy God?" (Micah 6:8).

V.) HOW CAN PASTORS PROTECT THEIR FLOCK FROM DIOTREPHES IN ALL HIS MANIFESTATIONS?

Protection from Diotrephes: Sola Scriptura

Following all of Scripture out of love for and humble trust in the Father, Son, and Holy Spirit is the best way to protect one's flock from Diotrephes. Someone with a genuine love for Christ and for His flock cannot have the heart of Diotrephes, and someone who knows and scrupulously practices Scripture cannot perform the actions of Pastor Diotrephes. Christian saints who themselves love Christ and know Scripture well will know that something is wrong when they come face-to-face with the ungodly actions of Pastor Diotrephes.

Pastors must make sure to ground their flock in Biblical ecclesiology. The saints must understand both what Scriptural submission to pastoral authority means and what the Scriptural limits to it are. An under-shepherd who properly leads the sheep does not beat them up, acting like a Diotrephes himself. Nor does he fail to actually lead, possibly setting up the next pastor to be Diotrephes in a future overreaction to a current denigration of pastoral authority. Commenting on Hebrews 13:17, John Owen notes:

[1.] It is with respect unto their teaching, preaching, or pastoral feeding, that [Christians] are commanded to "obey them [their pastors]." For the word [obey] signifies an obedience on a persuasion; such as doctrine, instruction, or teaching, doth produce. And,—

[2.] The submission required, "Submit yourselves," respects their rule, 'Obey their doctrine, and submit to their rule.' And some things must be observed, to clear the intention of the apostle herein.

1st. It is not a blind, implicit obedience and subjection, that is here prescribed. A pretense hereof hath been abused to the ruin of the souls of men: but there is nothing more contrary to the whole nature of gospel obedience, which is our "reasonable service;" and in particular, it is that which would frustrate all the rules and directions given unto believers in this epistle itself, as well as elsewhere, about all the duties that are required of them. For to what purpose are they used, if no more be required but that men give up themselves, by an implicit credulity, to obey the dictates of others?

2dly. It hath respect unto [pastors] in their office only. If those who suppose themselves in office do teach and enjoin things that belong not unto their office, there is no obedience due unto them by virtue of this command. So is it with the guides of the church of Rome, who, under a pretence of their office, give commands in secular things, no way belonging unto the ministry of the gospel.

3dly. It is their duty so to obey whilst they teach the things which the Lord Christ hath appointed them to teach; for unto them is their commission limited, Matt. 28:20: and to submit unto their rule whilst it is exercised in the name of Christ, according to his institution, and by the rule of the word, and not otherwise. When they depart from these, there is neither obedience nor submission due unto them. Wherefore,—

4thly. In the performance of these duties, there is

> *supposed a judgment to be made of what is enjoined or taught, by the word of God, according to all the instructions and rules that are given us therein. Our obedience unto them must be obedience unto God.*
>
> *5thly. On this supposition their word is to be obeyed and their rule submitted unto, not only because they are true and right materially, but also because they are theirs, and conveyed from them unto us by divine institution. A regard is to be had unto their authority and office-power in what they teach and do.*[194]

The saints must see godly shepherding preached, taught, and modeled. "Pastors must not go beyond the Word and require obedience in everything; neither may they allow their people to ignore the teaching of Scripture."[195] What Scripture clearly teaches must be obeyed, and shepherds must unapologetically call their sheep to follow Christ's Word. On the other hand, if neither the direct statements of Scripture, nor good and necessary consequences of Scripture, require a particular course of action, pastors may advise and offer their opinion (as may any other Christian), but not command.

> *[P]astors need to understand that advice is just that—advice. People are free to take or leave that advice! While [in a given situation] the pastor may have more insight into a circumstance than the people, ultimately they must be free to receive or reject advice. It is not to be equated with command.*[196]

This Biblical imperative exists because holy actions are not whatever a head pastor decides they are, but "good works are only such as God has commanded in His holy Word; and not such as without the warrant thereof, are devised by men, out of blind zeal, or upon any pretense of good intentions."[197]

Pro-Diotrephes writers transform pastoral advice and opinion in areas where Scripture is silent into commands which must be implicitly and unquestioningly obeyed. Simply by virtue of his pastoral office, independent of whether his position is actually stated in the Bible, the pastor (allegedly) has special insight and must be unhesitatingly followed.[198] Church members should be encouraged to seek wise counsel (Proverbs 11:14). A pastor is a great source for godly advice about the meaning and application of Scripture. But the flock must not be encouraged or allowed to turn their pastors into sources of infallible wisdom that they can trust implicitly and utterly the way that they must trust God's written Word and wisdom, the Bible, and His living Word and Personal Wisdom, Jesus Christ (John 1:1; Proverbs 8:22; Colossians 2:3). Nor can the flock be encouraged or allowed to abdicate their responsibility to be directly taught by Christ through the Holy Spirit and the Word (1 John 2:27) to make the pastor into an idol that provides infallible oracles. Pastors who refuse to require obedience to Scripture detract from the glory of Jesus Christ. Pastors who place obedience to their persons and opinions in the place of obedience to Scripture also detract from the glory due to Jesus Christ alone. Rejecting both of these errors, the glorious Biblical and Baptist principles of the priesthood of the believer and individual soul-liberty must be unhesitatingly affirmed.

Protection from Diotrephes: Mark And Avoid Him

Church members must understand what 3 John teaches about the negative model of Diotrephes. The church constitution should have a section explaining what should be done if an elder is accused of wrongdoing that both provides the Scriptural presumption of innocence that protects the righteous pastor and the Scriptural warrant and procedure for action against the unrighteous wolf in shepherd's garb. Modern sons of Pastor Diotrephes must have no place behind the pulpit of their church, and when the possibility of negative influence from Diotrephes exists, those who practice like that wolf should be exposed specifically, by name. Church members must be carefully instructed both that unverified accusations against anyone must not be received, especially against elders (1 Timothy 5:19) and that verified accusations must be both received and impartially acted upon (1 Timothy 5:20-21). Godly pastors do not need to fear what a church will do if congregants are taught God's truth that proven accusations against unrighteous elders must be received, such persons must be removed from the ministry and, in situations of serious sin, placed under church discipline. When, by the marvelous saving and sustaining grace of Christ, you are a "blameless" bishop (1 Timothy 3:2)[199] whose speech and actions "cannot be condemned" (Titus 2:8), a righteous flock will not receive as true a false accusation against you (1 Timothy 5:19).[200] You will also be less likely to fall from your own stedfastness (2 Peter 3:17) when you know that, if you do, your church will keep you accountable. You can trust the sovereignty of God if false accusations arise. You have the smile of the Almighty God, rich blessings from your Savior Jesus Christ, and the sweet comforts of the Holy Spirit. Do not fear what your congregation might do in some unknown future difficult day (Matthew 6:34)—submit in humble reverence to the Head of the Church, fear Him, and commit your affairs into His nail-pierced hands.

Protection from Diotrephes: Transparency

You must model transparency, not cover-ups and damage control, with your flock. God commands the congregation to "look at again and again … examine, observe carefully … give careful thought to, consider"[201] the conduct of their overseers, and by seeing their righteous, blameless example, to "use as a model, imitate, emulate, [and] follow"[202] their faith (Hebrews 13:7). You should be a well-known and public model of righteous living your congregation can imitate.[203] You should be able to say to your church, "[T]hou hast fully known my doctrine, manner of life, purpose, faith, longsuffering, charity, [and] patience" (2 Timothy 3:10) and "Those things, which ye have both learned, and received, and heard, and seen in me, do" (Philippians 4:9), not "Hide your eyes from and cover up for the heretics from whom I am secretly learning doctrine, my scandalous manner of life, my angry uncharitableness, my intemperance, and my other notorious sins; for I am the Lord's Anointed." You must love light, not darkness, and train Christ's sheep to do the same (John 3:19-21). A culture of Biblical transparency will contribute greatly to protect your church from Diotrephes, not only during your years of service, but for many years afterwards, if Christ has not yet returned.

Protection from Diotrephes: A Plurality of Pastors

A plurality of pastors is not essential to the existence of a church, but it is the consistent pattern in the New Testament, contributing to the well-being of the church. A godly overseer who is pastoring a church alone should seek, when possible, to move his congregation toward appointing a plurality of properly qualified pastors,[204] both for the increased present flourishing of the Lord's work and so that if God's providence takes a single elder away, the sheep are not left to wander without shepherds. It is harder for a single Diotrephes to raven the sheep when there are several other godly elders in his way—elders who know and love their Lord, their Bibles, and their flock, and who keep each other accountable to both Biblically pastor and individually walk with God, living for Him in a manner above reproach. Head pastors should make sure that assistant pastors are committed to supporting Christ and His Word first, and them only second. They must make sure that their flock knows how to distinguish between a Demetrius and a Diotrephes, and that they are committed in their souls to following the infallible apostolic witness in Scripture, no matter what the cost, if—may God forbid it—a Diotrephes in shepherd's clothing is able to sneak into their church's leadership. Finally, while the flock should be very far from a paranoid suspicion that their pastors are secret sons of Diotrephes, the congregation must know that if Satan could plant men like Diotrephes in churches where the Apostle Paul himself had pastored or where the Apostle John had ministered (Acts 20:28-32; 3 John), then after the departure of a godly overseer, his successor could indeed turn out to be Diotrephes. It happened after Paul left. It can happen after you leave. Therefore, like Paul, continually watch, remember, warn, and commend the knowledge of God and of the Word of His grace to your flock (Acts 20:31-32).

VI.) HOW CAN PASTORS PROTECT THEIR FLOCK FROM A PERVERT DIOTREPHES, IN PARTICULAR?

Pervert Pastors Rise When The Gospel Falls

To protect Christ's flock from a pervert Pastor Diotrephes, an understanding of the historical development of pro-Diotrephes ecclesiological praxis is warranted, for sexual immorality and the philosophy of Pastor Diotrephes are inextricably associated.

Jack Hyles, Hyles-Anderson College, and First Baptist Church of Hammond, Indiana, led a movement which spread a pro-Diotrephes pastoral philosophy through many Baptist churches.[205] Hyles combined this unbiblical, idolatrous philosophy of the head pastor with a corruption of gospel doctrine that denied Biblical repentance[206] and a corruption of evangelistic practice that employed salesmanship techniques to manipulate vast numbers of people to repeat a "sinner's prayer"[207] and then pronounced them regenerate, although 99% or more of them were just as lost as before they were so manipulated.[208] Hyles also seriously corrupted the Person of Christ and the gospel of Christ in other ways.[209] Along with others, the books of Roy L. Branson, Jr.[210] adopted the pro-

Diotrephes pastoral philosophy of Hyles and spread its corruption widely among Baptist pastors and leaders. The introduction to Branson's *Dear Abner*[211] was written by Joe Combs, Branson's pastor at Emmanuel Baptist Church in Bristol, Tennessee, and former head of the Bible department at Hyles-Anderson College.[212] Branson claims that his *Dear Preacher, Please Quit!* was endorsed by W. A. Criswell (who was twice elected as president of the Southern Baptist Convention) as "mandatory reading for every minister," and similarly endorsed by Southern Baptist leader E. J. Daniels, along with independent Baptist leaders such as David Otis Fuller, Baptist Bible Fellowship standard-bearer John Rawlings, Tennessee Temple University president Lee Roberson,[213] *Sword of the Lord* foundation president Curtis Hutson, and "a thousand other … preachers."[214] His books were read by and impacted others, such as the radical KJV-Onlyist Peter Ruckman.[215] Branson's works, such as *Dear Preacher, Please Quit* and *Dear Abner,* were "well received and highly praised," so that his works were "widely circulated[,] with young preachers swallowing [them] hook, line, and sinker."[216] In the shallow evangelistic trajectory of Jack Hyles, Branson believes one can explain the gospel in "twenty seconds to a minute," depending on whether one chooses to quote Scripture (one minute) or not quote any Scripture (twenty seconds), utilizing a presentation that does not mention the Trinity or mention repentance but adds the good work of asking to be saved to faith alone.[217] Branson claims to have had "over a thousand … saved in a single service."[218] However, he also thinks it probable that less than 25% of church members in the kind of Pentecostal, Presbyterian,[219] Southern and Independent Baptist churches where he preaches are saved,[220] while "well over 90 percent of church members" are "carnal, wicked Christians," "wicked, carnal, weak, rebellious, and unseparated," "spiritual incorrigibles."[221] Biblically speaking, those Branson identifies as "carnal Christians" are not really Christians at all,[222] although Branson's aberrant theology would view them as truly born again. If approximately 25% of those in Branson-type congregations are born again (according to Branson), and if 90% of these "Christians" are wicked, rebellious persons with no Biblical evidence of regeneration, then approximately 2.5% of church members in Hyles/Branson-type congregations are genuinely converted.[223]

Shallow evangelistic methods not only result in the vast majority of "converts" from the world never being truly born again, but also in a terribly high percentage of the second-generation in churches with the philosophy of Hyles never being born again. Many youth in Hyles-type churches will just repeat the "sinner's prayer" but never become new creatures, because their parents will sincerely employ the same salesmanship techniques upon their own children that they employ with the rest of the world. Similarly, Southern Baptist leaders admit that "shallow evangelism ... has filled our church rolls with unconverted members."[224] Much "SBC evangelism" really involves: "shallowness, emotional manipulations, and [a] distressing tendency of some SBC churches to baptize younger children, including even preschoolers. Some have described this trend as 'infant baptism with bigger infants.'"[225] Churches full of unregenerate people, lacking the new hearts of the New Covenant (Hebrews 8:8-12) and so dominated by their ungodly lusts, are the fearful result. When these unregenerate people receive the idolatrous preeminence and blind trust inculcated by Hyles' pro-Diotrephes philosophy, rampant sexual immorality among lascivious sons of Diotrephes is fearfully likely.

Pervert Pastors Rise When Blind Followers Cover Sin

However, Branson's pro-Diotrephes philosophy of the pastorate has spread even among those who repudiate the mockery of Biblical evangelism practiced by Jack Hyles and his disciples. For example, Baptist pastor R. L. Hymers, Jr., in two books specifically written to promote careful, Biblical evangelism and repudiate the shallow salesmanship of Hyles and others, nevertheless commends Roy L. Branson's works.[226] Hymers even preached messages such as "Lessons from Dr. Roy Branson" and "More Lessons from Dr. Roy Branson"; these messages (like others by Hymers) were translated into 46 languages. Hymers states: "Dr. Branson's (1) *Dear Preacher, Please Quit* and (2) *Church Split* ... [g]et them and read them! I am once again asking everyone who hears this message to read them all the way through."[227]

Those who repudiate the flagrantly unbiblical pseudo-evangelism of the Hyles movement but retain its Diotrephes-type model of pastoral leadership will not have as many problems, because they have seen through a major part of Hyles' false teaching, but the part that they continue to embrace still opens a dangerous amount of room for ungodly leaders to engage in immorality. By giving church leadership the kind of absolute confidence that pertains properly to Christ alone, pervert Pastors Diotrephes are given the leeway to ensnare and groom congregants and gradually prepare them to commit sexual sin.[228] Among those soft on Diotrephes, the possibility that an associate or head pastor could be a grievous wolf is not something warned about day and night with tears (Acts 20:29-31), but something that is almost inconceivable. Therefore, when a wolf does manage to get into the sheep pen, it can consume one trusting, blindly following wooly meal after another.

The shameful and rampant immorality in Hyles-influenced circles, in accord with the improper actions of Jack Hyles himself, is well-documented.[229] Hyles-influenced, pro-Diotrephes authors like Roy L. Branson, however, argue that "The accusation [against Hyles] should be ignored; Jack Hyles should be treated as if it had never occurred."[230] Branson illustrates his pro-Diotrephes view of the untouchable nature of even a pervert Pastor Diotrephes:

> *"Touch not Mine annointed [sic].[231] ... [P]astors are untouchable men, and we must not forget it. ... Preachers get out of the will of God, too. Leave the disciplining of God's man to God. ... God's preachers are untouchable. ...* ***Even when King Saul had rebelled against God and God had taken His hand off him, he was still untouchable.*** *[Bold in original. Note that Saul was literally committing mass-murder, wiping out entire towns of innocent and godly people, men, women, and children, e. g., 1 Samuel 22.] ... We're saying that if a man of God is out of the will of God, leave him to God to take care of; and believe it, God will take care of him. One may say, "Well, what if he's tearing up our church?" Either live with it or go to another church, but don't ever try to get rid of the preacher. You may be right and the preacher may be wrong, but, if he's*

called of the Lord, that's God's man ... [w]hen you try to do it, you put yourself in the position of Saul's Amalekite. **IN SUMMARY, WE CAN SAY A PREACHER IS CONSIDERED BY GOD TO BE UNTOUCHABLE ...** *[Bold and all caps in original.] ... [H]ow terrible in [God's] eyes is the sin of touching His annointed [sic]. ...*

The author [Branson] had preached on [this subject.] ... During the invitation one night a young woman came weeping to the front and requested counselling after [sic] service.

"You know," she sobbed, "You know!"

I did not know and told her I did not.

"But, [sic] I thought you were preaching at me!"

"That was the Holy Ghost speaking to you through the message. Why don't you tell me what's wrong?" I replied.

She then told me she was having an affair with a well known [sic] local pastor.

Many preachers secretly rejoice at getting such news and hasten to "expose the scoundrel." However, that is the wrong attitude. ...

What did the author do? He prayed with the young woman and she sought and received God's forgiveness. He told no one, not even his wife, about the problem. Leave God's man to God to straighten out.

By the way, the above affair was ended because the young lady got right with God and refused to continue it. [Note: the man continued to pastor as an unrepentant adulterer and was able to continue to prey on others. There was no investigation, nor was the adulterous pastor placed under church discipline and rebuked before all, 1 Timothy 5:20; Matthew 18:15-20.]

Finally, let us be sure we understand that God put no qualifications, no "unless" or "if," on the warning, "Touch not mine annointed [sic] and do my prophets no harm."[232]

Indeed, Branson claims that adulterous pastors need not be removed from the ministry. A "single tryst" is a "temporary aberration," and if one of the Lord's Anointed Ones sins like the adulterous felon and televangelist Jim Bakker, but admits it after he is caught, it is "far worse" to tell others publicly about what happened than to commit the adultery and the felonies; after all, "[n]ext to unbelief, no sin in the Bible is so condemned as gossip." What is adultery when compared to gossip? A pattern of not inviting people into one's home often enough, a pattern of being "inhospitable," is also a greater sin than the "single impropriety" of an act of adultery. Branson continues: "Peter's sin [in Galatians of temporarily not eating with Gentiles] ... was more serious than promiscuity." Since "Peter ..._continued in his ministry as before," despite having committed a sin (allegedly) worse than immorality, immoral preachers should likewise be allowed to continue in their position. "[T]here are no limits given, in reality ... [for] men who are genuinely called of God."[233] It is not surprising that Branson recognizes that for "preachers" (in the circles in which he runs) "adultery ... seems near epidemic," as those who view the pastor as the Lord's Anointed, the "most untouchable of men," have "their [sexual] passions ... inflame[d] ... more than for any other man."[234] Thus, for example, Dave Hyles abused his position to engage in serial immorality with dozens of women, being guilty of statutory rape as he committed immorality with underage girls,[235] and committed regular "adultery with girls from the time he was a teenager." But Jack Hyles and others with his pro-Diotrephes philosophy continually "covered [it] up."[236] Why? For Branson, "if ... wayward woman and girls ... are 'ruined,' it is because they thirsted to be ruined."[237] Perverted sons of Diotrephes are not abusing their power and committing the greater sin, but the women are "often more than equa[l],"[238] bearing the majority of the blame.[239] The introduction to Branson's *Dear Abner* was written by Branson's pastor, Hyles-Anderson College head Joe Combs,[240] concerning whom Sumner notes:

> *Joe and Evangeline Lopez Combs ... adopt[ed] ... a beautiful 4-month old girl. They signed an adoption agreement and took custody of her, naming her Esther Alice Evangeline Combs. ... The Combses made that precious soul their personal slave and subjected her to a life of horror and abuse – physical, mental, emotional and social – one that ended only when she went to authorities in Georgia and told her tale, bringing to termination nearly two decades of horror. ... Accused by siblings of jumping on a bed, Mrs. Combs hurled her against the wall and knocked out two front teeth, which were hurriedly placed back in their sockets and grew oddly spaced and crooked. On one occasion, in a fit of temper, Mrs. Combs threw a shoe at her, hitting her in the head and opening a bloody cut. Evangeline promptly sewed it up with needle and thread, then referred to the scars as "her marks of the beast." ... Esther was treated as a slave for the rest of the family her entire life, told by the Combses that this was God's purpose for her life. When she didn't finish her duties on time, she was beaten. ... Over the years she was burned with a curling iron, beaten with a baseball bat, and tortured in other ways. Altogether, there were 410 scars on the poor girl's body[.] ... While the other children were home schooled, she rarely got to attend. When a baby sitter taught her to write her name, Esther was beaten and ... told ... that Jesus didn't learn to read and write until He was 12 years old, and she shouldn't either. By the way, this [baby sitter] and another sitter testified that they suspected abuse, but were afraid of this highly revered Bible professor. The other girl did report her misgivings to the school president, but no action was taken. (The policy is, you may recall, If I didn't see it, it didn't happen; even if I did see it, I was probably mistaken; and even if I did see it and wasn't mistaken, someone else had to have seen it in*

> *order to confirm that I saw it!) ... As a teenager, Combs bound a rope around her neck, then draped her over his back, cutting off her air supply until she passed out. ... It was also as a teenager that the greatest Bible teacher in Christendom [according to Jack Hyles] raped her repeatedly, usually on church property (where they were living). ... Esther said Mrs. Combs repeatedly pulled chunks of her flesh out with a pair of pliers. ... On at least two occasions Esther ran away from home, not getting far either time and each time brought back by police – when she was severely beaten for her actions. ... Finally ... desperate and unhappy, she decided to end her life by drinking antifreeze. She was found unconscious and rushed by ambulance to an area hospital and the seeds for ending the abuse were planted. Physicians found layers of scar tissue from wounds and fractures than had not healed properly. She had no birth certificate, no school records, no medical records, and no Social Security. ... Joseph Combs was found guilty on 11 counts, namely, charges of especially aggravated kidnapping, aggravated assault, aggravated perjury, aggravated rape, and 7 other counts of rape. ... Evangeline Combs was found guilty on 6 counts, namely, charges of especially aggravated kidnapping, aggravated assault, and 4 counts of aggravated child abuse.*[241]

Sumner concludes: "[T]he full record of the damage done to Christendom and to individual Christians by Hyles and those in his orbit can never even be imagined – to say nothing of being told – this side of the Judgment Seat of Christ![242]

Protection from Perverts:
Separate Over the Gospel and Pro-Diotrephes Doctrine

To protect one's flock from a pervert Diotrephes, pastors should maintain clear lines of ecclesiastical separation from all those who endorse the corrupt anti-repentance gospel, shallow salesmanship for evangelism, and pro-Diotrephes, pro-cover-up philosophies associated with Jack Hyles. The Bible teaches the doctrine and practice of faithful independent Baptist churches,[243] and no Baptist confession of faith has ever endorsed Hyles' anti-repentance gospel heresy, his shallow "sinner's prayer" evangelistic methods, or his idolatrous pro-Diotrephes pastoral philosophy; Hyles' distinctive teachings are completely absent from Baptist confessional life.[244] Churches that adopt such teachings are repudiating their Baptist heritage, repudiating fundamental doctrines of Christianity, and ought to cease calling themselves "Baptist." But whether they do drop the name "Baptist" or not, Christ-exalting Biblical Baptist churches must maintain clear lines of ecclesiastical separation from such compromising religious congregations, for they are neither Biblical, Baptist, nor fundamentalist, even if they improperly insist upon calling themselves independent, fundamental Baptists. "[H]ave no fellowship with the unfruitful works of darkness, but rather reprove *them*" (Ephesians 5:11). When a spiritual leader was deceptively seducing[245] God's "servants to commit fornication," the resurrected Lord Jesus pointedly and specifically warned about this person (Revelation 2:20) in a document that was distributed widely among God's people (Revelation 1:4). It is insufficient to, as Eli, simply address a private reproof to spiritual leaders who are immoral (1 Samuel 2:22)—they must be publicly reproved and stopped when they make themselves vile in this way (1 Samuel 3:13). Marking and avoiding (Romans 16:17) the disobedient religious congregations that follow Jack Hyles and his heresies—along with all other spiritual wolves who cover up sin—is an important, though not in itself sufficient, method to significantly reduce the threat from a pervert Diotrephes.

Hyles' pernicious influence is easily identified if a congregation claims to be independent Baptist, has a doctrinal statement that affirms that the lost must only repent of unbelief, and keeps records of the numbers of people who repeat the "sinner's prayer" which validate that the overwhelming majority of these "converts" are not faithful to church and give no evidence of regeneration. An inquiring Christian can also see if members of church staff are graduates of Hyles-Anderson or affiliated educational institutions and ask if they still agree with the unbiblical doctrinal and practical positions of their *alma mater*. However, churches that repudiate these clear doctrinal and practical corruptions of the gospel may still manifest a pro-Diotrephes pastoral paradigm. Sadly, Hyles' pro-Diotrephes model has spread beyond those who avowedly affiliate with him. Indeed, the fearful corruption of the unregenerate human heart provides more than sufficient material to adopt the anti-Christian pastoral philosophy of Diotrephes—the actual first century Pastor Diotrephes had never read a work by Jack Hyles or Roy Branson. Furthermore, the indwelling sin within even a truly regenerate pastor can improperly hanker for the preeminence that Christ alone deserves. If the secondary sources affirming that Roy L. Branson's books were highly commended by Southern Baptist presidents like Paige Patterson and W. A. Criswell are correct,[246] Branson's pro-Diotrephes pastoral philosophy could have been a significant contributing factor in the hundreds of pervert Pastors Diotrephes who engaged in corrupt practices within the

Southern Baptist Convention.[247] However, even apart from the corrupt pro-Diotrephes influence of men like Hyles and Branson, shallow evangelistic practices and the neglect of Biblical church discipline provide wide avenues to fill Southern Baptist churches with unregenerate individuals who are still enslaved to sin and lust.[248] Furthermore, when pastors demand "blind trust and unquestioning loyalty," they "cultivat[e] the perfect atmosphere for sexual predators."[249] Defending a pure gospel, practicing careful Biblical evangelism, and avoiding those with pro-Diotrephes models of the pastorate are important factors in protecting congregations from perverted Pastors Diotrephes, but of themselves they are not sufficient protection. The Apostle Paul evangelized correctly, held to a pure gospel, and never taught anything like Hyles-Branson nonsense, but still warned that grievous wolves could enter Christ's flock (Acts 20:29-32). What else must be done?

Protection from Perverts: Knowledge is Power

As in all that the church needs for life and godliness, Scripture contains the answers (2 Timothy 3:16-17) for how to avoid a pervert Pastor Diotrephes. The Bible, perfectly balanced, avoids inappropriately graphic detail concerning sexual sin while providing enough information to equip youth and adults about how to "flee fornication" (1 Corinthians 6:18). Parents and pastors should recognize that those who are "young and tenderhearted" can have difficulty strengthening themselves to resist[250] sons of Belial (2 Chronicles 13:7) who may be filthy perverts (Judges 19:22), and should exert their utmost care to protect youth from such children of the devil. Part of that care includes teaching children the passages of Scripture that warn about immoral sexual activity. Parents must not avoid such texts out of a misplaced sense of over-protectiveness and prudishness, and so leave their young people unprepared for the snares of a pervert Diotrephes or other whoremongers. Not just adults, but also "children" must "hear" and "observe to do all the words of [God's] law" (Deuteronomy 31:12). Youth need to know the commands of Leviticus 18:

> *6 None of you shall approach to any that is near of kin to him, to uncover their nakedness: I am the LORD. [Many specific examples follow.] ... 22 Thou shalt not lie with mankind, as with womankind: it is abomination. ... 24 Defile not ye yourselves in any of these things: for in all these the nations are defiled which I cast out before you: 25 And the land is defiled: therefore I do visit the iniquity thereof upon it, and the land itself vomiteth out her inhabitants. 26 Ye shall therefore keep my statutes and my judgments, and shall not commit any of these abominations; neither any of your own nation, nor any stranger that sojourneth among you: 27 (For all these abominations have the men of the land done, which were before you, and the land is defiled;) 28 That the land spue not you out also, when ye defile it, as it spued out the nations that were before you. 29 For whosoever shall commit any of these abominations, even the souls that commit them shall be cut off from among their people. 30 Therefore shall ye keep mine ordinance, that ye commit not any one of these abominable customs, which were committed before you, and that ye defile not yourselves therein: I am the LORD your God.*

There is nothing inappropriate about children knowing that it is abominable to God to uncover the nakedness of others as described in this chapter, and that to do such a wicked thing makes those who engage in this activity worthy of being "cut off" or executed.[251] They should know that these strictures apply to "whosoever"—no exception is listed for trusted authority figures. Children are not defiled by knowing that God hates what Leviticus 18 describes. Children are defiled when, unprepared to resist such abominations because their parents and pastors withheld God's Word from them, they are abused by a pervert Diotrephes who commits filthy crimes with them.

Young people should know that within the one-flesh relationship of holy matrimony there is nothing shameful about a husband and wife being together naked (Genesis 2:23-25), for matrimony is honorable and the marriage bed undefiled (Hebrews 13:4); this relationship in the marriage bed results in children being conceived (Genesis 1:26-28). In matrimony a man goes in unto a woman with emission of seed that is received by the woman, sometimes resulting in the bearing of children.[252] This is God's good gift in marriage: but outside of marriage, "whoremongers and adulterers God will judge" (Hebrews 13:4). Outside of marriage, seeing the nakedness of another, or "lying carnally" (Leviticus 18:20; 19:20; Numbers 5:13)[253] with someone, is a great sin. Young people should know that they must not secretly look at someone who is naked or allow someone else to look at them when they are naked (2 Samuel 11:2), for this puts them in grave danger for further sexual sin (2 Samuel 11:2-4). Children should know that if an authority figure, even one well known to them, makes a sexual proposition, then they must refuse (Genesis 39:7), run away (Genesis 39:12) or in any other way get away (Genesis 19:10) and stay away (Genesis 39:10), saying, "[H]ow then can I do this great wickedness, and sin against God?" (Genesis 39:9). They should know that it is a grievous sin to behold the nakedness of an authority figure.[254] While the authority figure initiating the immorality has by far the greater sin, if youth permit him to get his way without resistance, they are also committing serious iniquity.[255] They must scream with a loud voice (Genesis 39:14-15). If they cannot immediately run away, they must fight back, as they would fight if someone were trying to kill them.[256] If they do not scream loudly and resist, they are consenting to this great sin (Deuteronomy 22:24, 27). They should know that while there is great joy in the physical aspects of marriage, if a wicked person plots to lie carnally with them and succeeds in his evil design, they will feel great "shame," will not be able to stop crying, and will have been harmed in a similar way to someone who is murdered (2 Samuel 13:1-19), for "as when a man riseth against his neighbour, and slayeth him, even so *is* this matter" (Deuteronomy 22:26); furthermore, the criminal deserves to be put to death (Deuteronomy 22:25). They should know that God rained fire and brimstone on Sodom for its homosexuality (Genesis 19) and that sodomites are disproportionally likely to rape others (Genesis 19:4-5). They should know that seductive people can employ seductive words as sweet-sounding as honey (Proverbs 5:3), but their "end is bitter as wormwood, sharp as a twoedged sword. [Their] feet go down to death; [their] steps take hold on hell" (Proverbs 5:4-5). Young people must listen to Scripture's wisdom from their godly parents (Proverbs 5:1, 7) rather than whatever sweetly deceptive poison-speech seducers give for why their violations of Scripture's teaching are really acceptable. Children must know age-appropriate information about what God has revealed about both the good gift of sexuality within marriage, its devilish distortion in sinful lust, and what wicked people will do as they seek to use others for their own ungodly and illicit pleasure.[257]

Proverbs contains sobering warnings—directed specifically to youth—about the danger from the strange, the heathen, the immoral woman: "Hear me now therefore, O ye children, and depart not from the words of my mouth. Remove thy way far from her, and come not nigh the door of her house" (Proverbs 5:7-8). Solomon specifically warned his son about the immoral woman who "cover[s] her lust with a religious motivation"[258] (Proverbs 7:14-16). Scripture likewise warns about "sodomites" who wanted to hang around and seduce by the "house of the LORD" (2 Kings 23:7). Young people should be instructed to delight in the large majority of people in faithful churches who have genuine spirituality and piety while also being aware that wolves may creep into the sheep-pen.

Protection from Perverts: Preserve Clear Boundaries

Furthermore, all Christians must not only flee from sexual immorality, but stay far away from the possibility of committing it. To "abstain from all appearance of evil" (1 Thessalonians 5:23)[259] is an important means through which the God of peace sanctifies His people and preserves them blameless (1 Thessalonians 5:24). Believers must avoid the appearance of impropriety and "giv[e] no offence in any thing, that the ministry be not blamed" (2 Corinthians 6:3). The wise man fears evil and turns far away from it (Job 28:8; Proverbs 14:16), keeping himself far away from falsehood and sin (Exodus 23:7). Scripture states:

"It is good for a man not to touch a woman" (1 Corinthians 7:1).[260] In general and among non-relatives, men and women should avoid physical contact with one another, or at least any possible contact that could cause stumbling or offence. Unfiltered, unmonitored electronic devices should be completely forbidden.[261] Christian leaders, churches as a whole, and individual believers should all maintain appropriate safeguards. Shiflett notes:

> *[If you] see something, say something. ... [If you see] things that constitut[e] a red flag ... respon[d] accordingly[.] ... Sexual predators have a specific and unique approach. ... They cultivate the respect and awe of their victims. They also groom the parents in many cases to build trust and cover their tracks. ... [Use] security cameras ... their existence is a tremendous deterrent. ... [They] have the capability to ... catch the perverts, and clear the innocent. ... [C]reate an atmosphere of transparency. ... One of the greatest deterrents to sexual abuse in the church is an environment of transparency. ... Any pastor or church leader who shies away from transparency may have something to hide. ... [This includes] transparency ... in financial reporting. ... I have found an astonishing correlation in men who have a sense of entitlement in the area of money, and a sense of entitlement in the area of sexual fulfillment. ... [E]ncourag[e] children and teenagers to tell someone if they are abused. Encouraging this type of environment will in itself be a deterrent. [Perverts] will not hang around a church where the victims are encouraged to speak out. ...*
>
> *Anyone who volunteers to serve in any area of ministry involving children should be required to submit to initial and subsequent periodic background checks. ... A person with any kind of sex crimes in his past [should be] banned from working with children at ... church. ... [A] man [should] not be with someone else's child alone[.] ... [Do] not travel alone in a vehicle with a member of the opposite sex ... the opportunities for temptation are too*

> *great. Furthermore, it is impossible to defend [one]self against a false accusation. ... [E]liminate the opportunity to sin [as much as possible]. ... [A] woman who communicates with [the pastor should be required to] include [his] wife in the text. ... Under no circumstances should [the pastor] take a woman or girl into a room and close the door ... [or] counsel ... a woman ... alone anywhere ... [or] talk to a woman [having marriage difficulties] about her marriage without [his] wife in the room under any circumstances. ... Sometimes, women feel that no one but their pastor can help them. ... [However,] Titus 2:4-5 admonishes the older women to teach the younger women. The older women are encouraged to help the younger women with their marriage and parenting, among other things. ... [A pastor or other Christian leader man must not] get too comfortable with an emotional and vulnerable woman.*[262]

God promises: "There hath no temptation taken you but such as is common to man: but God *is* faithful, who will not suffer you to be tempted above that ye are able; but will with the temptation also make a way to escape, that ye may be able to bear *it*" (1 Corinthians 10:13). God certainly does not cause His people to enter situations where irresistibly overpowering temptation exists. However, they may encounter such when they fail to "escape" from temptation (1 Corinthains 10:13) and "flee" from it (1 Corinthians 10:14).[263] Strong safeguards are one of the best ways both churches and individual Christians avoid sexual immorality.

Protection from Perverts: Put Policies in Writing

A church constitution should outline procedures for all cases of church discipline, both protecting the large majority of godly pastors from false accusations and impelling the removal of the minority of Diotrephes-wolves in all their manifestations. Churches could include statements such as the following:

> *At [Church Name,] we recognize that the large majority of Bible-believing Baptist pastors are godly men who must be esteemed very highly in love (1 Thessalonians 5:13), followed as they follow Christ (1 Corinthians 11:1), and their leadership obeyed as they call the saints to obedience to the Word of God (Hebrews 13:7, 17). However, as Christ had one Judas among His eleven righteous apostles, so Scripture warns that wolves can infiltrate a flock and even find their way into leadership positions (Acts 20:29-31; 3 John 9-11). Matthew 18:15-17 and 1 Timothy 5:19-21 outline the procedure that must be followed in case of an accusation of misconduct by a pastor or other church leader.*
>
> *First, God commands: "Against an elder receive not an accusation, but before two or three witnesses" (1 Timothy 5:19). Scripture emphasizes the requirement of multiple witnesses before the receipt of any accusation for all people (Deuteronomy 17:6; 19:15-20), and this requirement is emphasized for accusations against elders. Witnesses include both personal eyewitness and other types of witness (Genesis 21:30; 31:46-48; Exodus 22:13), such as written or video documentation. Elders, like all Christians, receive a presumption of innocence (1 Corinthians 13:5). To intentionally falsely accuse an elder is a serious sin worthy of bringing upon the false witness whatever punishment he sought against the church leader falsely accused (Deuteronomy 19:15-20).*
>
> *Second, Scripture requires "diligent inquisition" into credible accusations (Deuteronomy 19:18), including accusations against elders. Elders must not be improperly*

presumed guilty, nor must they receive preferential treatment that allows them to hide their sins. The same standard is applied to them as to any other accused person in the congregation: "I charge thee before God, and the Lord Jesus Christ, and the elect angels, that thou observe these things without preferring one before another, doing nothing by partiality" (1 Timothy 5:21).

Third, if multiple witnesses prove that an elder is guilty of a sin that disqualifies him from his office (1 Timothy 3:1-7; Titus 1:6-9), the congregation will not allow him to continue in that role. If he is guilty of a sin that warrants church discipline, he will be placed under discipline like any other person, following the procedures described elsewhere in this constitution. Those found guilty of sins that deserve church discipline will be "rebuke[d] before all, that others also may fear" (1 Timothy 5:20), for Scripture values light and transparency, not cover-ups and darkness (John 3:19-21).

Any person, including a pastor, who attempts to cast another person out of the church without following the steps mandated in Matthew 18:15-17 for most offences or 1 Corinthians 5 for known, public and scandalous sin, is himself committing serious sin worthy of church discipline (3 John 9-11).

Scripture likewise warns that Satan may on occasion succeed in placing vile persons who wish to seduce God's people into immoral acts into the membership or even the leadership of a church (Revelation 2:20). To protect our congregation from such wickedness, and to maintain a godly testimony before the saints and before the world, all church staff (paid and volunteer), particularly those working with minors or vulnerable adults, must submit to a thorough background check, including criminal and sex offender registry searches. Also, no adult other than a child's parent or guardian shall be alone with a minor or vulnerable person during any church-sponsored activity. At least two screened adults must be present at all times.

All allegations or suspicions of abuse shall be taken seriously and reported immediately to civil authorities as

> *required by law, reported to appropriate church personnel, and be the subject of "diligent inquisition" (Deuteronomy 19:18) to clear the innocent and uncover the guilty. The church will cooperate with civil authorities in investigating credible accusations of abuse, and will support legal civil sanctions (Romans 13:4) as well as church discipline and public rebuke for such wickedness (1 Timothy 5:20). Any individual found to have engaged in sexual abuse or misconduct will be immediately removed from his or her position, reported to law enforcement, and permanently disqualified from any position of leadership or trust in the church. Because children are a heritage from the Lord, they must be absolutely protected within the church from any form of abuse or molestation. The church has zero tolerance for any person, whether paid staff, volunteer, member, or visitor, who abuses or molests a child (Psalm 127:3-5; Matthew 18:6; 19:14; Mark 10:14). The church shall maintain secure records of background checks, training certifications, and reports and actions taken regarding abuse allegations.*
>
> *Any attempt at restoration for perpetrators of abuse who profess repentance and give clear and consistent evidence thereof shall only be pursued under strict oversight and never involve return to positions involving minors or vulnerable adults.*

Church constitutions must be doctrinally sound and Biblically, practically principled. Church members must know what their constitutions say. A church constitution that contains procedures for dealing with Diotrephes, including a pervert Diotrephes, provides significant protection from the depredations of that wolf. Strong, preemptive defenses help protect a territory from being attacked by an enemy army in the first place (2 Chronicles 11:5-12, 17). A pervert Diotrephes is likely to seek other sheep to prey upon when he discovers that a congregation is a strong-walled fortress rather than an unwalled and unguarded pasture.

Protection from Perverts: Love Jesus Christ

Even more crucial than installing safeguards is knowing, loving, and exalting Christ.[264] The book of Proverbs presents Jesus Christ as God's Personal Wisdom.[265] Young people, who are born as "simple" sinners,[266] must embrace Christ, who calls to them at the entry to the city (Proverbs 8:3), and so become "wise" before they enter the city and hear the seductive siren-song of the temptress. If they fail to embrace Christ and instead embrace the strange woman, they are in fearful danger of never coming to true conversion: "None that go unto her return again, neither take they hold of the paths of life" (Proverbs 2:19). To protect them from perverted sons of Diotrephes, and all other peddlers of fleshly lust, young people must embrace Christ and become truly wise as soon as possible. Both youth and adults must have a vibrant, growing fellowship with and love for Jesus Christ. More love for Christ, and more genuine delight in Him, means less love for all idolatrous and adulterous substitutes that vie for His preeminence in the human heart. Why do perverted sons of Diotrephes multiply in congregations that substitute cheap salesmanship for Biblical evangelism? The lack of careful, Biblical evangelism fills churches with unconverted people who do not know Christ. Why do man-exalting, man-centered ministries fall prey to pervert-Pastors Diotrephes? They give the "big man" the submission, affection, and absolute trust that is the sole prerogative of Jesus Christ. This is idolatry and spiritual adultery. It is often associated with physical adultery (Ezekiel 23:37).

VII.) WHAT SHOULD A PASTOR DO IF HE SUSPECTS A CO-PASTOR IS DIOTREPHES?

Potential Co-Pastor Diotrephes? Think the Best

The large majority of pastors are not Diotrephes but humble and godly, although imperfect, men. Christ had His Judas, but the eleven other apostles sincerely loved Him, and almost all of them died as martyrs for His sake.[267] Paul had his Alexander the coppersmith (2 Timothy 4:14), but he also had many faithful coworkers and co-laborers. Love "is not easily provoked, thinketh no evil; rejoiceth not in iniquity, but rejoiceth in the truth; beareth all things, believeth all things, hopeth all things, endureth all things" (1 Corinthians 13:4-7). You should be strongly biased toward assuming your co-pastor is *not* a Diotrephes. Differences in personality are far from meaning that a co-pastor is Diotrephes—the Apostles Peter and John had different personalities, with Peter more easily acting and speaking impetuously,[268] but both sincerely loved Christ. Godly pastors have many false and slanderous accusations made against them.[269] Nor are godly pastors sinless pastors—there are holy requirements for the holy pastoral office (1 Timothy 3; Titus 1), but sinlessness is not one of them. Scripture provides the correct balance:

> *Against an elder receive not an accusation, but before two or three witnesses. Them that sin rebuke before all, that others also may fear. I charge thee before God, and the Lord Jesus Christ, and the elect angels, that thou observe these things without preferring one before another, doing nothing by partiality. Lay hands suddenly on no man, neither be partaker of other men's sins: keep thyself pure. ... Some men's sins are open beforehand, going before to judgment; and some men they follow after. Likewise also the good works of some are manifest beforehand; and they that are otherwise cannot be hid.* (1 Timothy 5:19-25)

While no accusation should be received as true against any Christian, not just pastors, apart from multiple witnesses, Scripture reiterates this requirement for accusations against elders—unproven accusations against them must certainly not be received.[270] However, accusations with sufficient evidence must also be received, not rejected. The importance of impartiality—neither having improper bias for or against those bringing accusations, or for or against those accused—is emphasized by Paul's charge before Jesus Christ, who is God and Lord, and the elect angels.[271] You must think the best of every fellow Christian, and certainly must do so of a brother pastor. At the same time, Pastor Diotrephes will distort the Biblical requirements for an accusation into a standard that makes it impossible for him to be found guilty for any sin.[272]

When your fellow pastor is a holy, merciful, loving, forbearing, humble, and forgiving man, one who is open and honest, who has a sensitive conscience toward truth himself and honors the consciences of others, one who is bold for truth, one who does not cover his sins but confesses and forsakes them, and one who strengthens the weak, heals the sick, binds up the broken-hearted, brings again those driven away, seeks for the lost, and leads them with tender care and compassion (Ezekiel 34:4), you have no need to fear he is Diotrephes—he is a righteous servant of Jesus Christ. Do not apply an impossibly high standard of perfection to him that you would fail yourself, and which the apostles would fail, in order to falsely accuse him of being Diotrephes. Instead, rejoice at the wonderful blessing that Christ has given your church and go forward together in faith for the glory of God.

Potential Co-Pastor Diotrephes? Reasons for Concern

If, on the other hand, he has a truth-telling problem (3 John 10; Jeremiah 29:23), and you find out that he is using deceit to cover sin he has committed (2 Corinthians 11:13), acting with craftiness and cunning to hide wrongdoing (Ephesians 4:22), then you have reason for concern. The righteous have "renounced the hidden things of dishonesty, not walking in craftiness, nor handling the word of God deceitfully; but by manifestation of the truth commending [them]selves to every man's conscience in the sight of God" (2 Corinthians 4:2). Anyone can accidentally misstate or misunderstand something, and righteous people can even on occasion sinfully fail to tell the truth out of fear (Genesis 18:15; Matthew 26:69-75), but Diotrephes' lack of love for truth in his heart manifests itself in a pattern of truth-distortion—and Pastor Diotrephes' exaggerations and misstatements somehow seem to always tend either to make himself look better[273] or to make his enemies look worse.

Pastor Diotrephes may accuse others in order to cast them out, but a little scrutiny reveals that his accusations are false and inaccurate, collapsing under investigation. He is likely to want you to simply trust his accusations of others without any verification, while also trusting that he is innocent of any wrongdoing—including financial or lustful wrongdoing—without any need to investigate. The canonical context of the Johannine epistles[274] indicates that Diotrephes is one of the spirits Scripture requires Christians to "try" or "test." While Diotrephes wants you to just blindly believe and follow him, Scripture commands you to "make a critical examination ... to determine genuineness, put to the test, [and] examine" his life and teaching, and then "to draw a conclusion ... on the basis of testing."[275] Diotrephes wants your mindless trust, but God commands: "believe not ... but try" (1 John 4:1). Scripture repeatedly commands the entire church to "judge" with Scripture the preaching and practice of their leaders;[276] therefore the righteous overseer similarly commands: "judge ye what I say,"[277] not "blindly follow what I say." A godly pastor will pass the Scriptural test, and will encourage your obedience to these commands of Christ your common Lord. But Pastor Diotrephes, fearing what obeying 1 John 4:1 will uncover, discourages and takes offense at practicing its inspired mandate. The righteous elder wants you to believe God first, and then believe him after you verify his life and doctrine with God's word; the unrighteous elder demands that you mindlessly follow him. Godly shepherds want the sheep to use their Bible's wolf-detector test. The wolves have a different opinion.

Diotrephes may seek to manipulate your commendable desire to have unity among church leaders into a mandate that you violate 1 Timothy 5:21. He may claim that you know he has a good heart,[278] and therefore he could not possibly be guilty of what he is credibly accused of doing. He may claim that he has special "Divine insight ... special knowledge, [and] peculiar leadership of the Spirit"[279] by virtue of his office, so that other pastors—and certainly mere members of the congregation—must simply trust and follow what he says about casting out others without verification.[280] He may make such claims, not only for his practical advice, but even for his interpretations of Scripture, taking offence when questioned politely about what he claims the Bible teaches.[281] Denying in practice the individual priesthood of the believer, Diotrephes may believe that he must be preeminent in all Scriptural interpretation by members of his church; the words of the apostles must be filtered through him, not understood directly by every church member through the illumination of the Holy Spirit (3 John 9).[282] He may affirm that people are not encouraged to study the Bible independently; rather, the pastor studies the Bible and the rest of the congregation follows along. He may claim that one is supposed to just trust, not verify with Scripture in either English or the original languages, what he preaches and teaches. While anyone can commit the serious sin of misinterpreting Scripture, Diotrephes may also regularly say strange things[283] that just are not in the passages he references. While the Bible holds pastors to a higher standard (1 Timothy 3), Pastor Diotrephes wants anyone who crosses him judged very harshly while he himself is held to a much lower bar. He can berate, misrepresent, and falsely accuse—but this is fine, because he is the pastor. Yet if someone else treated him anywhere close to the way he treats others (which should not be done, because railing accusations[284] or abusive speech should not be employed even against Satan, Jude 9, and therefore not even against Diotrephes), he would have that person run out of church immediately. Diotrephes may be implacable—unwilling to reconcile, bringing up old offences that others have already repented of and received forgiveness for—and quick to unmercifully cast others out (Romans 1:31). Rather than exercising himself "to have always a conscience void of offence toward God, and toward men" (Acts 24:16), he may engage in actions that would trouble your conscience were you to do them while putting pressure on members of the congregation to violate their consciences.

If a co-pastor or head pastor distorts 1 Timothy 5:19-25[285] into a standard that would allow him to get away with just about any sin, you have a problem. A church member who has concerns about your co-pastor, has attempted but failed to resolve them with him privately, and then humbly brings those concerns to you for help, is not violating 1 Timothy 5:19.[286] If what the church member says is either slander or something that cannot be verified, then his claims must not be received as true, and if the member is either knowingly inventing falsehoods or repeating falsehoods that he could easily have known were false, he is sinning, and you should counsel him to repent of such sin. But if his concerns about the sin of your fellow-pastor involve reputable testimony from multiple witnesses, you cannot just dismiss it out of hand or refuse to listen and impartially investigate. Nor can you insist that only two or three living people are witnesses, refusing to consider hand written, recorded, or other sorts of non-living witnesses.[287] An email sent by one person to another has two witnesses to it—the sender and the one to whom it is sent.[288] A video recording substantiating a sin is a witness. Scripture employs the word "witness" for verbal testimony from eyewitnesses (Ruth 4:9), but not only for such witnesses: a heap of stones, a pillar, seven lambs, an altar, an animal carcass, physical facial features, necessary inferences from phenomena in nature, a written document, and improperly obtained wealth are all among what God designates as "witnesses."[289] If there are multiple, reliable witnesses to sin, that sin must be investigated and dealt with impartially. You cannot fail to obey 1 Timothy 5 out of fear, out of laziness, out of sympathy for Diotrephes' doctrine, partiality to the accused, ties by blood or by marriage, a desire for job security, or for any other reason. Not only the person bringing the verifiable evidence, but also God the Father, the Lord Jesus Christ, the Spirit of truth, and every member of the vast host of the elect angels call on you to act. You must—and must do so impartially, not with a bias in favor of (or against) your co-pastor (1 Timothy 5:21) other than the presumption of innocence due to anyone who is accused (1 Corinthians 13:5-7).

Potential Co-Pastor Diotrephes? Clear Evidence of a Wolf

The clearest evidence that a co-pastor is Diotrephes is if, while demanding an impossibly high bar of evidence to receive any accusation against himself, he fabricates accusations against godly members of your congregation in order to maintain his preeminence and cast them out, distorting Matthew 18:15-17 in order to accomplish his sinful goals. If a fellow-pastor tells you that a member of the congregation deserves to be excommunicated, the process of Matthew 18:15-17 must be scrupulously followed. An elder who seeks to cast out a church member based merely on his own authority, or who is willing to have a small number of hand-picked people, to whom he unilaterally spoon-feeds information and then discovers, lo, they agree with him that a sheep must be cast out, but refuses to allow the accused person a trial before the congregation, or who places his thumb heavily on the scale, refusing to allow a fair trial, so that even the secular, heathen courts would indicate that his meddling would necessitate a mistrial and that the accused is not guilty beyond reasonable doubt (cf. Acts 25:16), gives strong evidence that he is truly Diotrephes.

Thankfully, the large majority of head pastors in Biblical churches are not Diotrephes—but if some crept into the pastorate in even the apostolic era, you would be foolish to think that Satan does not work to bring them in today, when a Diotrephes in a pastoral position can cause such tremendous harm. The idea that a co-pastor may be Diotrephes may seem so horrible to contemplate that you may wish to just push it out of your mind, setting aside clear evidence that it is indeed the case—but if the evidence is there, you must not do so. You cannot, you must not, shut your eyes to compelling evidence and by refusing to investigate, pretend that Pastor Diotrephes is one of Christ's godly under-shepherds. Do not be an unfaithful watchman who shuts his eyes and remains in blind ignorance so that he may enjoy a nice nap—until the enemy comes in and kills those he was duty-bound to guard and warn (Isaiah 56:10).

Co-Pastor Diotrephes? Your Duty and Danger

You should also be clear-headed about the consequences of opposing Diotrephes. Godly pastors should be strongly defended and supported, but Pastor Diotrephes must be removed from his office and placed under church discipline. After a genuinely fair trial and after "diligent inquisition"—allowing Diotrephes the presumption of innocence due to anyone on trial—one who seeks to cast out righteous sheep from Christ's church by intentional deceit and false witness deserves to be excommunicated himself:

> *If a false witness rise up against any man to testify against him that which is wrong; Then both the men, between whom the controversy is, shall stand before the LORD, before the priests and the judges, which shall be in those days; And the judges shall make diligent inquisition: and, behold, if the witness be a false witness, and hath testified falsely against his brother; Then shall ye do unto him, as he had thought to have done unto his brother: so shalt thou put the evil away from among you. And those which remain shall hear, and fear, and shall henceforth commit no more any such evil among you. And thine eye shall not pity; but life shall go for life, eye for eye, tooth for tooth, hand for hand, foot for foot. (Deuteronomy 19:16-21)*

Diotrephes must neither be allowed to pastor in your church, nor be allowed to have his sins at your congregation covered up so that he can leave to prey on another church without any warning from you. You must not only remove the wolf from your sheepfold but do what you can to prevent the wolf from destroying your Lord's flocks in other places. Diotrephes' mouth must be stopped (Titus 1:11); his influence over others must be removed. The great Head of the church, Jesus Christ, who is God and Lord, as well as all the armies of holy angels, compel you to rebuke Diotrephes before all: "Them that sin rebuke before all, that others also may fear. I charge thee before God, and the Lord Jesus Christ, and the elect angels, that thou observe these things without preferring one before another, doing nothing by partiality" (1 Timothy 5:20-21). Diotrephes must be removed from the pastorate and placed under church discipline. If he repents of his sin and is born again, manifesting clear fruit of conversion over a significant period of time, then he can be allowed to become a member of Christ's church. Churches must be extremely careful before ever allowing any kind of Diotrephes back into the pastoral office; a pervert Diotrephes who abused his position of authority to commit adultery or other serious sexual sin is no longer "blameless" and is permanently barred from the office of a bishop (1 Timothy 3:2; Proverbs 6:33). That is the course of action that God the Father, the Lord Jesus Christ, the Holy Spirit who inspired the pastoral epistles, and all the elect angels call upon you to pursue. The fallen angels? They disagree—they want Pastor Diotrephes to stay in the pastorate, or if he leaves, to be back in it; the sooner, the better.

While your duty is clear, be aware that it is far from certain that you will be successful—from the perspective of this world—if you resist Diotrephes. Pastor Diotrephes will try to cast you out, too. He will use all the extensive powers of persuasion and trust that he has on account of his pastoral position to take away your office, take away your livelihood, harm your family, destroy your reputation, manipulate your psyche, and eliminate all your opportunities for service in God's work. Like Satan and the Antichrist, he wants preeminence, and he will destroy anyone or anything to grasp and maintain his grasp upon it. If you resist him, he will do everything he can to destroy you. He is willing to cheat and swindle, to lie and deceive,[290] to play dirty in order to win—and (from the perspective of this world) win he may. Judas turned the other apostles against a very godly woman (Matthew 26:6-13; John 12:4-6). False teachers were convincing enough to persuade people who were "devout and honourable" to be stirred up[291] against the apostles and support their being cast out (Acts 13:50). False teachers with plausible-sounding words were able to even (temporarily) lead godly Peter and Barnabas astray (Galatians 2:11-13).

Diotrephes may be able to deceive some of the truly godly to support his dissimulating hypocrisy, turning them against you. It can be shocking and disheartening to see someone who has been a Barnabas, a "son of consolation" to you and a spiritual guide and mentor (Acts 4:36), perhaps another co-pastor whom you deeply respect, led away by the hypocritical deceit of a Diotrephes (Galatians 2:13). But remember that some of God's servants, when they sacrificed all to live by faith, experienced great rewards even in this life; but others, similarly full of faith, were sawn asunder, tortured, and tormented, receiving persecution and suffering until their painful death (Hebrews 11). They also have their reward, for eternity is coming!

Commit yourself to Him who judgeth righteously (1 Peter 2:23). Do not cast your eye in fear upon Diotrephes with his power, position, and willingness to use them—cast your eyes in faith upon God your Father, Christ your Savior, the Spirit your helper, and the Word your guide. The power of Pastor Diotrephes is as nothing compared to that of God and of His holy angels, all of whom require you to act justly and without partiality. God swears that He will allow nothing in your life that is not for His glory and your good (Romans 8:28-39). Diotrephes may take a great deal from you if you do right. Satan took everything from Job—his property, his children, his health—except what is most important—Job's Redeemer, who could never be taken away, and whom Job refused to deny, no matter the cost: "For I know *that* my redeemer liveth, and *that* he shall stand at the latter *day* upon the earth: And *though* after my skin *worms* destroy this *body*, yet in my flesh shall I see God: Whom I shall see for myself, and mine eyes shall behold, and not another; *though* my reins be consumed within me" (Job 19:25-27).

If the Lord, in His sovereignty, permits Diotrephes to creep into your church unawares, and then calls on you to oppose him, you may face the most difficult trial of your entire Christian life. Settle in your heart now—before facing such a situation—what you will do. Decide now that you will strive to be on the same page and support your head pastor when—as the large majority are—he is a godly man. But if he turns out to be Diotrephes, decide now that you will support God and His Word, no matter the cost. Consider the seriousness of church discipline. It is the most serious act of judgment any of Christ's true churches can enact, and it results in the person placed under legitimate discipline being delivered to Satan (1 Corinthians 5:5; 1 Timothy 1:20)—a fate, for the godly, that is worse than physical death. When a sinner deserves excommunication, you must support it, out of love for Christ and for the sinning person. But if it is not justified, and the accused person cannot be proven guilty beyond a reasonable doubt after an impartial examination of all the necessary evidence, you cannot and must not support it.

Do not abdicate your responsibility by saying "it is a church decision, and so I will just go along with whatever the church decides," and then just let Diotrephes manipulate and deceive the flock. Roman Catholicism is not true[292] and the church is not infallible—Scripture is infallible. Furthermore, if you are one of the "two or three" witnesses of Matthew 18:16—as assistant pastors frequently are—you have a Biblical responsibility not just to go along, but to take a lead in both condemning the guilty and acquitting the innocent (Deuteronomy 17:7; John 8:7). If you have clear evidence of guilt beyond a reasonable doubt, you must speak up and encourage the church to cast out the unrepentant and flagrant sinner. If you do not, you must speak up and warn the church that they cannot and must not cast out someone not proven guilty. In either case, you cannot just coast along and follow the decision made by those who have less knowledge of the situation than you do.

You must use your position as an overseer to guide God's people towards making the correct decision. All Christians must obey John 7:24: "Judge not according to the appearance, but judge righteous judgment." How much the more must pastors? All Christians must obey Exodus 23:1-2: "Thou shalt not raise a false report: put not thine hand with the wicked to be an unrighteous witness. Thou shalt not follow a multitude to *do* evil; neither shalt thou speak in a cause to decline after many to wrest *judgment*." How much the more must pastors? If Diotrephes raises a false report, you cannot repeat it; you cannot raise your hand to agree to convict[293] a righteous person, but must raise your hand to vote against such a sin, even if you are going against a multitude that is following Diotrephes to countenance an evil action and twisting righteous judgment. If the other pastors of a church abdicate their responsibility or refuse to oppose Pastor Diotrephes, it is highly unlikely that any opposition of ordinary church members will be successful. Therefore, by just silently going along, you will be contributing to your church's loss of its candlestick or lampstand—if you are a silent watchdog who does not bark (Isaiah 56:10), you will, to keep the Diotrephes whom you see happy, lose the spiritual presence of the holy Christ whom you cannot now see (Revelation 1; Isaiah 56:10)—but will see one day. If Diotrephes is able to deceive other saints into supporting his casting out of a righteous person, you must lift your voice in protest against this egregious sin, this attempted soul-manslaughter, and the subsequent murder of a righteous person's reputation and ministry which Diotrephes will surely enact after he succeeds in casting him out. You must use the weight of trust and authority which Christ has entrusted to you in the pastoral office for what is holy, just, and true. Paul spoke up when Peter and Barnabas were deceived by false teachers (Galatians 2). You must speak up when Diotrephes is deceiving the saints. While the result of your speaking up must be left in the hands of God, who does not guarantee that you will succeed in leading the church to follow Christ and Scripture against Diotrephes, you also should not despair. Paul, during his personal time at Ephesus, was successful in keeping wolves out of the pastoral office (Acts 20:29-31)—God may bless your faithfulness to His Word, and you may be able to either keep Diotrephes from ever coming to your church (which is far better) or have him removed if he is able to creep in unawares (which is much harder, but absolutely necessary). You must also beware lest you also be deceived. You are not better than the eleven apostles, who were deceived by Judas. Do not let Pastor Diotrephes' persuasive words, manipulation, pressure tactics, and psychological warfare cause you to fall from your own stedfastness (2 Peter 3:17), but cleave to and rest on Christ, and follow His Word, and His Word alone. It may be very, very hard, but on judgment day—and probably far before then, even in this life—you will look back and thank God that, by His grace, you did what was right, with a pure conscience and with no regrets.

Furthermore, if you realize, after the fact, that your church has improperly cast out a righteous sheep under the influence of Diotrephes' deception, you must use all your influence in the church to guide it to repent of this sin. Simply deciding that you will do no such thing a second time is insufficient. While private sin can be simply confessed to God and repented of privately, public sin must be repented of publicly. Could publicly admitting that a church pastor, or the church as a body, grievously erred cause short-term harm to the reputation of the congregation? Perhaps—but it will please God. Perhaps Pastor Diotrephes' sin pushed the person he cast out to inappropriately lash out. If both the church and the person cast out sinned, you must lead the church to confess its sin, regardless of the future course pursued by the person who was cast out. Do you want to be highly esteemed in God's eyes, or in the eyes of other fragile fleshly men, who will soon pass away?

VIII.) WHAT SHOULD A CHURCH MEMBER DO IF HE SUSPECTS HIS PASTOR IS DIOTREPHES?

Is My Pastor Diotrephes? Think the Best

What should a church member do if he suspects one of his pastors is Diotrephes? First, he should be strongly inclined to assume his pastor is *not* Diotrephes.[294] Church members must "esteem" their pastors "very highly in love for their work's sake" (1 Thessalonians 5:13), and that sort of love includes thinking no evil and hoping and believing the best of the one loved (1 Corinthians 13:4-7). This kind of love involves not being easily provoked (1 Corinthians 13:5) upon discovering that, just like the Apostle Paul was still a sinner (Romans 7:14-25), so is your pastor (and so are you). When David initially told Jonathan about a grievous sin of Saul, Jonathan's initial response was "God forbid ... it is not so," along with reasons why Saul would not do such a wicked thing (1 Samuel 20:2), even though Jonathan was already fully aware of the sinful tendencies of his father (e. g., 1 Samuel 14:29, 43-44). However, when investigation provided clear evidence of Saul's guilt, Jonathan sided with David against his own father, the king (1 Samuel 20:4-42). Jonathan was hesitant to believe David's accusation, but he did not close his eyes, refuse to investigate, and then seize David and bring him to Saul for execution. Seek to esteem your pastor highly, and yourself lowly. Could you be wrongly putting a sinful interpretation on his statements? Could you be misinterpreting his actions—could there genuinely be justification for them? Could they even be unjustifiable and sinful, but his sins be the struggles of a righteous man who meets pastoral qualifications (1 Timothy 3) against his flesh—as you yourself experience and groan under indwelling sin (Romans 7:14-25; 8:23)—rather than the rampaging of an unregenerate Diotrephes? As 1 Timothy 5:19-25 requires, set aside defamatory hearsay against your pastor (as you ought to set aside such hearsay against any Christian). Who cares if "Gashmu saith it" (Nehemiah 6:6)? Where is the proof? The large majority of pastors in Bible-believing churches are *not* Diotrephes, and it is a great sin to falsely accuse such righteous men—it is doing the work of Satan, not of God.

Your pastor is not Diotrephes if he takes stands for Biblical doctrine, nor is he Diotrephes if he applies Scripture in a stronger, more conservative way than you currently understand the need for. The Apostle John did not warn that Diotrephes was too conservative in his doctrine. Diotrephes was not too bold in preaching against sin or too detailed in his application of Scripture. Pastor Diotrephes was both corrupting Biblical doctrine for a form of hierarchicalism where he idolatrously took preeminence away from Christ, and corrupting Biblical practice by casting out righteous people while maliciously slandering those who stood in his way. You should thank God if He has provided your church a bold preacher who plainly and specifically warns against sin and carefully and practically applies Scripture to daily life—not slander him as a Diotrephes.

Is My Pastor Diotrephes? Seek Resolution Privately

But what if, despite, in love, extending deep, Spirit-produced longsuffering and grace, honesty with the teaching of Scripture and the clear testimony of multiple lines of evidence bear witness to Diotrephes-type attitudes and actions, not as a sinful slip of a godly man who sincerely seeks to tenderly care for his flock—but in a repeated, persistent pattern? After all, while the Christian implicitly trusts Christ, and knows, without question and doubt, that his Lord is sinless and perfect, only the sinless Son of Man is worthy of this sort of trust among all the sons of men. The preeminent Christ is worthy of such unwavering and undoubting trust, but none of the fallen children of Adam are (Jeremiah 17:5-8). The Christian knows Christ has not and cannot do wrong—he does not know that for even the godliest pastor. If it seems clear to you that your pastor has sinned, you should speak to him privately about the situation (Matthew 18:15).[295] Approach him in a humble, self-deprecating spirit, wanting what is best for God's glory, your church, and for him as a person. Genuinely esteem him very highly in love for his work's sake. Be genuinely open to the possibility that you are the one who is wrong or who has misunderstood. Mention what you appreciate in him and are thankful for about him (Philemon 4-7; Romans 16:3-15). Pray that God will help you to see any beam in your own eye (Matthew 7:3-5). Even if you are not the one who is wrong, do not rebuke the pastor, but intreat him as a father (1 Timothy 5:1; 2 Kings 5:13). Say nothing in anger or in bitterness. Humbly confess anything you have done wrong—even if you think you are only partially wrong, and you think he is partially, or even mainly, wrong. With a godly man, the vast majority of the time the same Holy Spirit that dwells in him and in you will be able to bring you both to resolution and agreement. If he does not see the problem you bring up right away, you can still exercise godly forbearance (Ephesians 4:2; Colossians 3:13), trusting that Christ will help you to grow more like Him as you practice this glorious virtue.

Nothing in Matthew 18:15-17 requires that a Christian make only one attempt to deal with a sin privately. If you try one time, but resolution is not achieved, try repeatedly. As you would want others to honor your reputation, seek to do the same with him. "[W]alk worthy of the vocation wherewith ye are called, with all lowliness and meekness, with longsuffering, forbearing one another in love; endeavouring[296] to keep the unity of the Spirit in the bond of peace" (Ephesians 4:1-3). You can also ask a godly close friend—such as your spouse, or another righteous person whom you are close to—for confidential advice.[297] If you do this, as part of thinking the best, you should present your pastor's actions and statements in the best light possible (without distorting reality or being dishonest). The point is not for you to hear advice that you want to hear, but to hear good advice (1 Kings 12:7-16). Does this godly counselor see something that you are missing? Is there a beam in your eye? If there is no beam, how can you in the most respectful and compassionate way help your pastor with a mote in his eye? If he is a wise man—as you should properly be heavily biased to think—even if it is not always immediately a comfortable topic, in the longer term he will be thankful that you brought the matter up with him (Proverbs 9:8). By speaking to him, you are showing him love, for love not only avoids vengeance and grudges, but also helps one's neighbor not to sin. Not a difficult conversation, but sin itself, is the evil of evils (Leviticus 19:17-18).

But what happens if when you go privately, and humbly, to the pastor, seeking on multiple occasions to get resolution, his answers to you are consistently hard and harsh, answering you roughly (1 Samuel 20:10, 30)? What if, to him, the problem is not the clear sin that you are bringing up, but the fact that you dared to bring up anything? What if he claims to be the Lord's Anointed, the "Untouchable Man," and that you are like Dathan, Abiram, and Korah for daring to say anything?[298] What if his counsel seems to consistently support his preeminence and the need for blind loyalty, but does not consistently seem to be what passages he references themselves actually mean in their context, so that his talk makes no sense (3 John 10)? What if he is "unstable," confusing, and crazy, saying one thing at one time and then something radically different another time (James 1:8; 2 Peter 3:16)? What if the more seriously you take his words, the more messed up you get? What if he seems to have a truth-problem,[299] so that, in striking contrast with other godly pastors you have had, with him you feel that you need to start documenting your conversations, keeping exact records of his and your emails and other written communications, because somehow what really happened keeps getting twisted in his mind into something very different—the only consistency being that the distortions result in allegations made against you but enforce preeminence for him? What if, instead of being thankful for accurate documentation of what actually happened, he fears it and views a paper trail as a threat? It is very right to practice forbearance, but if you come to a point where it is clear that you cannot get resolution privately, you must bring it up to two or three. If your church has multiple elders, the two or three are very likely to be them.

Is My Pastor Diotrephes?
Seek Resolution With Two or Three

What happens if attempts to get resolution privately fail? You can certainly ask your pastor for forgiveness for any element of that failure that is your fault. But Scripture does not teach that such situations should be left unresolved (Ephesians 4:26); they should be resolved "quickly" (Matthew 5:25). If attempts at private resolution fail, you can seek to involve two or three godly people for help (Matthew 18:16). In the large majority of cases, if you think sin has been committed by a pastor in your church, the two or three would be other elders, if your congregation has a plurality of overseers.[300] Throughout the church age, Christ has resolved countless seemingly impossible situations through the prayers, fasting, and godly counsel and fellowship of several wise pastors. Your all-wise God is He with whom "all things are possible" (Matthew 19:26). Furthermore, just as with addressing a fellow Christian brother alone one can attempt on numbers of occasions to resolve situations privately, so with two or three it is lawful and often wise to have multiple meetings, seeking resolution. If you have not already made the situation a matter for fasting as well as prayer, consider Christ's commendation for fasting in resolving spiritual problems (Matthew 17:21). If even repeated attempts to seek resolution with two or three fail, and the issue is a serious one for which simply exercising forbearance would be wrong, it may be necessary to seek the guidance of the whole church on the matter (Matthew 18:17), again seeking for resolution, not conflict or separation. In such a situation, it would very likely be wise to have the other pastors initiate bringing the situation to a larger audience. When everyone involved is a godly person, going to the whole church will rarely be necessary.

When bringing the situation up to the two or three, approach them with the same lowliness that you did when you brought the problem up to the pastor privately. Seek not only to put the pastor with whom you have concerns in the best light that you honestly can, but also to make sure that you are scrupulously accurate with truth. It may not necessarily be wrong to bring up something that the pastor said to you in private without any witnesses, but in such a case there is much room for either your memory or his memory to be in error. Something that is written—where both of you are witnesses to what was said and done—is far better. If, seeking to be sure you accurately understood and could take seriously his counsel, you took notes from verbal counseling sessions with him, and the pastor with whom you have concerns verified in writing that your notes were accurate, that is better than a situation where it is your memory against his. If something concerning was said publicly in a sermon that the church records online, the exact words in question are available and can be accessed without any question.[301] A conversation where both the pastor's and church members' wives are present with them, so that four witnesses exist, is better to reference than something done in private that cannot be proven. The other pastors may be able to provide helpful perspective—perhaps you were wrongly understanding what was being said or done, and there was no sin involved. Alternatively, perhaps there was a sin such as very harsh speech, but there were also mitigating circumstances—perhaps apart from your knowledge, the day the elder with whom you have concerns spoke roughly to you he had just dealt with an extremely difficult and confidential church situation with some other persons after getting only two hours of sleep for three straight days because he had been caring at home for a sick child who had been up all night, and in the same situation you might have said the same thing he had said, or worse.

Is My Pastor Diotrephes? Failure With Two or Three: Then What?

But what if the other pastors seem to care little about the clear and serious sins committed by the pastor with whom you have concerns—what if the pastor's sins mean very little, but the fact that you dared to bring them up means very much, and, to them, means that you are the problem? In such a situation you should first seriously consider whether they are right. Every Christian, although born again (John 3:3), still has indwelling sin within that can deceive him (Jeremiah 17:9; 1 John 1:8-10). No man or group of men is infallible, and so several pastors in a godly church are not infallible—but very often they are right. If they are taking Scripture out of context, you must not follow them: "To the law and to the testimony: if they speak not according to this word, *it is* because *there is* no light in them" (Isaiah 8:20). Barnabas and Peter were wrong (Galatians 2:11-13); James and John were wrong (Luke 9:54-56); all twelve of the apostles were wrong (Matthew 26:8-10); and several pastors in your church could also be wrong. As a spiritual priest and an adopted son of God (Galatians 4:5; 1 Peter 2:5), you have the same access to God that they do, the same indwelling and guiding Holy Spirit (Romans 8:9), and the same Bible. But if you are going to disagree, you had better be 100% sure that Scripture and its Divine Author are on your side. The Bible alone is your final authority (2 Timothy 3:16-17), and Scripture is self-authenticating and self-interpreting (cf. 2 Peter 1:20), so there are times when a godly person may truly say, "I have more understanding than all my teachers: for thy testimonies *are* my meditation" (Psalm 119:99). But it is certainly much more common that all your teachers are wiser than you are. You can easily sin and easily go astray. Are you truly alone in what you are standing for, or are there wise Christians who agree with you? Are you standing for something the Spirit has led many godly churches to recognize throughout history? If you disagree with your church's pastors on whether burgers or burritos are better fast food, it does not matter. If you disagree with them on something as serious as whether what they are teaching and practicing is Biblical or is actually sinful, that matters a great deal. So take the possibility that they are right, and you are wrong, very, very seriously. But what do you do if it is, indeed, clear that the pastor with whom you have concerns is indeed sinning and is wrong, and the other pastors either refuse to see the problem or refuse to deal with it? What do you do if at least one of your pastors is a Diotrephes, and the other pastors are fine allowing him to usurp the preeminence that properly belongs to Christ alone?

My Pastor Is Diotrephes! What Do I Do?

If Pastor Diotrephes has taken control of your church, either he needs to leave, or you need to leave. If there is a strong possibility that Diotrephes can be removed from his position, as the Apostle John was prepared to lead in the removal of Pastor Diotrephes (3 John 10), remaining in your church and following the steps of Matthew 18:15-17 to have Pastor Diotrephes dismissed is a right decision. Christ loved the church and gave His life to purify her (Ephesians 5:25-27); if you can stop a church of Christ from becoming a church of Diotrephes, you do well. If you can get the wolf out of the sheep pen before it eats all of the sheep, should you not do it? If your congregation has multiple pastors, and if they recognize Pastor Diotrephes, you may be able to deliver your church from a dangerous wolf. There is a time for godly men to fight Diotrephes. If you do, you must use only the truth of the Word and the strength of the Spirit, avoiding anything underhanded, dishonest, disreputable, or shady, no matter how twisted the depths of dishonesty and depravity are that Diotrephes uses to fight back—and fight back he will as he grasps for preeminence. Even if Pastor Diotrephes fights for himself in ways that shockingly violate Scripture and would leave your conscience screaming, you cannot respond in kind. You must obey Matthew 18:15-17, 1 Timothy 5:17-25, and all other relevant passages of Scripture, remembering that your responsibility is not to achieve a specific outcome, but to honor Christ, who exercises sovereign control over all events (Ephesians 1:11) and especially guides His church as her Head (Ephesians 5:23).

If, however, the other pastors either are themselves men like Diotrephes, or are righteous men whom Diotrephes has deceived,[302] the likelihood that Diotrephes will be removed is not very high (although every church's situation is different). Likewise, if a church has only one pastor—Diotrephes—and everyone else in a leadership capacity supports him, you are quite unlikely to have him removed, and you should just leave. If the wolf cannot be taken out of the sheep pen, at least you and the other sheep in your family can get out.

If you need to leave, there are certainly situations where leaving quietly without telling anyone else is the right thing to do. But there are also situations where it is right to try to tell others and seek to get other sheep out of the pen where a wolf has lodged itself. On one extreme, if a pastor is an immoral monster like Dave Hyles,[303] but church leadership refuses to believe the proven facts and place the wolf under church discipline, it is right to seek to get as many sheep out of that congregation as possible. Furthermore, whoremongering is not the only sin where the Bible would support your encouraging other sheep to leave a church that has departed from the faith to enthrone Diotrephes. On the other hand, if a pastor has evidenced spiritual immaturity that you are concerned has hurt your family spiritually, or he evidences Diotrephes-type tendencies but there is no unambiguous proof that he is actually Pastor Diotrephes, and you hope he may simply be immature and can grow stronger and successfully pastor for the glory of God, there may be a place to quietly leave while encouraging others to stay there and help this simply immature but righteous pastor grow stronger in the faith. If a pastor has too soft a spot for Diotrephes but is not himself Pastor Diotrephes, it may be appropriate to seek a letter of transfer[304] from a church that you need to leave so that you can more effectively serve the Lord. If Pastor Diotrephes has already taken over the congregation and controls it with an iron fist, on the other hand, you should leave whether he is willing to give you a letter of transfer or not.

Whether you need to leave a church because of Diotrephes or seek to preserve a church and have Diotrephes removed, you must not take your decision lightly. You must be 100% sure that you are obeying Scripture. You should have the support of godly counselors (Proverbs 11:14; 15:22). Your decision should be made with serious prayer and fasting. You must be able to claim God's promises: "Trust in the LORD with all thine heart; and lean not unto thine own understanding. In all thy ways acknowledge him, and he shall direct thy paths" (Proverbs 3:5-6). You must not stay, long-term, in a church where Pastor Diotrephes maintains preeminence. The preeminence Diotrephes claims is idolatry, and you must not support such idolatry—even if others, indeed, many others, tolerate it.[305] But it is no small sin to misidentify a godly man as Pastor Diotrephes, and it is no small sin to tear sheep away from a Biblically sound church because you misidentify a righteous person as Diotrephes. You should expect both that making a right decision to forsake Pastor Diotrephes and making an evil decision to slander a godly shepherd as Diotrephes will have profound consequences—for good or for evil—for you personally, for your family, and for many others for generations to come, if Christ does not first return.

IX.) WHAT SHOULD A CHURCH MEMBER DO IF PASTOR DIOTREPHES IS CASTING HIM OUT?

Diotrephes Is Casting Me Out! Be Sure You Are Not the Problem

What should you do if Pastor Diotrephes is in the process of casting you out? First, you should make 100% sure that the problem is not you, but Pastor Diotrephes. The large majority of people who are removed from the membership of a Biblical church through discipline deserve it. If you have sinned and acted foolishly, you have no business accusing a righteous man of being Diotrephes as an excuse to cover your sin. Instead, you should repent and be reconciled with God, with the church, and with its godly pastoral leadership.

Diotrephes Is Casting Me Out! Draw Near to Christ

Furthermore, if you are in the process of being cast out by a genuine Diotrephes, you may be about to go through what could be the most difficult trial of your Christian life. There could be meetings where Satan's devils are clearly present. You could be the recipient of astonishing depths of hatred, slander, spite, and perhaps even physical harm at the hand of Diotrephes and those whom he has deceived. Unless you are walking closely with Christ, the weight of this kind of trial could easily swallow you up. You must be able to bless those who will curse you, pray for those who persecute you, love those who hate you, and speak kind words of loving truth to those who will speak harsh and malicious lies against you (Matthew 5:44). You must be able to pray: "I have done judgment and justice: leave me not to mine oppressors. Be surety for thy servant for good: let not the proud oppress me" (Psalm 119:121-122). If you rely on the strength of Christ through the Spirit, and the promises of God in His holy Word, then you will be able to honestly pray with the psalmist:

> *If it had not been the LORD who was on our side, now may Israel say; If it had not been the LORD who was on our side, when men rose up against us: Then they had swallowed us up quick, when their wrath was kindled against us: Then the waters had overwhelmed us, the stream had gone over our soul: Then the proud waters had gone over our soul. Blessed be the LORD, who hath not given us as a prey to their teeth. Our soul is escaped as a bird out of the snare of the fowlers: the snare is broken, and we are escaped. Our help is in the name of the LORD, who made heaven and earth. (Psalm 124)*

You can pray: "*It is* time for *thee*, LORD, to work: *for* they have made void thy law" (Psalm 119:126). If Jehovah is with you, then you will be able to look back on your trial with a pure conscience and upright heart after He assists you through these troubled waters. You will be able to offer your Good Shepherd thanks for His sustaining and delivering goodness. But if you are not close to Him, you stand in grave danger of being swallowed up.

Diotrephes Is Casting Me Out! Expect Violations of Matthew 18

Pastor Diotrephes may seek to simply compel you to leave without pursuing any of the steps of Matthew 18:15-17. He may preach messages that are full of hint-dropping and harshness. He may use extremely rough words to you in private, tearing into you with his wolfish claws, while in public he maintains the appearance of a kind and caring shepherd. He may simply abruptly command you to leave the church property and not come back. He may, in his insecurity, fear that he might not succeed were he actually to pursue the steps prescribed in Matthew 18 and may therefore, like a wolf leaping suddenly upon its unwary prey, bring you before some panel to cast you out without first coming to you privately, then bringing two or three, and finally having a fair trial before the entire congregation; one week you may think that you are a member in fine standing, and the next you may be either already cast out or just about to be cast out. Employing the methods of ungodly corporations (Mark 10:42), he may prefer the heathen and worldly business model where employees are suddenly terminated without warning to the pattern of Christ, where excommunication pertains only to persons who knowingly and stubbornly resist repeated admonishment and loving attempts at restoration. You should expect Pastor Diotrephes to fail to fully follow the steps of Matthew 18:15-17 and also expect that for whatever portion of those steps he follows he will have a very heavy thumb on the scale. Diotrephes will treat you as fairly and kindly as a wolf does the sheep it is eating for lunch.

No Violations of Matthew 18? Could You Be The Problem?

On the other hand, if the steps of Matthew 18:15-17 are scrupulously followed, and not only the pastor on his own speaking to you privately, and not only the two or three witnesses, but also the entire congregation after a fair trial conclude you are guilty, you should search the Scriptures and examine your heart and conscience.[306] What if not only the pastors, but also the whole church, is right, and you are wrong? If they are—as they are in the large majority of church discipline situations—you have been delivered to Satan. You are in a very dangerous place. You should immediately repent and seek reconciliation with your church. Is it possible that the whole congregation is wrong? This is possible, but not probable. What if you attempt to join another Biblical church, they fairly investigate, and they also conclude that the church was right and you are wrong? Is it possible that this second congregation is also mistaken? This is again possible, but is becoming more and more improbable. You had better be truly 100% sure—not 75%, not 80%, not 95%, but 100% sure—that you are in the right and that Jesus Christ and His Word are on your side. You want Christ by your side to bless you, not Satan by your side to curse you, but you have the latter, not the former, if you have been legitimately excommunicated. Unless the situation is crystal-clear and Scripture is without any doubt on your side, rather than "church shopping" until you find a spiritually weak congregation that does not care to investigate before receiving you into membership, you must humble yourself and be reconciled to the faithful church of Christ that sorrowfully placed you under righteous discipline.

Diotrephes Is Casting Me Out! Do I Resist?

If you are being cast out by Diotrephes, there may be a place to just quietly leave and let him get his way, allowing him to cast you out without a fight. However, if he allows you even a show-trial before some portion of the congregation or some panel, if righteous people are on that panel or that select fragment of the congregation, you should seriously pray about attending and offering a defense. If Diotrephes is in control of the proceedings, you are not likely to be successful in vindicating your innocence—but attempting to deliver one of God's adopted sons over to Satan (1 Corinthians 5:5) is a fearful sin, and if such an abomination is happening in a church that used to be a stronghold of Biblical faithfulness, lawful resistance to such a heinous crime is right and God-glorifying, even if it is unsuccessful. It would be honorable for a man to seek to protect His wife's purity and honor from a criminal who would seek to assault her, even if her husband failed and died in the attempt to protect his wife. It is likewise honorable to seek to protect the purity of Christ's bride, the church, from the defilement and abominations of Pastor Diotrephes, even if your attempts to do so are not successful and you are greatly bruised and battered as a result.

Diotrephes Is Casting Me Out! Guard Your Heart

If Pastor Diotrephes is in the process of casting you out, it is crucial that you guard both your attitude and your actions. You must not be bitter or allow Diotrephes' slanders and attacks on you and your family to lead you to harbor hatred for him in your heart. You should the rather pity Diotrephes because of the eternal damnation that is coming to him. Your heavenly Father knows the hurt and harm Diotrephes is inflicting on His beloved children. Your Father will repay Pastor Diotrephes a hundredfold in His good time. Let the lion-like vengeance remain with the Lord your God (Hebrews 10:30), while the lamb-like meekness remains with you. Go out of your way to show kindness and respect to Pastor Diotrephes and those he is turning against you—do not let him overcome you with evil, but overcome his evil with good (Romans 12:20-21). The Lord Jesus was not bitter with Judas, but He washed His betrayer's feet (John 13:2-12) and showed him other acts of kindness (John 13:26), fully aware that it would have been better for Judas to never have been born (Mark 14:21). If you are "now for a season ... in heaviness through manifold temptations," let "the trial of your faith, being much more precious than of gold that perisheth, though it be tried with fire ... be found unto praise and honour and glory at the appearing of Jesus Christ" (1 Peter 1:6-7). Fill yourself with God's sanctifying Word more than ever, so that instead of giving in to hatred or bitterness, you can pray: "Trouble and anguish have taken hold on me: *yet* thy commandments *are* my delights. ... I *am* small and despised: *yet* do not I forget thy precepts" (Psalm 119:141, 143). God has allowed this trial in your life for His glory and your good (Romans

8:28-39) and will always provide a way for you to gain the victory in whatever temptation He permits (1 Corinthians 10:13). Do not waste the opportunity to walk with the Son of God in the fiery furnace (Daniel 3:25), but guard your heart so that it is full of Spirit-wrought love for God and for all men—including Diotrephes himself. Guard your attitude!

Diotrephes Is Casting Me Out! Guard Your Speech

As you guard your heart-attitude, you must also guard your speech. You can expect Diotrephes to speak many words of malice and slander against you (3 John 10), berating you, prating against you, and spreading lies. He may blast and berate you personally; he may slander you secretly to others, stealing their hearts and turning them against you (2 Samuel 15:1-6); he may paint you as evil publicly from the pulpit. Whatever sorts of malicious prating he uses, do not use the same towards him. Even under the strongest provocations, you must still "speak evil of no man ... be no brawle[r], *but* gentle, shewing all meekness unto all men" (Titus 3:2)—even to Diotrephes.[307] He loves to have preeminence—do not give him Christ's preeminence, but show him the greatest respect, not because he deserves it, but because of his pastoral office, because he is created in God's image, and because he is your brother in Adam, even if not your brother in Christ. You will have to give account for your words at the judgment seat of Christ (2 Corinthians 5:10), and your reward for infinite ages will be influenced by your overcoming in this trial. Diotrephes will have to give account, in terror, for every malicious syllable he has spoken when he is brought before the great white throne judgment of Christ (Revelation 20:11-15) and will have an eternity in the lake of fire, with the devil and all other liars (Revelation 21:8), to lament and wail over every one of his malicious words, as the smoke of his torment ascends for ever and ever. He may succeed in casting you out now, but the whole universe will know he is a liar when every single one of his lies is exposed in that day. Speak in light of the fact that you are in the very presence of the holy God who hears all of Diotrephes' words, and all of yours (Jeremiah 23:24-25). Diotrephes may think he is in control, but he is not—the Triune Jehovah is the One who is truly in control.

It is appropriate to share with co-pastors clear proof that exposes Pastor Diotrephes, or if there are no co-pastors, to share clear proof with deacons or other church leadership. But you must be extremely careful to make no false accusations. You must be conscientious and careful with truth. You must not return evil for evil, even when Diotrephes is doing whatever is necessary, out of his seared conscience, to slander you and accuse you. Pastor Diotrephes will play dirty because he does not really believe Christ is Lord of His church, nor that the risen and ascended Christ acts as the living Head of His body. But you know Christ is truly the ascended King and Holy One—you must not play dirty. It could be best to make not only no false accusations, but no accusations at all, even the most obviously true ones—simply point out undeniable facts, and let the facts speak for themselves (John 9:32).

When you are at the point of being cast out by Diotrephes, there is likely little value reproving him personally for his sins. "He that reproveth a scorner getteth to himself shame: and he that rebuketh a wicked *man getteth* himself a blot. Reprove not a scorner, lest he hate thee: rebuke a wise man, and he will love thee" (Proverbs 9:7-8). The Lord Jesus warned His true disciples about Judas, but He did not direct a sharp, pointed rebuke individually to the traitor (Matthew 26:24). The Apostle John wrote to Gaius (3 John 1), not to Diotrephes. If you have done right up to this point, then you initially assumed Pastor Diotrephes was a wise man. Only with great reluctance, based on overwhelming evidence to the contrary, did his sinful deeds and words compel you, in sorrow and shock, to change your mind. Diotrephes does not care about sinning against God. (He may care about getting caught sinning if it threatens his preeminence, but the sin itself is not his concern, because he is not born again.) He knows the conclusions he needs to reach—you must be out, and he must be preeminent. The means to get there, whether lawful or not, the accusations to use, whether true or false, are much less important to him. Whatever you say is going to be used against you—and even what you never said is probably going to be placed into your mouth as if you had said it. If you reprove Diotrephes, all you will be doing is giving him evidence which he will use against you (John 9:30-34). If you are brought before a panel, in many situations it is also better not to reprove those on it, but to intreat them as fathers (1 Timothy 5:1). Diotrephes has almost surely connected his casting you out to some sins that affect his preeminence and honor, so anything you do that could even remotely cast dishonor on him or upon those whom he has prejudiced against you will be used against you. But if you did sin against Diotrephes—or against anyone else—confess it, even if you know it will be used against you. You are seeking to please God, not to achieve worldly success. Even if huge and heavy timber beams in Diotrephes' eye smack you, taking your breath away and leaving your sides black and blue every time he turns around, and he never says a syllable about them, if you nevertheless have a tiny speck in your eye, repent of your speck, confess the speck as sin, and ask both God and all those against whom you sinned for forgiveness (Matthew 7:3-5). Pastor Diotrephes may not forgive you but instead use your confession against you—nevertheless, you must still do what is right in the sight of God.

Diotrephes Is Casting Me Out! Prove Your Innocence

If Diotrephes mistakenly allows you to provide clear proof that you are not guilty to either a panel or to the congregation, you should take the opportunity. Since his casting you out is itself an egregious sin and is likely connected to other sins that Pastor Diotrephes is hiding, proving your innocence also shows his guilt. Nevertheless, you should follow Scripture, only pointing out proven facts rather than unprovable extrapolations (1 Timothy 5:19), and you should be careful to obey all procedures in both Scripture and in your church constitution, even if Diotrephes is violating them right and left—although you can also politely ask questions when Pastor Diotrephes does so.[308] Do the best you can, even if you are given an egregiously biased trial, but enter the trial with your eyes both fixed on

Christ and open to what is very likely predetermined to happen—you are going to be found guilty of something—anything—and then cast out. Disregarding the solemn warning of 1 Timothy 5:21, Pastor Diotrephes has likely greased the wheels for your condemnation ahead of time by pre-poisoning the minds of the judges on your panel with accusations that you never get to hear about or defend against; perhaps he has even pressured them into promising to find you guilty before your show-trial even begins. Whoever he allows to be on a panel will enter the hearing extremely sympathetic to him and hostile to you. The people on the panel may not be sons of Diotrephes themselves—even righteous Peter and Barnabas were "carried away"[309] by dissimulating hypocrisy and lies (Galatians 2:13), by the unprincipled deceit[310] of the wicked, and temporarily fell from their steadfast[311] adherence to the truth (2 Peter 3:17). Not everyone who supports casting you out is necessarily wicked; Pastor Diotrephes may have simply stolen their trusting hearts with his lies. Having been subject to his falsehoods and emotional manipulation,[312] they are very likely to find you guilty, no matter what a dispassionate examination of the evidence would indicate. Furthermore, Diotrephes may have a kind of courage and valiantness in doing evil (2 Samuel 13:28; contrast Joshua 1:6-9) and have very subtle and slick advisors who can help him manipulate events to fulfill his plots (2 Samuel 13:3-5), both factors which strongly mitigate against your being cleared from his accusations. In a situation of emotional group-frenzy against you, do not assume that anyone will stop to ask rational questions at that time. However, if some or all of the people Pastor Diotrephes has manipulated into casting you out are righteous, they may rethink the situation later when the emotional fervor has worn off. The Holy Spirit may lead them later to privately reconsider the facts in light of Scripture, when they are not under pressure from Diotrephes to suppress their doubts, or when they see a similar pattern played out again after Pastor Diotrephes picks his next victim. Do not be bitter against the people on the panel who believe the lies of Diotrephes and cast you out. After you are cast out, you are free to join a truly Biblically faithful church, while the people on the panel are not free—they have chosen the devil's wolf over God's sheep, the preeminence of Diotrephes over the preeminence of Christ, and will reap bitter fruit from it. The wolf will not be satisfied with just one sheep. It will strike again and again. Diotrephes is loose with his words to get what he wants, and those whom he does not cast out may find that he is equally loose with the money or the purity of others when he wants them. It is far better to be you than to be them.

Diotrephes Is Casting Me Out! Document the Proceedings

Try to get Diotrephes' accusations against you in writing, as well as whatever you are found guilty of, and the evidence alleged for your condemnation. Because Diotrephes prates, speaking nonsense (3 John 10), his accusations, like many lies, can often fall under their own weight; the false accusations he makes at one time may contradict those he makes on other occasions (Mark 14:56), although a more subtle and smart Diotrephes will seek to guard against this method of being discovered (2 Samuel 13:3). A Biblically faithful congregation takes church discipline very seriously and will not want to receive into its membership an unrepentant person who has truly been delivered to Satan. A faithful assembly will agree with Edward Hiscox's *Standard Manual* that "the *presumption* is that the church has done right, and is justified in its action, [but] the *possibility* is that the church has done wrong, and is censurable for its action."[313]

If you are cast out, a good church will presume you are guilty unless you can prove your innocence. Furthermore, you can expect Pastor Diotrephes to continue to reject and slander you after he has cast you out, covering his wrongdoing by seeking to destroy any ability you have to reunite with a faithful church elsewhere. If your church constitution requires Diotrephes to give you his accusations in writing before initiating discipline against you, ask that this take place. If he is required to provide you written statements of what you are allegedly guilty of after casting you out, ask for that to take place. If Diotrephes ignores his church constitution the way he ignores Scripture, make sure that your requests for what the constitution requires are themselves documented. For the evil deeds of Diotrephes to be remembered (3 John 10) accurately, written documentation is very helpful. He may ensnare himself by his own words (Proverbs 12:13; 18:17), throwing out accusations that are so wild that they make the wise skeptical even before you offer any rebuttal, or are self-defeating. He may also trap himself with his own unrighteous deeds (Psalm 9:16); in God's good providence, sin regularly brings its own snare to catch the wicked.[314] If what he accuses you of before casting you out is different from what he accuses you of before a panel, and that is different from the slander he spreads about you after casting you out, a church that is willing to hear both sides of the matter (Proverbs 18:13-17) will see that something is not right. Furthermore, if his written accusation explains that an alternative process, not the steps of Matthew 18:15-17, is going to be followed, then you have in his accusation itself evidence that he is Diotrephes. If you apply for membership at a Biblically faithful Baptist church, and that church asks Pastor Diotrephes for his side of the story (as they should), but he refuses to provide the evidence upon which you allegedly deserved to be cast out, simply insisting that all other churches should just trust him, in the minds of Biblically-guided and righteous people the presumption of your guilt will seriously waver.[315]

Thus, you should do whatever you can to get documentation about what Diotrephes is doing. If the congregation from which he casts you out allows him to continue to tyrannize them, Pastor Diotrephes may seek to pursue you with his corrupt and false charges the rest of your earthly pilgrimage. If the events are simply his undocumented word against yours, or if what took place is simply based upon the memory of eyewitnesses, it will become harder as time passes to prove your innocence and to show that he is guilty of slander and deception.

Diotrephes Is Casting Me Out! Reject His Prating

Finally, remember that what Diotrephes says is nonsense—"prating" (3 John 10). When you believed Pastor Diotrephes was a godly man, full of knowledge of Scripture and of the Holy Spirit, you rightly took his words very seriously. Once he exposes himself as a wolf, you no longer need to take his words to heart. "To the law and to the testimony: if they speak not according to this word, *it is* because *there is* no light in them" (Isaiah 8:20). Spend enough time on his accusations to prove your innocence to a faithful church after you are cast out, but do not let his words tear you up on the inside any more, nor waste unnecessary time on them. Diotrephes does not care if what he says is truth—you should not care about what he says, either. Diotrephes does not care if he wastes your time—he is willing to destroy your life and cares about his preeminence, not about the cause of Christ, about truth, or about you. Indeed, his corrupt mind leads him to "perverse disputings" (1 Timothy 6:5);[316] he will "waste ... time in unimportant matters."[317] He is perfectly willing to wear away vast quantities of your time[318] striving about his "evil surmisings"—whether a word you said here derogated from his honor, or whether a deed you did there implied disrespect to him if one squinted at it with enough suspicion and from just the right angle (1 Timothy 6:4). He does not care if you fail to accomplish important ministries the Lord has given you for His kingdom because all your time is worn away and wasted[319] in fruitless efforts to please him. Instead of meditating on the words of Diotrephes, meditate on the words of God, so that "the trial of your faith, being much more precious than of gold that perisheth, though it be tried with fire, might be found unto praise and honour and glory at the appearing of Jesus Christ" (1 Peter 1:7).

X.) WHAT SHOULD A CHURCH MEMBER DO IF PASTOR DIOTREPHES HAS CAST HIM OUT?

Cast Out? Examine Yourself

What should you do if Pastor Diotrephes succeeds in casting you out of the church? First, again, you must make 100% sure that you did not actually deserve it. You do not want to compound some serious sin that made you justly worthy of excommunication with the additional sin of blind hard-heartedness to your guilt and the sin of slandering a righteous pastor as Diotrephes. If you were not cast out because of your guilt, but because of the maliciousness of a Diotrephes, how was he able to convince others in the congregation that you deserved to be cast out? Were there at least elements of truth in his accusations, or were they completely false? If there were elements of truth, did you confess them as sin to God and deal with whatever in them relates to others? Diotrephes is an evil man, and a Pastor Diotrephes can at times successfully manipulate even righteous people into supporting his casting out of an innocent sheep. But be very sure that this is indeed what took place. It is a grievous sin for Pastor Diotrephes to cast out a righteous sheep—and it is also grievous sin for someone who deserves excommunication to falsely accuse a godly overseer.

Unjustly Cast Out? Remember Christ's Words

If you are certain that you were innocent and were cast out by Pastor Diotrephes, then "Let not thine heart envy sinners: but *be thou* in the fear of the LORD all the day long" (Proverbs 23:17). Do not wish that you were the one who was still in the congregation instead of the one who was unjustly cast out. You may have patiently endured the wounds of Diotrephes for a long time, seeking resolution and peace with him; he may have taken your kindnesses and turned them into knives with which to stab you. Diotrephes may have, at least temporarily, destroyed your opportunities to minister for Christ as godly people in other churches assume he must be right because he is the pastor. Diotrephes may have shattered close friendships. He may have caused awful sorrow and anguish to you and your family, and then brought his wolfish animosity to a climax by casting you out. It may look as though he has won while the cause of God and truth has lost. But this is not truly so, and you must not think it so. God allowed the abomination of desolation to defile His temple in the days of the Maccabees for only a short time (Daniel 8:14), and He will allow the Antichrist to usurp power in the coming Tribulation for only a short time (2 Thessalonians 2:3-15). Instead of grieving over the temporary success of Diotrephes, remember Christ's words:

> *Blessed are they which are persecuted for righteousness' sake: for theirs is the kingdom of heaven. Blessed are ye,*

> *when men shall revile you, and persecute you, and shall say all manner of evil against you falsely, for my sake. Rejoice, and be exceeding glad: for great is your reward in heaven: for so persecuted they the prophets which were before you. (Matthew 5:10-12)*

Under tremendous pressure, you refused to compromise on Scripture or on your conscience. You refused to disobey Christ or renounce His sweet voice for the harsh commands of Diotrephes. It will be easy for your heart to grieve; but remember Christ's promises: great is your reward in heaven. Rejoice, and be exceeding glad!

Unjustly Cast Out? Resist Bitterness

Continue to resist the sin of bitterness. You will have the joy of living with your upright conscience and the smiling face of Christ, while Diotrephes will need to live with his seared conscience and heart hardened in sin, and any righteous people in the church whom he convinced to go along with his program will themselves also need to live with a wolf, not a shepherd, tyrannizing them. Thank God that he has delivered you from the snares, lies, and control of Pastor Diotrephes, and pity and pray for those still held in his claws—for a wolf will not rest content with one sheep alone. Others that are left behind will reap the whirlwinds of the loss of blessing from Christ, or of themselves becoming the next victims of Diotrephes, or of the loss of their children to the world, as their next generation sees through the hypocrisy and pride of Pastor Diotrephes, or of the loss of their children's purity, as Pastor Diotrephes fulfills his lusts upon them. It is far better to be cast out by Diotrephes than to have his favor and company while sharing in his sins—your state is far better than theirs. The curses of Diotrephes, but the smiles of Christ, are immeasurably superior to the smiles of Diotrephes, but the curse of Christ. Christ will turn the curses against you into a blessing, because He loves you (Deuteronomy 23:5). Your heartbreak has come, and Christ stands by you to tenderly bind up your bleeding wounds. Their heartbreak is yet to come, and with someone other than Christ as preeminent to them, what balm will heal their wounds?

Unjustly Cast Out?
Remember Christ and His People's Example

Remember that as Diotrephes cast you out, so did wicked spiritual leaders cast out the godly in Biblical times, and so was Christ your Savior cast out:

> *And rose up, and* ***thrust*** *him [Christ]* ***out*** *of the city, and led him unto the brow of the hill whereon their city was built, that they might cast him down headlong. (Luke 4:29)*

> *And they caught him, and* ***cast*** *him* ***out*** *of the vineyard, and slew him. (Matthew 21:39)*

> *And they took him, and killed him, and* ***cast*** *him* ***out*** *of the vineyard. (Mark 12:8)*

> *And again he sent a third: and they wounded him also, and* ***cast*** *him* ***out****. ... So they* ***cast*** *him* ***out*** *of the vineyard, and killed him. What therefore shall the lord of the vineyard do unto them? (Luke 20:12, 15)*

> *Blessed are ye [God's people], when men shall hate you, and when they shall separate you from their company, and shall reproach you, and* ***cast out*** *your name as evil, for the Son of man's sake. (Luke 6:22)*

> *And **cast** him **out** of the city, and stoned him: and the witnesses laid down their clothes at a young man's feet, whose name was Saul. (Acts 7:58)*
>
> *But the Jews stirred up the devout and honourable women, and the chief men of the city, and raised persecution against Paul and Barnabas, and **expelled** them out of their coasts. (Acts 13:50)*[320]

The prophets and godly servants of Christ were cast out throughout the Old Testament (Luke 20:12). The godly preachers of the New Testament were cast out by the wicked (Acts 7:58)—and the wicked were even able to persuade some who were "devout" and "honorable" to join in the unjust judgment (Acts 13:50). Christ Himself was cast out from the synagogue specifically because of truth that He had told them (Luke 4:29) and then was cast out of Israel and cut off in the most humiliating way on the cross (Matthew 21:39; Mark 12:8; Luke 20:15). And for those who are identified with Christ, He does not say that they are blessed "if" men cast their names out as evil, but "when" they cast their names out as evil.

When Diotrephes usurps Christ's preeminence, and then casts out Christ's sheep, not only do the sheep go out, but Christ Himself goes out with them: for He will not give His glory to another (Isaiah 48:11). Like Moses, "estee[m] the reproach of Christ greater riches than the treasures in Egypt," and have "respect unto the recompence of the reward" (Hebrews 11:26). Cheerfully join Christ in leaving the church of Diotrephes for the church of Christ, where He alone is preeminent: "Let us go forth therefore unto him without the camp, bearing his reproach. For here have we no continuing city, but we seek one to come" (Hebrews 13:13-14).

Unjustly Cast Out? Remember Christ's Zeal

The church where Diotrephes is preeminent is a dangerous place to abide—it is far better to be cast out of it than to remain in it. Recall how "Jesus went into the temple of God, and cast out[321] all them that sold and bought in the temple, and overthrew the tables of the moneychangers, and the seats of them that sold doves, and said unto them, It is written, My house shall be called the house of prayer; but ye have made it a den of thieves" (Matthew 21:12-13). John's Gospel explains:

> *Jesus went up to Jerusalem, and found in the temple those that sold oxen and sheep and doves, and the changers of money sitting: and when he had made a scourge of small cords, he drove[322] them all out of the temple, and the sheep, and the oxen; and poured out the changers' money, and overthrew the tables; and said unto them that sold doves, Take these things hence; make not my Father's house an house of merchandise. And his disciples remembered that it was written, The zeal of thine house hath eaten me up. (John 2:13-17).*

The Lord Jesus, burning with holy zeal for the purity of His Father's house, drove out with a whip those who were corrupting the purity of the place of God's special presence. The same holy zeal burns in His holy heart today. Sometimes in this life, and always in the day of judgment, He will wreak horrible devastation on those who contaminate the purity of His New Testament temple, the church (1 Timothy 3:15; Ephesians 2:21-22). That holy zeal both protects His holy people, redeemed freely and in a holy way by His grace and His cross, and brings wrath on His enemies, whom He will "cast out into outer darkness: there shall be weeping and gnashing of teeth."[323] He tenderly comes to and cares for those unjustly cast out in their time of forsakenness and need (John 9:34-35), for "a bruised reed shall he not break, and smoking flax shall he not quench" (Matthew 12:20). While they are cast out by men for His name's sake, He swears to them in His everlasting love: "[H]im that cometh to me I will in no wise cast out" (John 6:37). Were you "sorrowful for the solemn assembly," finding "the reproach of it *was* a burden"? Jehovah swears: "I will gather [thee] ... I will undo all that afflict thee: and I will save her that halteth, and gather her that was driven out; and I will get them praise and fame in every land where they have been put to shame." Sinful men may have hated you and cast you out, but a time is coming when "[t]hou shalt no more be termed Forsaken ... for the LORD delighteth in thee" (Isaiah 62:4). Indeed, the "LORD thy God in the midst of thee *is* mighty; he will save, he will rejoice over thee with joy; he will rest in his love, he will joy over thee with singing" (Zephaniah 3:17-19).

Unjustly Cast Out? Seek for Grace

Seek the Spirit's grace to have the Christ-like attitude of the martyr Stephen, who, when cast out and stoned, "kneeled down, and cried with a loud voice, Lord, lay not this sin to their charge" (Acts 7:58-60). Casting out a righteous person for something he did not do is a grievous sin, and you should pray for those who committed it. Remember your Lord's words, and follow His example:

> *But I say unto you, Love your enemies, bless them that*

> *curse you, do good to them that hate you, and pray for them which despitefully use you, and persecute you; that ye may be the children of your Father which is in heaven: for he maketh his sun to rise on the evil and on the good, and sendeth rain on the just and on the unjust. (Matthew 5:44-45)*

Do not forget that your heart was as bound by sin before your regeneration as Diotrephes' heart still is, and God's grace alone has broken that dominating slavery to sin (1 Corinthians 4:7). Be humbled by the fact that, apart from grace, you yourself could easily be Diotrephes, instead of being the one cast out by him.

Unjustly Cast Out? Pray

You can offer God all sorts of prayers for the righteous people deceived by Diotrephes who will have to live with the fearful consequences of allowing a wolf to remain in the sheepfold. You can pray for Diotrephes in particular both the sorts of prayer that Stephen prayed for his persecutors and those of the Apostle Paul for Alexander: "Alexander the coppersmith did me much evil: the Lord reward him according to his works" (2 Timothy 4:22). Like God, you must wish for Diotrephes' repentance and salvation (2 Peter 3:9), but you can also pray for the coming day when God will vindicate the righteous and give the wicked their due (Matthew 6:10; Psalm 109).[324] It is lawful to both petition the Lord to reward Diotrephes according to his works and to ethically do what you can to be God's instrument for the answer to that prayer. You also must certainly thank God for His grace, which alone enabled you to overcome in your extremely difficult trial (John

15:5). Apelles was "approved in Christ" (Romans 16:10)[325]—he was found "genuine on the basis of testing, approved (by test), tried and true, genuine,"[326] and, having "endured temptation," could look forward with joyful faith to "the crown of life, which the Lord hath promised to them that love him" (James 1:12).[327] Thank God if, through His glorious grace, you also have been found genuine on the basis of testing, and look forward to joining Apelles in receiving the crown of life that the Lord gives to those who genuinely love Him. However, there are numbers of Biblical reasons not to look back the rest of your life and focus your prayers on that past situation (Philippians 3:13; 1 John 5:16).[328] As you move forward serving the Lord, let the focus of your prayers move forward as well.

Unjustly Cast Out? Remember Victory Follows the Cross

Never forget that by remaining faithful to Christ, His Word, and your conscience, at tremendous cost, you have not just hung on and avoided defeat. You have won a great and glorious victory. God promises those who deal properly with false teachers (Romans 16:17-18) and remain obedient to Christ (Romans 16:19) that "the God of peace shall bruise Satan under your feet shortly" (Romans 16:20). You may have been cast out—but you actually won, because you obeyed God, while Diotrephes lost, because he sinned. Even in this life, you may see Satan crushed under your feet in this situation, and at the coming judgment you will certainly see this victory. Even more important than having Satan trampled under your feet, you have "the grace of our Lord Jesus Christ ... with you," and the sweet smiles of the "God of peace" (Romans 16:20). Like the saints who resist the future Antichrist, all those who resist the many antichrists that seek even now to usurp Christ's place (1 John 2:18) have Christ's strengthening promise: "Fear none of those things which thou shalt suffer ... ye shall have tribulation [for a short time]: be thou faithful unto death, and I will give thee a crown of life" (Revelation 2:10). Satan's servants "shall make war with the Lamb, and the Lamb shall overcome them: for he is Lord of lords, and King of kings: and they that are with him *are* called, and chosen, and faithful" (Revelation 17:14). Seven years of tribulation under the rule of Antichrist will be followed by the reign of Jesus Christ for ever and ever and ever. As the cross—followed by the resurrection!—was not Satan's victory, but the supreme victory of Jesus Christ over sin, death, and the devil, so Christ calls us through a brief cross to receive an eternal crown from his nail-pierced hand. You may have lost an earthly church home, but you still have an eternal heavenly one in your Father's house (John 14:1-2). If a few men, who are but dust and ashes, have cast you out and slandered you, everyone whose opinion really matters either knows already that you were in the right—as do God the Father, Son, and Spirit, the holy angels, and the saints in heaven—or will know soon enough—as will all the saints on earth at the end of their earthly pilgrimage, alongside any saint on earth now who is willing to objectively evaluate both sides of the issue. You have not suffered a terrible defeat by being cast out. You have not just fought a battle to a draw. Having taken up your cross and followed Christ (Mark 8:34), you have won a wonderful and eternal victory, by the grace and for the glory of your Lord, Jesus Christ. Hallelujah!

Unjustly Cast Out? Join a Biblical Church

You should immediately apply for membership in a Biblical, Baptist church that holds to every truth you mistakenly thought the church of Diotrephes held to when you united yourself with it. Do not blame Biblical separatism, Biblical fundamentalism, strong historic Baptist beliefs, or any truth associated with earnestly contending for all the faith (Jude 3) and militant, Christ-exalting separation from all disobedience to it (1 Timothy 1:3). The problem with the church of Diotrephes was not that it was too militant, too conservative, and not weak-kneed or wishy-washy enough. The Biblical "brand" that the church of Diotrephes claimed was not the problem, any more than the apostolic "brand" caused false teachers to arise up among elders trained by Paul (Acts 20:29-30) or caused Judas to mingle with the apostles trained by Christ Himself. The problem was not that the church of Diotrephes believed in excommunication. The problem was that it tolerated Diotrephes' sinful and cultic dictatorship, which is in no wise part of the faith Christ delivered once for all to the saints (Jude 3), and practiced an ungodly, unbiblical form of church pseudo-discipline (Matthew 18:15-17).

If you turn to the soft, mushy world of neo-evangelicalism, join an "emerging" church full of disobedience and compromise, or unite with a congregation that rejects the infallible Word for theological liberalism, you will displease Christ, fail the test that you have been put into, and justify Diotrephes. You do not want your good Shepherd to be displeased when you give an account to Him; nor do you want Pastor Diotrephes to be able to say, "See where they are going to church now? I was right—look at the disobedient compromisers they are!" much less, "See how they have dropped out of church completely? I was right—look at the disobedient sinners they are!" The problem was not with God's church or God's truth, but with sin. If you turn from churches with Biblical doctrine to ones that are full of disobedience, that do not even claim to earnestly contend for all the faith, you will not be free from Diotrephes, either—in an environment that is more tolerant of sin of all kinds, you should expect to find an even greater crop of Pastors Diotrephes than in the churches from which you departed. Non-fundamentalists in the evangelical Southern Baptist Convention, which has largely stopped practicing church discipline,[329] recognize:

> *Southern Baptists ... are giving meager evidence of having today an ordered, disciplined churchmanship. ... Moral failures, which often are crimes as well as sins, increasingly occur among members ... and are reported in the public press. Even ordained ministers and other church leaders may experience such failures and no action by the congregation or by denominational bodies be taken.*[330]

Many non-separatist, non-militant evangelicals think that taking a man who committed adultery with a double-digit number of women over thirteen years in four churches, not removing him from church membership but only having him resign his ministerial credentials, and then re-ordaining him one year and three weeks later, is a great model of how to deal with pastoral immorality.[331] In such non-fundamentalist, neo-evangelical circles many pastors would agree:

> *The church is notoriously weak in disciplining its sinning pastors. ... The sinner is uncorrected ... [and] the first concern is to remove them quickly and as far away as possible [while allowing them to pastor again.] ...*

> *[Situations occur such as] a prominent pastor [who] was discovered in a compromising situation that suggested moral impurity. He was confronted. He admitted to indiscretion but refused to accept any responsibility for his actions. He was asked to resign. He left guilty, but he left behind him a totally bewildered church family whose feelings ranged from anger to guilt. He assumed a pastorate in another church and soon revealed again that he was morally irresponsible. That man has had five short-term pastorates in as many years, and has been forced to leave each one for reasons of moral impurity. His departures were not disciplinary in nature. The church just got rid of its problem. He was able to transfer his problem to another unsuspecting congregation.*[332]

Do you think there is less immorality in evangelical denominations that almost never practice church discipline? Is there less child abuse among clergy in modernist denominations that officially sanction the abomination of homosexuality or that officially condone fornication? Outside of Christendom, the wicked world swarms with hordes of ruthless, autocratic, and filthy Diotrephes-type people. Should faithful Jews who saw sin in other Israelites have abandoned Jehovah's tabernacle and temple to gather with those who claimed to worship the LORD but did so with golden calves? Or should they have abandoned the LORD entirely and joined themselves with worshippers of Baal or Moloch? You do not help anyone or anything if you yourself sin by failing to assemble with faithful saints (Hebrews 10:25) because an unfaithful pseudo-saint cast you out.

Unjustly Cast Out?
Be Ready to Prove Your Innocence

Expect that just as Diotrephes would not receive you, but cast you out, so he will do all in his power to prevent others from receiving you (3 John 10). "Prating"[333] and "tattling"[334] are related. Having cast you out, Pastor Diotrephes' malicious words have not come to an end—indeed, he will likely be encouraged by his success (in this world, and in this short life) in casting you out to exert even harsher dictatorial control over those he has left, while spreading the leaven of his prating and malice against you to others. Saul was not content with having driven David away—the seared conscience and the fearful darkness of sin that had settled over Saul urged him forward to continued depredations (1 Samuel 22:16-19) while, deceiving and being deceived (2 Timothy 3:13), he spread delusional slanders in which he himself was the victim and David the oppressive wrongdoer (1 Samuel 22:8). Sheep's blood arouses Diotrephes' wolfish hunting instinct. So you should be ready with clear, unambiguous proof that you were not justly excommunicated, but rather were wickedly devoured by a spiritual carnivore. A good church will properly be biased in favor of the decision of a whole congregation over the claims of one individual, while also recognizing that congregations can err.[335] Good churches will presume a cast-out person is guilty unless he can prove his innocence—while some who have a blind spot for Diotrephes-type leadership will assume you are guilty even if you can prove your innocence, for they will not only assume that the church and its pastor are (rightly) *presumed* right in such situations, but (wrongly) assume that they are *always* right. A good church will be fearful of taking in someone delivered to Satan (1 Corinthians 5:5; 1 Timothy 1:20); the last thing they want is people in Satan's realm in their membership instead of people under Christ's authority. They want to receive true and visible saints and to keep out the wicked. Before they give you consolation as an unjustly cast out sheep, they may ask many hard questions to make sure you were not a justly excommunicated goat—rightly so. So you should be ready, when Diotrephes continues to follow you with his malicious words, to be able to kindly, respectfully, and completely refute them. Also, when some people simply assume Diotrephes is right in his accusations without hearing both sides of the matter, do not let your heart be troubled. The Apostle Paul's loving heavenly Father allowed His adopted son to experience a "messenger of Satan to buffet" him, "lest [he] should be exalted above measure" (2 Corinthians 12:7); your Father will only allow you to have a messenger of Satan like Diotrephes buffeting you if it is for His glory and your good. Receive His sovereign disposition with lowly humility as from His loving hand, trusting that He knows what is best and what you need.

Unjustly Cast Out?
Repent of Sin

If, being surrounded by a sea of malice and slander, you failed to endure it like a meek lamb brought to the slaughter (Isaiah 53:7) but lashed out, giving back some of the bitterness and sinful language that you were getting, you must confess that sin to God and to those whom you sinned against. If you sinned, even against Diotrephes or a panel he brought together to cast you out, confess it and ask for forgiveness from God and from him or them. It was a sin when the Levite in Judges colored the facts to make himself look better (Judges 20:4-6; cf. 19:18), even though he and his concubine had truly been sinned against in a horrifying way (Judges 19). If it is wrong to speak abusive, railing speech even against Satan (Jude 9), although that fallen angel is the absolute master of abusive and slanderous speech, then you must not let one word of such Satanic-type speech come from your lips, even if you were condemned with hundreds of such words. If you did not so sin, rejoice that God strengthened you in the trial, and that, although you are cast out of the church of Diotrephes, you will not, like Diotrephes, be cast into hell fire (Luke 13:28).

Unjustly Cast Out?
Remember Your Relatives

If you have relatives in the church from which you were cast out, Pastor Diotrephes may make life difficult for them. He may already have attempted to set family members or relatives against each other through fear and other manipulation tactics (John 9:19-23). To help secure his preeminence, he may attempt to coerce relatives to agree with your being cast out, threatening to crush and cast them out as well unless they consent to his unjust actions. He may threaten to hold family members hostage to prevent you from warning others about his evil deeds: "If you say anything about what I did, you will never talk to your grandkids again." If your relatives are well-trained in

Scripture and can discern between a righteous overseer and Pastor Diotrephes, his fulminations and threats may be largely ineffective. But if they have a blind spot for Diotrephes-style leadership, they may be susceptible to his feigned but fair-sounding speeches (2 Peter 2:3; Romans 16:18). You will need great wisdom about the right course of action in such situations. Thankfully, God promises: "Trust in the LORD with all thine heart; and lean not unto thine own understanding. In all thy ways acknowledge him, and he shall direct thy paths. Be not wise in thine own eyes: fear the LORD, and depart from evil. It shall be health to thy navel, and marrow to thy bones" (Proverbs 3:5-8).

Unjustly Cast Out? Learn Christ-like Ministry

Isaiah sings concerning Christ, the Good Shepherd: "A bruised reed shall he not break, and the smoking flax shall he not quench" (Isaiah 42:3). Your Jesus "shall feed his flock like a shepherd: he shall gather the lambs with his arm, and carry *them* in his bosom, *and* shall gently lead those that are with young" (Isaiah 40:11). Let these words not only be sweet in your ear and comfortable to your heart, but let them deeply affect how you minister to others. You have experienced the bitter pain of rejection; you have experienced how awful it is not to be received. Let this difficult trial mold you into a fountain of Christ-like receiving, hospitality, and kindness. Were you never received into others' homes, as Diotrephes set the example of not being given to hospitality (1 Timothy 3:2),[336] but of being given to harshness? Be someone who is overflowing in hospitality, who delights to entertain others in a friendly, hospitable way (Acts 28:7).[337] Were you shunned specifically because of a conscientious, Christ-like stand for truth? Be ever the more a "lover of good men" (Titus 1:8).[338] Learn from the bitterness of being cast out how important it is to carry Christ's little lambs in your own bosom; learn from the harshness you experienced how you must gently lead His sheep. Satan wishes for you to be swallowed up in overmuch sorrow (2 Corinthians 2:7)—but instead allow the trial to be a purging fire that makes you more like Christ. It will be abundantly, everlastingly worth it!

It is right to learn spiritual lessons from such a trial—indeed, that is certainly one of God's purposes in ordaining it for you (Romans 8:28-37). But do not dwell upon the injustices you experienced. You serve a God who delights to bring good from evil. Be able to say with Joseph, "[Y]e thought evil against me; *but* God meant it unto good, to bring to pass, as *it is* this day, to save much people alive" (Genesis 50:20). Rather than constantly dwelling upon the past, "forgetting those things which are behind, and reaching forth unto those things which are before ... press toward the mark for the prize of the high calling of God in Christ Jesus" (Philippians 3:13-14). Go forward in faith in your new, Biblically faithful congregation.

Unjustly Cast Out?
Learn When to Speak and When to Move On

Also, after your new, Biblically faithful church has determined that you were not justly excommunicated, but unjustly cast out, there may be situations where you are ethically obligated to let others know about how you were sinned against. However, Scripture does not obligate you to always tell the wolf's spin on the facts, repeating lies Diotrephes spread about you to others as well as the truth, out of a scrupulous desire for fairness. Joseph did not believe it was necessary to repeat and then refute the slander of Potipher's wife—that he was an attempted rapist—even though her slander had successfully landed him in prison. The godly man believed it was sufficient to say that he had "done nothing that they should put me into the dungeon" (Genesis 40:15). There is a time to expose Diotrephes, a time where vindicating one's actions is necessary (2 Corinthians 11), and also a time to just move on, serving the Lord.

XI.) WHAT SHOULD A CHURCH DO IF SOMEONE SEEKS MEMBERSHIP, CLAIMING TO HAVE BEEN CAST OUT BY DIOTREPHES?

Admit a Cast-Out Person? Exercise Great Caution

As already noted, in the large majority of instances, churches act correctly in their acts of excommunication, lawfully binding their members to obey the truths of Scripture and pronouncing Word-based censure on those who sin.[339] Another congregation would be very unwise to receive into its membership someone who has been lawfully excommunicated by a sister church of like faith and practice. Why would you want to bring into your congregation's membership someone who has been delivered to Satan (1 Corinthians 5:5; 1 Timothy 1:20)? Do you want to bring Satan into your church? Such an action neither demonstrates love and reverence for Christ, the Author of the commands in Matthew 18 about excommunication and the holy Head of the church, nor does it show love for the excommunicated person, whose repentance will be hindered by your justification of his sin, nor does it show love for the other members of your flock, as you bring danger into the sheepfold instead of keeping it out. Why would you side with the wicked instead of with a righteous church and people who were sinned against? "He that justifieth the wicked, and he that condemneth the just, even they both *are* abomination to the LORD" (Proverbs 17:15). Will you make yourself and your congregation into an abomination? Church discipline is not child's play. It is a solemn, serious act of eternal significance. You must take the legitimate acts of discipline by other Bible-believing and practicing churches very seriously.

Admit a Cast-Out Person? Investigate Carefully

However, the acts of other congregations are not infallible, and the infallible Word indicates that while most acts of church discipline are legitimate, there are some sinful situations where Pastor Diotrephes unjustly casts out righteous sheep, instead of godly pastors sorrowfully leading the assembly of saints to remove unrepentant sinners from their membership. "Edward Hiscox," the "author of the most popular Baptist church manual ever written,"[340] explains:

> *1. First step.—The member who considers himself injured must go to the offender, tell him his grief, and between themselves alone, if possible, adjust and settle the difficulty. "If thy brother shall trespass against thee, go and tell him his fault, between thee and him alone." This must be done, not to charge, upbraid, or condemn the offender, but to win him. "If he shall hear thee, thou hast gained thy brother."*
>
> *2. Second step.—If this shall fail, then the offended member must take one or two of the brethren with him as witnesses, seek an interview with the offender, and, if possible, by their united wisdom and piety, remove the offense and harmonize the difficulty. "But if he will not*

hear thee, then take with thee one or two more, that in the mouth of two or three witnesses, every word may be established."

3. Third step.—If this step should prove unavailing, then the offended member must tell the whole matter to the church, and leave it in their hands to be disposed of, as to them may seem wisest and best. "And if he shall neglect to hear them, tell it to the church." He has done his duty and must abide by the decision of the body which assumes this responsibility.

4. The result.—If this course of kindly Christian labor proves finally ineffectual, and the offender shows himself incorrigible, excision must follow. He must be cut off from fellowship in the church whose covenant he has broken, and whose authority he disregards. "And if he neglect to hear the church, let him be unto thee as an heathen man, and a publican." However painful the act, the church must be faithful to its duty, and to its God. ...

[The person accused] should be allowed to hear the evidence against him, know the witnesses, and be permitted to answer for himself. If the accused disproves the charges, or if he confesses the wrong, makes suitable acknowledgment, and, so far as possible, reparation, with promise of amendment, in all ordinary cases, this should be deemed satisfactory, and the case be dismissed. But if, after patient, deliberate, and prayerful labor, all efforts fail to reclaim the offender, then, however painful the necessity, the church must withdraw its fellowship from him, and put him away from them. ...

All discipline should be conducted in the spirit of Christian meekness and love, with a desire to remove offenses and win offenders. It must also be done under a deep sense of responsibility to maintain the honor of Christ's name, the purity of His church, and the integrity of His truth. ... If any member shall persist in bringing a private grievance before the church, or otherwise make it public before he has pursued the course prescribed in the eighteenth chapter of Matthew, he becomes himself an offender, and subject to the discipline of the body. ... Any member tried by the church has the right to receive copies of all charges against him, the names of his accusers, and the witnesses, both of whom he shall have the privilege of meeting face to face, hearing their statements, bringing witnesses on his side, and answering for himself before the body. ... Every member on trial or excluded, shall have furnished at his request, authentic copies of all proceedings had by the church in his case, officially certified. ... In every case of exclusion, the charges against the member, and the reasons for his exclusion, should be accurately entered on the records of the church. ... If at any time it shall become apparent, or seem probable to the church that it has for any reason dealt unjustly with a member, or excluded him without sufficient cause, it should at once, and without request by concession and restoration, so far as possible, repair the injury it has done him. ... The church should hold itself bound to restore to its fellowship an excluded member whenever he gives satisfactory evidence of repentance and reformation consistent with godliness. ... Nothing can be considered a just and reasonable cause for discipline, except what is forbidden by the letter or the spirit of Scripture. And nothing can be considered a sufficient cause for disfellowship and exclusion, except what is clearly contrary to Scripture, and what would have prevented the reception of the person into the church, had it been known to exist at the time of his reception. ...

[A] case of discipline undertaken under excitement is almost certain to be wrongly conducted. ... Any person who believes himself wronged by church action has the inalienable right to appeal to the church for a new hearing, and, failing in this, to ask the counsel and advice of brethren, should he see fit to do so. ... If they refuse him ... he could apply to some other church to be received to its fellowship, on the ground that he had been unjustly excluded. Should he be received to another church, that would give him church standing and fellowship again, and vindicate him so far as any ecclesiastical action could vindicate him. ... [T]he presumption is that the church has done right, and is justified in its action [of excommunication], [but] the possibility is that the church

> *has done wrong, and is censurable for its action. ... Any church has the right to receive a member excluded from another church, since each church is sole judge of the qualification of persons received to its fellowship. But any church so appealed to [should] use great caution, and with due regard to its own peace and purity, ascertain all the facts in the case before taking such action.*[341]

It is wrong to assume that a person removed from membership is telling the truth without checking with the excommunicating church (Proverbs 18:13), but it is also wrong to assume that a person cast out is always wrong, listening only to the side of the church or pastor that issued the discipline without hearing the side of the person who was removed, and in that way possibly providing cover for Pastor Diotrephes. Both sides should be fairly heard and the evidence should be evaluated fairly, with a presumption in favor of the decision of the entire congregation (if Diotrephes allowed the entire church to have any voice at all). A sinner who is delivered unto Satan is nobody one would want to be in fellowship with—but neither is Pastor Diotrephes one to fellowship with, as Satan is Diotrephes' lying master.

Receive the Righteous Cast-Out Person

If the person seeking admittance has strong evidence that he was cast out by Diotrephes' personal authority, the steps of Matthew 18:15-17 not having been followed, after giving the congregation from which the person was removed ample opportunity to justify its actions, the cast-out member should be received into your church, and the congregation that cast him out should be called upon to repent. If they refuse, and longsuffering attempts to help them change fail, they should be disfellowshipped themselves.[342] If evidence proves that the accused person was innocent and was only found guilty because of an egregiously biased "trial," he should be received. If the pastor who cast out the sheep refuses to share proof of the guilt of the person he cast out, instead claiming that your church should just trust his unverified accusations, or refuses to share the certified records of the proceedings, while it is possible that you may be dealing with someone who simply needs to understand better Biblical, Baptist ecclesiology and polity, a real danger exists that you are dealing with Pastor Diotrephes. If the pastor of the other church refuses to interact with you directly, only communicating with you indirectly through third parties so that it is impossible to ask and get answers to difficult questions or discover potentially incriminating information, you may be dealing with Pastor Diotrephes. You should have serious concerns if either the person excommunicated or the pastor who led in the excommunication seems intent on hiding evidence, or is offended that you intend to fairly hear both sides of the matter, instead of welcoming an open and unbiased investigation.

Receive the Righteous, Reject the Rogues

Both a sinner justly excommunicated and a Diotrephes unjustly casting out the righteous may have "very subtil" friends (2 Samuel 13:3) who can craftily distort facts in their favor. Like the serpent in the garden, they may both also be very subtil themselves (Genesis 3:1). You cannot make a decision based upon who has more convincing friends, which side of the story you heard first, or which side you want to believe is right. "*He that is* first in his own cause *seemeth* just; but his neighbour cometh and searcheth him" (Proverbs 18:17). Rather, you must evaluate the facts dispassionately with Scripture as your guide, the illuminating Spirit as your confidence, the Father as your reverend Judge, and Christ as your all-seeing Lord. "Ye shall do no unrighteousness in judgment: thou shalt not respect the person of the poor, nor honour the person of the mighty: *but* in righteousness shalt thou judge thy neighbour" (Leviticus 19:15). Do not respect the person of the individual cast out—if he is a big giver, or would be a great help as a hard worker in the ministry, yet if he is a big sinner who was justly placed under discipline, do not receive him in. Do not respect the person of the pastor who led in the excommunication—if he is a very well-known and prominent person, or a dynamic speaker, or a leader at a Christian college, he must still provide the same kind of clear evidence of guilt for a person placed under discipline that would be necessary if he were the pastor of a congregation of a handful of people with no fame in this world. "Judge not according to the appearance, but judge righteous judgment" (John 7:24), and Christ will protect your church by His Word and Spirit from both the spiritual harm that arises from receiving justly excommunicated sinners and the spiritual harm that arises from receiving the slanders of Pastor Diotrephes while turning away the wounded and needy sheep of Christ.

XII.) CASE STUDIES

A.) People Like Diotrephes Who Exerted Control over Other "Congregations" or "Assemblies"—Aristotle on Tyrannies in the Greek City-State (*Ekklesia*)[343]

As to tyrannies ... the old traditional method ... [in which] they are preserved ... [is the way] in which most tyrants administer their government. Of such arts Periander of Corinth is said to have been the great master, and many similar devices may be gathered from the Persians in the administration of their government. ... [F]or the preservation of a tyranny, in so far as this is possible ... the tyrant should lop off those who are too high; he must put to death men of spirit; he must not allow common meals, clubs, education, and the like; he must be upon his guard against anything which is likely to inspire either courage or confidence among his subjects; he must prohibit literary assemblies or other meetings for discussion, and he must take every means to prevent people from knowing one another (for acquaintance begets mutual confidence). Further, he must compel all persons staying in the city to appear in public and live at his gates; then he will know what they are doing: if they are always kept under, they will learn to be humble. In short, he should practice these and the like Persian and barbaric arts, which all have the same object. A tyrant should also endeavour to know what each of his subjects says or does, and should employ spies, like the "female detectives" at Syracuse, and the eavesdroppers whom Hiero was in the habit of sending to any place of resort or meeting; for the fear of informers prevents people from speaking their minds, and if they do, they are more easily found out. Another art of the tyrant is to sow quarrels among the citizens; friends should be embroiled with friends, the people with the notables, and the rich with one another. Also he should impoverish his subjects; he thus provides against the maintenance of a guard by the citizens, and the people, having to keep hard at work, are prevented from conspiring. The Pyramids of Egypt afford an example of this policy; also the offerings of the family of Cypselus, and the building of the temple of Olympian Zeus by the Peisistratidae, and the great Polycratean monuments at Samos; all these works were alike intended to occupy the people and keep them poor. Another practice of tyrants is to multiply taxes, after the manner of Dionysius at Syracuse, who contrived that within five years his subjects should bring into the treasury their whole property. The tyrant is also fond of making war in order that his subjects may have something to do and be always in want of a leader. And whereas the power of a [righteous ruler] is preserved by his friends, the characteristic of a tyrant is to distrust his friends, because he knows that all men want to overthrow him, and they above all have the power.

Again, the evil practices of the last and worst form of democracy are all found in tyrannies. Such are the power given to women in their families in the hope that they will inform against their husbands, and the license which is allowed to slaves in order that they may betray their masters; for slaves and women do not conspire against tyrants; and they are of course friendly to tyrannies and also to democracies, since under them they have a good time. For the people too would fain be a monarch, and therefore by them, as well as by the tyrant, the flatterer is held in honour; in democracies he is the demagogue; and the tyrant also has those who associate with him in a humble spirit, which is a work of flattery.

Hence tyrants are always fond of bad men, because they love to be flattered, but no man who has the spirit of a freeman in him will lower himself by flattery; good men love others, or at any rate do not flatter them. Moreover, the bad are useful for bad purposes; "nail knocks out nail," as the proverb says. It is characteristic of a tyrant to dislike everyone who has dignity or independence; he wants to be alone in his glory, but anyone who claims a like dignity or asserts his independence encroaches upon his prerogative, and is hated by him as an enemy to his power. Another mark of a tyrant is that he likes foreigners better than citizens, and lives with them and invites them to his table; for the one are enemies, but the others enter into no rivalry with him.

Such are the notes of the tyrant and the arts by which he preserves his power; there is no wickedness too great for him. All that we have said may be summed up under three heads, which answer to the three aims of the tyrant. These are, (1) the humiliation of his subjects; he knows that a mean-spirited man will not conspire against anybody: (2) the creation of mistrust among them; for a tyrant is not overthrown until men begin to have confidence in one another; and this is the reason why tyrants are at war with the good; they are under the idea that their power is endangered by them, not only because they will not be ruled despotically, but also because they are loyal to one another, and to other men, and do not inform against one another or against other men: (3) the tyrant desires that his subjects shall be incapable of action, for no one attempts what is impossible, and they will not attempt to overthrow a tyranny, if they are powerless. Under these three heads the whole policy of a tyrant may be summed up, and to one or other of them all his ideas may be referred: (1) he sows distrust among his subjects; (2) he takes away their power; (3) he humbles them. This then is one of the two methods by which tyrannies are preserved[.][344]

B.) Catholic Submission to that False Prophet and Antichrist the Pope, and other Diotrephes-like Leaders in the Jesuit Order: Ignatius of Loyola's *Letter On Obedience*

[A]lthough I wish you all perfection in every virtue and spiritual grace, it is true (as you will have heard from me on other occasions) that it is more particularly in obedience than in any other virtue that God our Lord gives me the desire to see you distinguish yourselves. ... We may let other religious orders outdo us in fasting, night-watches, and other austerities which each one, following its own institute, holily observes. But in the purity and perfection of obedience, with genuine resignation of our wills and abnegation of our judgment, I am very desirous, dear brothers, that those who serve God in this Society should distinguish themselves, and that its true sons may be recognized by this[.] ...

For the superior is not to be obeyed because he is highly prudent, very good, or qualified by any other gift of God our Lord, but rather because he holds his place and authority—as eternal Truth has said, "He who hears you hears me, and he who despises you despises me." Nor, on the other hand, should he be any less obeyed in his capacity as superior if he is less prudent, for he represents the person of him who is infallible wisdom and who will make up for any shortcomings in his minister; nor if he is lacking in goodness or other excellent qualities, since Christ our Lord, after saying, "The scribes and Pharisees have sat on the chair of Moses," expressly adds, "Do all that they tell you, but do not act according to their works." ... From this you can infer, when a religious [Jesuit] takes someone not only as his superior but expressly in the place of Christ our Lord to direct and guide him in his divine service, to what degree he ought to hold that person in his soul, and whether he should look upon him as a man, and not as the vicar of Christ our Lord instead.

I also desire it to be firmly fixed in your souls that the first degree of obedience, which consists in the execution of what is commanded, is quite low. It does not deserve the name of obedience or attain the worth of this virtue unless it rises to the second degree, which consists in making the superior's will one's own, in such a way that there is not just effective execution but a conformity of wish, an identical willing and not willing. This is why Scripture says, "Obedience is better than sacrifices[.]"[345] ... What a great and dangerous deception it is for persons to think they may lawfully deviate from their superiors' will[.] ... And so, my dear brothers, try to make the surrender of your wills complete. ... And so I conclude that anyone who wants to rise to the virtue of obedience will have to ascend to this second degree, which, over and above the execution, consists in making the superior's will one's own[.] ...

But whoever aims at making a complete and perfect oblation of himself must, in addition to his will, offer his understanding. ... It is certain that ... obedience ... must also include the judgment's thinking the same as the superior commands[.] ... [S]ubjection and subordination cannot be had without conformity of the inferior's understanding and will to the superior's ... judgment ... whom he has taken to govern him in God's place as interpreter of the divine will. ... Hence Cassian says in the "Conference of Abba Moses:" "By no other fault does the devil so draw a monk headlong to his death as by persuading him to ignore the advice of his elders and trust to his own conclusions and judgment."

[One can and ought] ... to obey ... against one's judgment ... obey even when commanded amiss ... [despite] doubts about the rightness of doing what is commanded. [But one needs to get beyond even this to] [t]he much-extolled simplicity of blind obedience ... [not even] debat[ing] whether the command was good or bad[.] ... Thus, while obedience is properly a perfection of the will that renders it eager to fulfill the will of the superior, yet it must also, as we have said, extend to the understanding, inclining it to think what the superior thinks, so that in this way one can proceed with the full strength of the soul—will and understanding—to a prompt and perfect execution. ... So do not consider the voice of the superior, insofar as he gives you a command, as anything but the voice of Christ ...

A ... means for subjecting the understanding is ... employed by the holy fathers. It is this: taking for granted and believing—very much as we do in matters of faith—that whatever the superior enjoins is the command of God our Lord and his holy will, one proceeds blindly to the execution of the command, without any inquiry and with the force and promptitude of a will eager to obey. This is how we are to believe Abraham obeyed when commanded to sacrifice his son Isaac. Similarly, in the new covenant with some of those holy fathers mentioned by Cassian, like Abba John, who did not examine whether what he was commanded was worthwhile or not, as when he laboriously watered a dry stick for a whole year; or whether it was possible or not, as when he strove so earnestly, when so commanded, to move a rock which a large number of persons could not have moved. ... My point is that this manner of subjecting one's own judgment without further inquiry, taking for granted that the command is holy and in conformity with God's will, is in use among the saints and ought to be imitated by anyone who wishes to obey perfectly in all things where no manifest sin is evident. ...

What I have said about obedience applies to individuals with reference to their immediate superiors, to rectors and local superiors with reference to provincials, to these with reference to the general, and to the general with reference to the one God our Lord has given to him as superior, his vicar on earth [namely, the Pope, that Man of Sin, False Prophet, and Antichrist]. In this way subordination will be fully preserved[.] ... we see the same on earth in well-ordered states, and also in the hierarchy of the Church, brought under the one universal vicar of Christ our Lord [the Pope]. The better this subordination is kept, the better the governance. ... [I]n this society, over which our Lord has given me some charge, I want the perfection of this virtue to be pursued as if the Society's entire well-being depended on it.[346]

The Jesuit dogma of blind obedience stands in the sharpest contrast to the declarations in Biblical Christian confessions of faith. For example:

> *God alone is Lord of the conscience (James 4:12; Romans 14:4), and has left it free from the doctrines and commandments of men, which are in any thing contrary to His Word, or not contained in it (Acts 4:19; 5:29; 1 Corinthians 7:23; Matthew 15:9). So that to believe such doctrines, or obey such commands out of conscience, is to betray true liberty of conscience (Colossians 2:20, 22–23); and the requiring of an implicit faith, and absolute and blind obedience, is to destroy liberty of conscience and reason also (1 Corinthians 3:5; 2 Corinthians 1:24).*[347]

C.) Classic Diotrephes: A Modern Situation Where Pastor Diotrephes Casts Out the Righteous[348]

Joining the Church!

Mr. and Mrs. Sheep were excited to join Bovine Baptist Church in the town of Sheep, Penn. Mr. Sheep had known of this faithful church for many years, and both Brother and Sister Sheep had been positively impacted by the faithful service of both the head pastor and other pastors at Bovine Baptist Church. They had moved to Pennsylvania with the strong encouragement of the head pastor of BBC in order to engage in greater ministry in areas where both Mr. and Mrs. Sheep had been gifted by the Lord. However, shortly after their arrival, the previous head pastor had resigned from the church. A church member at BBC with no previous experience in the pastorate, but years of experience in the business world, was elevated to be the head pastor. Mr. and Mrs. Sheep did not know the new pastor, Mr. D., very well, but they wished him well and looked forward to joyfully serving the Lord together.

Things Are Different Now.

Mr. Sheep had loved talking about the great Biblical messages the previous pastor had preached with that man of God and other saints in the church after services. They would gather near the entrance of the church building afterwards and discuss the Word that had been preached, asking questions, making application, clarifying teaching, being built up. However, things were different with Pastor D. He viewed such questions as a threat; Bro Sheep was insulting him when he asked questions. Mrs. Sheep, who had not known BBC as well as Mr. Sheep, also had questions, and Mr. Sheep had encouraged her, before they came, that BBC was a place where one could ask and have questions answered. However, that was no longer the case under Pastor D. When Mrs. Sheep asked questions, she was trying to teach men, Pastor D. asserted. Indeed, not only was she trying to teach him, but she was trying to teach the other pastors and deacons as well, and deserved to be put down harshly. Sister Sheep found this accusation shocking and disheartening, as she had never wished to do anything of the kind. However, the Sheep family recognized that people are different; not everyone is as outgoing as the previous pastor at BBC had been, and they thought it made sense that Pastor D., as a new pastor, might not be able to give answers as clearly as the previous pastor, who had been privileged to receive extensive seminary training, knew the Biblical languages, had decades of pastoral experience, and had preached verse-by-verse through the entire Bible. Pastor D. would not give detailed and careful answers to questions from Scripture; rather, his answers were shallow and dubious. He explained that, for guidance, he leaned heavily on his wife's womanly intuition. He would make doctrinally dubious affirmations, introducing into BBC's evangelistic literature the affirmation that "On the cross, Jesus was separated from His Father." Brother Sheep was concerned that their church was now telling the world that at one point the second Person in the Trinity was "separated" from the other two, contrary to Scripture and the classical doctrine of the Trinity.[349] Pastor D. also did not like Brother Sheep's belief that the lost could be saved simply by grace alone through repentant faith alone in Christ alone without repeating the sinner's prayer—but Pastor D. did not show that Brother Sheep's position was not taught in the Bible, nor deal with the fact that the "sinner's prayer" method of evangelism did not even exist for the vast majority of church history.[350] Rather, Pastor D., not even opening the Bible, pulled out instead a book written by a sincere man, and used that uninspired work as proof that the lost not only frequently do pray at the moment they trust in Christ, but they literally must confess and pray in order to be justified. While the Sheep family wished that they could get questions answered in the way it used to be possible, they determined that they would do their best to just accommodate Pastor D. and not worry about these things.

Nothing to Contribute

Pastor D. had a very different idea about what Mr. and Mrs. Sheep should be doing at BBC. The ministry that the previous pastor had encouraged them to move to Sheep, Penn. to lead was not something Pastor D. thought was important. Although it was a type of ministry that Bro Sheep had extensive training for and experience in, Pastor D. thought he should just abandon it. Whatever previous experience the Sheep family had in serving the Lord did not matter—they were to consider themselves like new Christians. They had nothing to contribute, but needed to simply be quiet and fit in. Indeed, even suggesting that they engage in the ministry that the previous pastor had strongly encouraged them to move to BBC to head up was now rebellious. Yes, they had moved to Sheep, Pennsylvania, specifically for that purpose; but now that he was the pastor things were different. Their ministry was no longer needed in Sheep, Penn. Indeed, there was antagonism between Pastor D. and the previous pastor—Pastor D. made many accusations against him, which the congregation was supposed to simply trust were valid. Mr. Sheep was saddened to think that the previous pastor, whom he had looked up to and who had impacted his life in many positive ways, was all the things Pastor D. said. He did not think to question if what Pastor D. said was accurate—he trusted him as the new pastor.

Unstable Accusations

Pastor D. would sometimes preach good messages. However, he would also sometimes preach troubling things that did not seem to be what the passages he quoted meant in their context. However, because asking about these things was viewed as insulting, Bro Sheep generally just let them go. Pastor D. had encouraged Brother Sheep to follow him without understanding.

"If you have a question about something in a message, just think about it for a while without saying anything to anyone. Then, say 'I'm not going to let this bother me,' and drop it without saying anything." Furthermore, "a good tree cannot bring forth evil fruit," Pastor D. explained, referencing Matthew 7:18. "I have a good heart, so what I say is going to be good—you can trust it, even if you don't understand why, and just follow."

However, one week, in the context of warning against sinful speech, Pastor D. repeated from the pulpit multiple times a minced oath, an expression that is a form of God's holy name taken in vain.[351] Brother Sheep could not believe his ears. He would never use such an expression himself, and when on one occasion a member of his family had used a similar expression at home, not thinking about what it meant, he had taken it very seriously, confessing it to God as sin with tears, and spending time in fasting and mourning over its use, beseeching God for mercy for his family's iniquity and his as the head of the home. It was not something that he had heard on the lips of other pastors of BBC.[352] He recognized that the New Testament church is the equivalent of the Old Testament holy of holies (1 Corinthians 3:16-17), and what one said in such a place, especially during the holy ordinance of preaching God's Word, was very, very serious. He was convinced that love for Christ's holy name required him to say something. He therefore, having complemented Pastor D. on many good things in that message, then asked, without offering any criticism, if he could kindly explain why he used the oath. This question did not go well.

"You are censorious and using entrapment," Pastor D. said.

Brother Sheep was shocked. Entrapment? What? The thought had never entered his mind and he had no idea how Pastor D. had drawn that severe conclusion. He sought to apologize for whatever he could see that was possibly wrong in what he said. Brother Sheep's apology seemed to improve things. Pastor D. said that he changed his mind.

"It's possible that what you said was bordering on disapproval and I got defensive. I thought I deserved more benefit of the doubt. I took it personally," he said. "That period was a dark time in my life, and I remember times of immense discouragement thinking that I should not be a pastor or preach at all. Your question was used of the devil (through no intent on your part) to cause me to think that I should not be behind God's holy desk speaking to God's holy people," confessed Pastor D. Pastor D. explained later that what had encouraged him to stay in the ministry was the book *Dear Preacher, Please Quit!* by Roy L. Branson, a book Brother Sheep had never heard of and (at that time) knew nothing about. Brother Sheep was shocked that the sort of communication that he had regularly engaged in with many Christian brethren would be so destabilizing to Pastor D., but he was glad that the harsh accusations of censorious entrapment had been taken back.

"Pastor D. was just very new pastoring and was having a hard time," thought Bro Sheep. Bro Sheep thought the issue was over—but it was not. Pastor D. changed his mind again. He started to avoid Brother Sheep, not talking to him except to say "Hi" or "Bye," something Brother Sheep found very strange and unbiblical. Pastor D. brooded over Brother Sheep asking about the minced oaths for over a year—Brother Sheep having no idea that Pastor D. had withdrawn from his view that he should not have taken offence at all—and became re-offended. Thus, one day, more than a year later, Pastor D. told Brother Sheep:

> *"You offended me, and I am still offended. You should be in trouble with God for communicating with me like that. The world will spin off its axis if we allow that kind of*

> *speech to pastors. God sets up authority and hierarchy, and it is not true that if what you say is right it makes it OK, for the pastor is like the Lord's Anointed. Church discipline proceedings should have begun for what you communicated. You are a 'vessel unto dishonor' (2 Timothy 2), and the 'great house,' the 'church' must be purged of people like you. You never listened when I confronted you—that was when our relationship ended. Do you want to be disciplined out of the church?"*

Bro Sheep had no idea that Pastor D. had changed his mind, moving from his questions being something that should not have been taken personally to being so radically sinful that they would drive the world off its axis and deserved excommunication. (Pastor D. certainly never agreed that he was wrong to take God's name in vain multiple times from the pulpit—the only question was whether Brother Sheep was sinning to ask about it.) Pastor D. stated that even though Mr. Sheep had no idea Pastor D. was still offended, nevertheless Mr. Sheep had been in sin for over a year, with all of his prayer and worship rejected by God, because Pastor D. had felt offended. (Brother Sheep was shocked at how Pastor D. had turned the teaching of Matthew 5:23-24 on its head, but he said nothing about it, as such questions were not welcome.)

Furthermore, Pastor D. had started avoiding Brother Sheep because there were certain people in the church who are "vessels of dishonor" from whom the pastor must "purge" himself. Brother Sheep was dumbfounded by the severe conclusions Pastor D. had come to and the allegorical interpretations of Scripture used to justify them. He was terrified by Pastor D.'s threat to excommunicate him and flabbergasted that Pastor D. could have so radically changed his opinion of what had happened. Brother Sheep apologized for whatever he could see fell short of Christ's perfection in his previous communications from a year earlier for a second time (now that he knew that Pastor D. was still offended) and, for a second time, Pastor D. said he was forgiven—but this also was taken back again later. Pastor D. explained later that Brother Sheep asking about minced oaths was proof that he was a rebel—and, as Pastor D's spiritual guide, Roy L. Branson, explained, "Rebels like Mr. Sheep don't change."

Get Off the Property, Right Now!

Sister Sheep had, for several years, tutored Pastor D's children in an area where she had significant expertise. However, that suddenly changed. Never having received one negative word or suggestion on anything that needed to change from Pastor D. in that entire time, he quickly drew the conclusion that something she was saying was not right. He then hastily walked in on and interrupted their tutoring session, abruptly ended it, rebuked Sister Sheep openly before the child, and then, following his practice in the business world, walked away. Sister Sheep, shocked by this explosion, reached out to the wife of Pastor D., seeking to get resolution before the sun went down (Ephesians 4:26)—but this was also rebellious, because Pastor D believed (as the Sheep family did not know at the time) that the word "quickly" in Matthew 5:25 should be "de-emphasized" in conflict resolution—it was better to wait and not deal with problems right away. Pastor D. explained that Sister Sheep trying to resolve the situation the same day was proof that she "could not contain herself, was not self-controlled, but was in self-righteous vindication mode." She did not want to solve anything, but was full of pride, and wanted to verbally assault Pastor D's wife and daughter—that was her motive for reaching out the same day. Brother Sheep needed to follow Pastor D's example, and start strongly rebuking Sister Sheep, bringing her low.

The next day Pastor D. called Brother Sheep on the phone while Mr. Sheep was at work and commanded him to have Sister Sheep leave the church property immediately, and not come back—that was the abrupt end of her work with Pastor D's children. Although the Sheep family had never heard of anyone being forbidden from being on church property except people like sexual perverts, Brother Sheep dutifully called his wife and told her to leave the property immediately. While Pastor D. lifted this prohibition several days later, he also spent approximately six hours, over several days, explaining why Sister Sheep was so bad, Brother Sheep not disagreeing or giving explanation, as Pastor D. had made it clear that there would be no back-and-forth—the pastor's view of things was the right one, and that was all there was to it.

"Sister Sheep needs to be brought low," Pastor D. explained. "I don't get leadership and orders from subordinates."

Get Over Your Conscience and Follow Without Understanding!

Furthermore, Pastor D. explained, "Sister Sheep needs to get over her conscience." Rather than proving with Scripture what he wanted to have done, Pastor D. said: "The only answer to her conscience issues is to trust leadership—she is not submissive." Whether she saw it or not, she must overcome her conscience and obey what Pastor D. wanted, following him without understanding, even if it required her to violate what she believed were Biblical principles. "Not doing so shows that she thinks she is the standard. Who made her the standard? If leadership says something is right, it is right. Nobody wants Mrs. Sheep's opinion, and nobody is asking her. She isn't in charge. She needs to take it on herself to just fit in."

Bring Your Wife Low!

Brother Sheep was overwhelmed by the severity that was pouring out of Pastor D., but he wanted to respect his new pastor's opinion. He therefore shared with his wife as much of Pastor D's severe judgments as he could—bringing Sister Sheep so low that he became concerned that she was literally going to snap mentally, something that had never even crossed his mind as a possibility at any previous point in their many years of marriage. As Sister Sheep sought to take Pastor D.'s harsh statements very seriously, his words led Sister Sheep to question truth at the deepest level. Could she herself have a relationship with God, or did God only guide and relate to the pastor, whom she needed to follow without understanding and even against her conscience and what she thought Scripture required? Did Pastor D. mediate between her and God? Was she really a miserable, proud, flagrant rebel for fearing to violate her conscience?

Brother Sheep was extremely concerned when he saw how low Pastor D's pattern of harsh advice had brought Sister Sheep. Bringing it up to him, Pastor D. said that what Mr. Sheep had seen in Mrs. Sheep was not happening—Mr. Sheep was making it up, claimed Pastor D. Even though he rarely even spoke to her, Pastor D. knew what was going on in Mrs. Sheep's life better than Mr. Sheep did. Besides, if Mr. Sheep was not making it up, it was not the fault of the harsh advice, but it was Mr. Sheep's fault.

"Mrs. Sheep is having trouble because you are rebellious; you are not listening," he accused. "You have never listened to me once the whole time you have been here." Furthermore, Mrs. Sheep did not need to be built up—she needed to be brought lower.

Brother Sheep was dumbfounded by these declarations. How much lower could Mrs. Sheep get before she literally snapped? He had never listened to Pastor D. one time? But they sought to take everything he was saying extremely, extremely seriously. They were striving to please him harder than they had just about any person in their entire lives. What was he talking about? But both Mr. and Mrs. Sheep knew that they had blind spots. What if Pastor D. was on to something? Was there some truth to what he said? They thought very, very carefully about his words. The more seriously they took them, the lower they sunk, as Pastor D.'s words and actions tore into their souls.

"I Do Not Encourage Individual Study of Bible Doctrine."

Brother Sheep had known the assistant pastors at BBC for a long time. They had been at Bovine Baptist in the days when Brother Sheep was encouraged to discuss Scripture at the church building's door. The assistants had never given Bro Sheep anything but support in his study of Scripture. Pastor D. had explained that his decree, that "nobody asked, and nobody wanted" the opinion of Sister Sheep did not apply to her only, because she was a woman. It applied to him as well, because he was not in leadership—for him as well, offering his opinion was proud, rebellious, and setting himself up as the standard of excellence. Brother Sheep, wanting the opinion of the assistant pastors, and seeking to respect the decree of Pastor D. that nobody cared about what he thought, when he studied Scripture and put his thoughts together on it, would occasionally email the assistant pastors to get their view on the matter. After Pastor D. had insisted that nobody asked, and nobody wanted Bro Sheep's opinion, Brother Sheep sought to respect Pastor D's decree by no longer adding Pastor D. on such emails. Furthermore, Pastor D. had said that Brother Sheep was "free to call or talk to the assistant pastors anytime; I 100% support it, without any reservation." But this also changed very suddenly. After sending the assistant pastors a study of Scripture, the fact that Brother Sheep did not send it first to Pastor D. was evidence of rebellion:

> *"You have a tendency to always put yourself in the midst of controversy. You lack mercy and love, and are not listening. You need to think that the pillar and ground of the truth is the church, not Mr. Sheep. You are unruly, out of line, not in sync. It is not your place to send people studies of doctrine. People are not encouraged to study doctrine individually, but the whole church studies doctrine together, following the lead of the head pastor. You must send to me first any new or revised original theological, doctrinal, or Bible studies before they are sent to other church members, even the other pastors. Confess that sending the studies to the other pastors was wrong."*

Brother Sheep was flabbergasted. Pastor D. had explicitly said that sending studies of Scripture to the other pastors was 100% acceptable, without any reservation—but when he did it, Pastor D. said that Mr. Sheep had sinned, and that he needed to confess that it was a sin. Pastor D. had explicitly stated, and confirmed in writing, that he did not want Brother Sheep's opinion—but now Bro Sheep had sinned by not sharing his opinion with him. This new decree was no passing fad, either—Brother Sheep asked if it was acceptable to even share an edifying quote from a commentary by Charles Spurgeon with a deacon he had known for many years. This request was rejected. Not only his own thoughts, but even edifying, non-controversial quotations from classic Christian authors could not be shared. Did not Scripture teach the priesthood of the believer, a core Bible doctrine and Baptist distinctive? Did not the Holy Spirit lead every Christian, not the pastor alone? How could Pastor D. state that individual Christians are not encouraged to study Bible doctrine, but the head pastor studies the Bible, and then everyone else just follows? Were the other BBC pastors—men who had been in full time Christian service for decades longer than Pastor D.—Christians of so little understanding of Scripture that they could not be trusted to have the discernment to even read a study of Scripture by a church member? What was going on here? Brother Sheep was shocked. He did not know what to make of all this—but so arrived the abrupt end of his asking the assistant pastors their thoughts on passages of Scripture. Pastor D. had suddenly and explosively brought to an end many years of edifying interaction with these other pastors. Brother Sheep was greatly saddened. He wanted to be pastored. How could that take place if he was forbidden from discussing Scripture with the pastors of his church?

"Discipline This Family Out—No Investigation Allowed."

Pastor D. called a meeting of the men in the church. A church family, he explained, needed to be placed under church discipline. Pastor D. said that this family had written a letter to the pastors giving reasons why they wanted to leave and asking for their membership to be transferred to another Baptist church. However, their letter was not open for examination, and what they had done was not right, Pastor D. affirmed.

"Whatever two witnesses agree to must be believed by everyone else, without any further investigation," Pastor D. claimed Matthew 18:15-17 taught.

Therefore, because Pastor D. and at least one other person agreed that this family needed to be cast out, the church was required to vote for their removal. The gathering of men dutifully voted as Pastor D. had instructed. Brother Sheep was troubled by this procedure, as it simply did not seem at all like what Matthew 18:15-17 taught, and seemed very open to abuse. However, Pastor D. had made it very clear that he needed to simply be obeyed.

Brother Sheep offered no objection, but, kept his concerns to himself, never telling anyone his concerns other than Sister Sheep.

"I hope that never happens to us," the Sheep family thought. "If Pastor D. ever decides to cast us out, we don't stand a chance."

"I Know Your Problem—You Are Ignorant!"

One day Pastor D. called both Brother Sheep and an assistant pastor into his office. Pastor D. began to read a pre-written, detailed and lengthy condemnation of Brother Sheep for disobeying Scripture in a particular area—both he and Mrs. Sheep were said to be grievously sinning by failing to do what Pastor D. said was necessary in this area. Pastor D. had never spoken to Brother Sheep about this matter before calling him in for lengthy condemnation before the assistant pastor.

"You do not love God and do not love your pastors," Pastor D. said; Mr. Sheep, he claimed, was not obeying this basic area of the Bible. However, Brother Sheep was actually sacrificially involved in this area of Biblical practice to an extent that went beyond what Pastor D. claimed was necessary; Pastor D. had never taken the time to find this out before calling Brother Sheep in for condemnation.

In reality, Brother Sheep was going far above the standard Pastor D. required. Furthermore, a few years after his conversion to Christ, Brother Sheep had been kicked out of his family's home and disinherited for refusing to compromise in conscientious obedience to the very practice Pastor D. was now condemning Brother Sheep for (allegedly) failing to follow. Brother Sheep had been given an ultimatum by his unbelieving family to stop obeying Scripture in this area or move out in thirty days, in the middle of a college semester.

Remembering the words of Christ, "He that loveth father or mother more than me is not worthy of me: and he that loveth son or daughter more than me is not worthy of me" (Matthew 10:37), Brother Sheep had moved out, accepted being disinherited, and began to live in a tiny single room not much bigger than his small bed. While the persecution he had endured for Christ's name was nothing in comparison to what many Christians endured in other countries, God had given Brother Sheep the privilege of suffering out of conscientious and loving obedience to Christ in the very area Pastor D. now claimed Brother Sheep was not practicing. Pastor D. had not known any of this—he did not know Brother Sheep, nor did he care to know him.

Pastor D. did not apologize once he found out that he had condemned Brother Sheep for the supposed crime of failing to follow a Christian practice that he not only was doing, but was doing greatly and sacrificially at the time, and had even been disinherited and persecuted for practicing in the past. "I don't care what you did in the past!" Pastor D. declared. Rather, he demanded that Brother Sheep adopt the lower standard in this area which Pastor D. himself followed. This lower standard would violate the conscience of Brother Sheep, but that did not matter. Brother Sheep had practiced the higher standard for many years. He had both in churches and in writing preached and taught on it for a long time—including with the approval of the previous head pastor of BBC. But Pastor D. (who did not know these facts) claimed that nobody practiced the way that Brother Sheep both had taught and also modelled in his own life.

"I know your problem—you are ignorant!" Pastor D. fulminated.

Pastor D. described how he had great understanding from his years in the business world, while Brother Sheep, Pastor D. declared, did not even understand basic mathematics.[353] Brother Sheep needed to adopt the lower standard, Pastor D. declared—or else. After much time spent reviling and berating Brother Sheep, insisting that he adopt the lower standard, the assistant pastor—who had essentially listened to the entire long session without saying anything—proposed a solution that would not involve violating Brother Sheep's conscience, but would require an even higher level of sacrifice from the Sheep family. Brother Sheep was glad that the assistant pastor had proposed this option—Pastor D.'s only option was for him to violate his conscience by adopting the lower standard. The Sheep family began to practice the even higher standard suggested by the assistant pastor that incorporated Pastor D.'s demands and also went beyond them. Brother Sheep was thankful for the counsel the assistant pastor had offered.

"Tell Mrs. Sheep that she has been in deep sin for practicing the way you have, Mr. Sheep," Pastor D. commanded, as their meeting ended.[354] Pastor D. also ordered Brother Sheep not to tell anyone about how he had hastily condemned him for (supposed) lack of love in this area of Biblical practice. After all, if they knew Brother Sheep had been persecuted and disinherited for obeying this very Biblical truth, it would make Pastor D. look bad. Both during the long, harsh meeting, and afterwards, Pastor D. could not bring himself to say a single positive word about Brother Sheep's suffering for Christ, nor did Pastor D. ever offer a word of apology for his astonishingly inaccurate assessments, false accusations, or explosive condemnations—but he made sure to mandate that his own reputation was protected.

"Submit, Submit, Submit!"

Pastor D.'s constant theme with the Sheep family was that they were not submissive. He tore down Mr. Sheep so strongly to Mrs. Sheep that she thought, "If he is right, I should never have married Mr. Sheep. I thought he was a godly man, but if Pastor D. is right, boy, was I wrong!" Mrs. Sheep also was full of pride, self-righteous vindication, and all sorts of other sin, and needed to be brought low, Pastor D. explained, and counseled Mr. Sheep that he needed to follow his pastor's example and begin to harshly criticize his wife to bring her low. Any problems were because they were not taking what he said seriously enough and were just rebellious. As each of them sought to take seriously Pastor D's explosive criticisms of both themselves and their spouse, he began to drive Mr. and Mrs. Sheep apart from each other. What could they do? This could not continue.

Slavish Service: Could it Suffice?

Brother Sheep suggested to Sister Sheep that, since Scripture uses the word *doulos,* "servant" or "slave," for believers and since Christians are commanded: "by love serve [*douleuo*] one another" (Galatians 5:13), they should try to be as submissive and respectful to Pastor and Mrs. D. and their children as black slaves would be to their white masters (and the master's children) in the antebellum south. There were black slaves who had faithfully served the Lord in churches in the Old South and honored God despite their status. They would try to put Pastor and Mrs. D. that high above them. Were they slaves in the antebellum South, it would be clear why nobody would ask and nobody would want their opinion. It would be clear why someone would take another person's word—even that of a child who had problems with exaggeration—against their word and why there would be no need to carefully review facts to see what had happened. Nobody would care if they lived, and nobody would care if they died, but they could still serve the

Lord and not worry about it, just casting their care on Him. Of course Pastor D. would not want to hear anything the Sheep family had to say if they were slaves—why should they expect anything else?

"If we say we are *douloi*—slaves—why should we be distraught at getting treated like *douloi?*" asked Brother Sheep. But they could still be lowly and serve them and others in love. They would not tell anyone what they were trying to do in terms of putting themselves that low down below them, and would see if it would help, if that would be lowly enough submission to satisfy what was being unceasingly demanded. They constantly thought about how they could seek to please Pastor D. and have a good relationship with him. Getting on his good side was in their minds when they woke up and when they went to bed. How they could please him was on their lips around their dinner table at home and when they were on vacation. How could they take what he said more seriously? How could they make him happy? They spent more time trying to figure out how to make him happy than they did almost anyone else in their entire lives.

However, even attempting to be as lowly as antebellum slaves failed, as had all their other attempts to please Pastor D. He still thought they were too high and were not submitting. He told Brother Sheep that they needed to be brought lower. After all, as Roy L. Branson had explained, rebels never change—so once the Sheep family was in the "rebel box"; they were not getting out. When Brother Sheep explained that he did not even know what they were not submitting to and that they had been trying for many months to be as lowly as antebellum slaves, even this was not acceptable—it was offensive for them to try to be that way. No explanation for what else they could do was provided.

"I have nothing more to say," Pastor D. explained. "It is all on you. Will you finally repent and start to listen?"

Listen to what? No specifics were given. Pastor D. continued to avoid them in services, not speaking to them for month after month after month. It was so strange, so grievous to their spirits. The Sheep family did not know what to make of it or what to do.

"If You Don't Want To Be Here, Get Out!"

Brother Sheep did not know how to explain all these things. "This is crazy," he thought, "but it has to get worked out somehow." The Sheep family assumed that these acts by Pastor D. were simply inexperience. They hoped that when Pastor D. said that he essentially agreed with Jack Hyles's view of the pastor that this was just a rhetorical overstatement that arose from Pastor D.'s Hyles-influenced background. They thanked God that the trial was happening to them, not to someone else, because what they were going through would have driven many others away from the church. They had moved to Sheep, Penn. with the intention of serving Christ there the rest of their lives. All of this seemed like it was just crazy stuff from Satan that simply had to get resolved. Furthermore, they deeply respected the assistant pastors at BBC, who had never said any of this sort of craziness. Surely there would be a way to work this all out.

Then, however, Pastor D. put a new thought in Brother Sheep's head.

Pastor D. told Brother Sheep, "If you don't want to be here, get out." Pastor D. said he was sick of what they would say and do; besides, they had never given themselves to serve the Lord at the church. (The Sheep family attended every service, were part of weekly evangelism, and were engaged in many other ministries of the church. Nobody else ever suggested that they had never given themselves to serve the Lord.) Brother Sheep asked about it, and Pastor D. confirmed that he meant these things—he was not kidding. Brother Sheep began to seriously think about this statement—something he never thought would happen at this church that they loved. Should they get out?

Request for a Letter of Transfer

The Sheep family spent a great deal of time praying and fasting about what to do. Many attempts to reconcile one-on-one with Pastor D. had failed miserably, and what had happened in those meetings had frequently morphed into something completely different from reality, becoming something for Pastor D. to brood upon for months and months and then bring down on them in an explosive outburst of anger. What happened in the real world, and what Pastor D. would claim afterwards had happened, were different so frequently that the Sheep family wondered if he might have some kind of early-stage Alzheimer's or some other physical malady[355] that led him to distort and color facts—although the distortions always seemed to make Pastor D. look better but Brother and Sister Sheep look worse. The thought began to force itself into their minds—could Pastor D. be Diotrephes? But they did not want to think this way about him—they strove to think the best (1 Corinthians 13). But with one harsh meeting after another, with very obvious pulpit "hint-dropping" to warn about the Sheep family that regularly drove Sister Sheep to tears and was very disconcerting to Brother Sheep, they did not know what to do. Pastor D. continued to avoid them in church, not speaking to them except for "Hi" or "Bye" with a fake smile. They wrote a letter asking for their membership to be transferred, and then sat upon it for a few months, wanting to be sure that they were not acting out of emotion. In the strictest confidence, they shared their letter with two godly friends who had never been to BBC and did not know Pastor D., wanting to make sure that they were thinking Biblically and that in their letter they were speaking respectfully and self-depricatingly. They believed the church was the place of God's special holy presence on earth and did not want to leave without clear Biblical justification.

Finally, after over half a year of "silent treatment" from Pastor D, during which he continued to avoid them as "vessels unto dishonor" but hint-dropped harshly at them from the pulpit in a way that would have led many people to just walk out of the church building and never come back, they finally mailed their letter of transfer request to the three BBC pastors.

Ban the Bible

The Sheep family waited to see what would happen after their letter was received. For a while, there was just eerie silence—nobody said anything. Then things became even more unbelievable. Pastor D. (whose knowledge of Greek and Hebrew was minimal) forbade Brother Sheep from looking at the Bible in its original languages in church.

"You do not need to verify what I am preaching," he said. "You need to trust what I am preaching."

Brother Sheep thought, "This cannot be right. How can the actual words that fell from Christ's holy lips when He was on the earth be forbidden from being in Christ's holy house, the church, during Christ's holy ordinance of preaching?" What about the principle set forth in 1 Corinthians 14:29; 1 John 4:1-3; 1 Thessalonians 5:20-21, and other texts that indicated that the saints should evaluate everything, including preaching, from Scripture? Furthermore, Brother Sheep had often been blessed and strengthened during preaching as the Holy Spirit illuminated truth in the original language text. Must his growth in understanding of the mind of Christ in Scripture be slowed? Pastor D's decree was very troubling to Brother Sheep, but he complied. He no longer brought his physical copy of the actual holy words Christ spoke with him into the church building.

The Pastor, An Untouchable Man: Even if Unregenerate

Pastor D. went on from harsh pulpit hint-dropping to preach things that the Sheep family found simply unbelievable. He proclaimed that God's servants in Matthew 24 are not all Christians, but pastors alone. The "evil servant" of Matthew 24 is a pastor who is not saved. Even if the pastor is unregenerate, and begins to "smite *his* fellowservants, and to eat and drink with the drunken" (Matthew 24:48-49), the normal church members needed to just stay in the church and take it, not leave the church; they should just wait for God to take care of the unsaved pastor, even if this only takes place years later. "The church is not a democracy," he taught. Anyone who wanted to have an unregenerate pastor step down in favor of one who was born again was like Dathan, Abiram, or Korah, for they were laying hands on the Lord's Anointed. Pastor D. got these opinions from Roy L. Branson's book *Church Split*, statistics from which he also quoted in the message. The Sheep family was filled with consternation. Leave an unregenerate man in the pastorate who is smiting the sheep and eating and drinking with the drunken? What? Brother Sheep asked Pastor D. for clarification.

Pastor D. responded: "I am satisfied with what I preached. I will not add to or take away from what I said. The real question is—how does what I preached apply to Mr. Sheep? Did you sin in sending your letter of transfer request, where you gave other people very damaging information about me?" Pastor D. explained that their letter of transfer request should not have been given to anyone, not even the other two pastors of BBC—he alone should have heard their reasons why they wanted to leave.

"Yikes!" thought Mr. Sheep. "Preaching publicly that an unregenerate man should be left in the pastorate is fine—but explaining in private to the three pastors of one's own church why we want to quietly transfer is not! We have to get out. This is not Biblical!"

Warning About Diotrephes Not Welcome

One of the assistant pastors was preaching through the Johannine epistles, and in God's good providence the assistant came to 3 John's passage on Diotrephes. This assistant pastor, who normally made strong applications, was unwilling to even say that Diotrephes was an overseer; supposedly Diotrephes was someone else who somehow had the ability to cast people out of the church on his own authority. Despite the assistant pastor treating the passage with uncharacteristic kid gloves, the message was too strong for Pastor D. Evidently displeased, after the message was over he got up and said that the assistant pastor had attacked the King James Version in the message (something that had not happened, and which probably not a person in the congregation even had as a thought in his mind after the sermon—the assistant pastor was zealously committed to the Received Text and the Authorized Version, and knew more about the issue of texts and versions than did Pastor D.). Nevertheless, based on this excuse of an alleged attack on the KJV, the assistant pastor's message never got up on the church's website—the other messages through the Johannine epistles were there, but that one was not. Out of many, many messages from the assistant pastor, why was the one on 3 John 9-11 the only one that never made it on the church website?

"I Said And Did It All: But I Was Wrong."

The Sheep family had great respect for the other two pastors of BBC. After getting their letter of transfer request, one of them initiated meetings for reconciliation. While a BBC pastor, he was helping with a church-planting effort in a different state and traveled a long distance to facilitate the meetings. Bro and Sis Sheep were deeply touched by his sacrifice. However, for most of the meetings, Pastor D. did not even attend, although he lived close to the church property. Instead of the three BBC pastors and Bro Sheep, most of the time the assistant pastors were present with Mr. Sheep, but Pastor D. did not even come—he would, instead, just pass messages on to the assistant pastors. When they met, the assistant pastors spent most of the time, not on the serious violations of Scripture Brother Sheep had brought up and plainly documented in their letter of transfer request, but on the fact that he had sent the letter at all, and about the need to protect Pastor D's reputation. Bro Sheep thought this was imbalanced, but if he actually had sinned by sending the letter, he wanted to hear how. He did not want to have a sinful mote in his eye, even if another party had a beam in his eye. Was there anything inaccurate in the letter? Nothing was shown to be out of context. Instead, the letter was supposedly sinful because "It was just not who Pastor D. is."

"Pastor D. has a good heart and is a good man," they said. "Pastor D. told us that he had apologized for every one of the situations mentioned in the letter," they said.

This was surprising to Bro Sheep, as he could not recall Pastor D. doing anything of the sort. Pastor D. had also told the assistants many other things that, to Bro Sheep's recollection, did not correspond with reality. Finally, Pastor D. came to one of the meetings with Bro Sheep and the assistant pastors. Pastor D. admitted that he had sinned in many of the situations recounted in the Sheep's letter of transfer request, and confessed them as sin. What about the threats to discipline them out?

"It never even entered my mind that you would need to be disciplined out," he said.

While Brother Sheep did not know how that fit with the multiple situations where that threat had indeed been made, he did not worry about it. It was very comforting to hear that this was not something Pastor D. had even thought about—whatever he had said before, he must have just meant something else. Brother Sheep forgave Pastor D. for everything that Pastor D. asked forgiveness about. Furthermore, the actual words of Christ in their original languages would be permitted in the church building again. What about leaving an unregenerate man in the pastorate?

"Around half a year after I preached that I concluded I was over-reading that narrative," Pastor D. explained.

Brother Sheep was very glad that Pastor D. claimed to no longer think an unregenerate pastor should be left in the pulpit. (Pastor D. never made any public correction of his message.) While taking approximately half a year to come to such an obvious conclusion seemed like serious pastoral inexperience,[356] and the fact that Pastor D. still seemed offended that Brother Sheep ever asked about it was still concerning, Brother Sheep would overlook these things and attribute them to mere inexperience, not to being Diotrephes. There were serious issues that were explicitly tabled indefinitely in these reconciliation meetings, and other statements that were still troubling—Pastor D. still affirmed that he was not interested in the opinions of Brother Sheep or Sister Sheep, and he continued to believe that his allegorical interpretation of Scripture, where certain church members were "vessels unto dishonor" who needed to be avoided, was correct. However, the Sheep family would not worry about those things, because there did seem to be genuine progress, which the Sheep family rejoiced in.

Promised a Letter of Transfer!

"Pastor D. said he never wanted to put us under discipline," Brother Sheep explained to Sister Sheep. "Romans 14 indicates that with a weaker brother one does not engage in doubtful disputations, but just offers kindness and words of support. Let's treat Pastor D. like that; let's give him nothing but positive words and encouragement, so he can grow stronger in the faith."

Sister Sheep was surprised. They both knew he had made threats of excommunication. How could he now say he had never even thought about it?

"I don't know the answer to that," Bro Sheep responded, "But let's think the best."

Perhaps the incredibly difficult trials Pastor D. had put them through might be evidence, not that he was Diotrephes, but only that he was a brother who was weak and who needed support. However, it did not make sense to stay in a church where the pastor was a weaker brother, even if they could rejoice that he was not Diotrephes. Furthermore, in another church they would be able to pursue the ministry to which they had dedicated their lives and which the previous pastor of BBC had specifically said they were going to be able to do, but which Pastor D. had shut down. The Sheep family looked forward to being able to transfer their membership in good order, putting all the troubles with Pastor D. in the past. They would not tell anyone else about what Pastor D. had done, since he had confessed that at least some of it was sin—they would continue to protect his reputation, as they had done through many months of brutal spiritual suffering. Pastor D. and the other BBC pastors promised the Sheep family a letter of transfer, and they looked forward to the church business meeting where it would take place. They looked forward to putting this very harsh trial behind them.

Pastor Diotrephes Springs His Snare

The week before the business meeting, however, there was another shocking surprise. Brother Sheep was called into Pastor D's office. Instead of voting for Mr. and Mrs. Sheep to have their membership transferred, Bro Sheep's transfer request was rejected, Pastor D. said. Instead, he was going to be placed under church discipline!

"You are a liar! You are a scorner!" Pastor D. shouted at Bro Sheep.

Why did Mr. Sheep need to be disciplined out?

"Your letter asking for a transfer of membership was 100% lies!" exclaimed Pastor D. "Your letter is the main reason why you need to be excommunicated. None of the things you wrote in there were true."

Brother Sheep asked about the documentation of their discussions, which Pastor D. had validated afterwards, in writing, as accurate. How could he now say that the severe and threatening decrees that he had forced them to live under for months had never happened?

"I don't care what your written notes say!" Pastor D. fulminated. Before, Pastor D. had confessed as sin many things Brother Sheep had documented in his letter of transfer request. Now, however, things had changed. He had never done any of them. His new position was complete denial. What he had said before, and what he had written, and what he had confirmed as accurate, and what overwhelming evidence confirmed as having taken place in the real world, was now said to be 100% lies—just lies.

For the first time, Brother Sheep knew for certain what he had only suspected before, and had striven hard not to believe was the case: Pastor D. was Diotrephes.

"You Are a Scornful, Contemptuous, Malicious, Misleading, Hubristic, Libelous, Disrespectful, Dishonoring, Unrepentant Talebearer, And You Have Persisted in This Sin For Years. Someone Sent Me a Text!"

Pastor Diotrephes did not talk about the letter of transfer request by Brother Sheep in the excommunication document—Diotrephes was afraid of the facts in that letter. He needed to cast out Mr. and Mrs. Sheep to protect his reputation, so that nobody would believe the facts in their letter if they ever shared it with others—destroying the Sheep family in order to preserve his preeminence was worth it. Roy L. Branson had explained that even if a church was destroyed to protect a preacher, it was worth it. If a whole congregation could be destroyed to protect one of the Lord's Anointed Ones, then two mere sheep could certainly be destroyed.

Thus, afraid of the facts in the letter of transfer request, other slanders were fabricated. Supposedly Brother Sheep had been speaking evil of the three BBC pastors to another pastor. The evidence for this was a (completely unrelated) text message from that pastor to Pastor Diotrephes. Also, Mr. and Mrs. Sheep had wished to show kindness to Pastor Diotrephes, and so had given him a gift and complimented him on some things in an accompanying letter; what they said was 100% positive, but even this letter found its way into the discipline document, along with out-of-context fragments from two emails. The one text message from the other pastor, combined with fragments of two emails and a fragment of a completely complimentary note, were all the "proof" needed that Brother Sheep was a "scornful, contemptuous, malicious, misleading, hubristic, unrepentant talebearer," employing "words of libel" in a "persistent pattern of dishonor and disrespect" that had lasted "years," according to Pastor Diotrephes.

"A Deacon Panel Is The Church."

Brother Sheep had never heard these accusations before—and, for that matter, the assistant pastor present when Brother Sheep was given the discipline letter acknowledged that he had not heard about them either—but nevertheless the assistant said that he would support the accusation. Pastor Diotrephes never approached Brother Sheep about them privately, and then with two or three witnesses—he suddenly sprang his accusations on Brother Sheep, like a snare, so that he could cast him out instead of transferring his membership. Had Pastor Diotrephes wanted reconciliation, the alleged evidence supplied in the letter of discipline could have been resolved in five minutes.

The BBC constitution declared that for "[d]ifferences between individuals or sins not generally known, the wronged party shall follow Matthew 18:15-17. A person bringing a matter into the public before the church, before following this Scripture, shall be subject to rebuke." Pastor Diotrephes, however, set this provision of the BBC constitution aside.

Furthermore, Pastor Diotrephes changed the definition of the church in his discipline document. There would be no trial before the congregation as a whole; indeed, the congregation was distinguished from the "church," which allegedly consisted of a panel of deacons with the pastors. This panel was the "church." If the panel assembled by Pastor Diotrephes agreed with him, Brother Sheep would be excluded from the congregation, which would then validate, without trial, what the "church"—that is, the pastors and deacons—agreed upon.

"Your Judges Will Be Partial."

Brother Sheep discovered that Pastor Diotrephes had called numbers of meetings where he had made many accusations about Mr. Sheep to the deacons. Diotrephes had sought to prepare his snare well before he sprang it on Brother Sheep.

Brother Sheep asked if he could find out what he had been accused of in those meetings, as the deacons would be his judges. This request was rejected. He would not be allowed to find out what he had been accused of or what prejudices against him had been placed beforehand in the mind of his judges. The BBC constitution stated that someone accused could have an advocate, a "lawyer" as it were, to act on his behalf. Brother Sheep asked if he could have such an advocate. That request was also rejected. Brother Sheep said that there were a lot of accusations made. Could he find out the specific evidence that he was a scorner, as well as contemptuous, as well as malicious, as well as hubristic, as well as libelous, etc.? He would be willing to have as many meetings as it took to get to the bottom of these accusations. This request was also rejected.

Pastor Diotrephes—who would moderate the meeting—would require that all the accusations be considered together, and even if it was obvious that there was no evidence for some, most, or even all of his wild accusations against Brother Sheep, Pastor Diotrephes would make sure that Brother Sheep would still be found guilty.

Preparation for Defense

Brother Sheep knew that the meeting would be very heavily stacked against him. Nevertheless, he thought that the assistant pastors and the deacons were sincere men. The accusations were so egregiously false that it should be easy to prove his innocence, even if he were deemed guilty until proven innocent. He prepared a careful statement of defense with Mrs. Sheep, one in which he made no accusations against anyone, but simply and clearly rebutted the false charges. When Pastor Diotrephes gave Brother Sheep the letter to cast him out,

Brother Sheep finally realized that Pastor D. was not an extremely inexperienced yet godly pastor but was, in fact, a genuine Diotrephes. Nevertheless, he decided he would not make any accusations against Pastor Diotrephes, because Brother Sheep thought that the Biblical way of doing this would be to address them privately, and then with two or three, not to immediately bring them to a larger group. Even if Pastor Diotrephes rejected Matthew 18:15-17, Brother Sheep could not and would not. Therefore, he would simply defend himself before the panel against the egregiously false accusations made by Pastor Diotrephes, knowing that they would fall apart under the smallest impartial examination.

Brother Sheep visited the pastor to whom Diotrephes claimed Brother Sheep had been spreading slander. He asked for permission to record (without explaining in advance why he was asking, to prevent any distortion or bias in the responses) this preacher's answers to some questions. The pastor gave his permission.

Brother Sheep asked this preacher, "Have I ever said anything negative to you about the three BBC pastors?"

The pastor said he had not, and that it was surprising that Brother Sheep would even need to ask the question. The other pastor said that the text message Pastor Diotrephes was using to slander and cast out Brother Sheep was not even about BBC—it was about some churches in a different city! Pastor Diotrephes had never sought for clarification on the words of this other pastor—he just wanted something so that he could cast out Brother Sheep and try to keep his own sins covered, fearing the documentation in Mr. and Mrs. Sheep's letter of transfer request.

Brother Sheep was thankful—the recorded words of this other pastor supplied unambiguous, incontestable proof that what Pastor Diotrephes had accused him of was false. Excommunicating him because of a text message that was not even about BBC was crazy, and surely it would not succeed. Brother Sheep also had other clear documentation that proved that the second section of the accusation was false. Concluding someone was a "scornful, contemptuous, malicious, misleading, hubristic, unrepentant talebearer," employing "words of libel" in a "persistent pattern of dishonor and disrespect" that had lasted "years" based on out-of-context fragments of two emails and a text message Brother Sheep did not even know about and which was not about BBC was outrageous.

Surely the other pastors and the deacons would listen! At this point, the assistant pastors were just assuming that what Pastor Diotrephes had told them was true. They were trusting his accusation and assuming Brother Sheep's guilt. But surely things would be different in the discussion before the panel. Brother Sheep would point out how Matthew 18 was not being followed. He would show them the unambiguous proof that the accusations were false.

The Kangaroo Court Commences

When the panel convened, Pastor Diotrephes gave an opening statement. He accused Brother Sheep of many things that were not in the written document that was supposed to supply the only topics of discussion for why Brother Sheep (allegedly) deserved to be cast out and for which Brother Sheep had no ability to prepare a response. As both the moderator and his accuser, Pastor Diotrephes determined that Brother Sheep would not be allowed to cross-examine him. As the moderator, Pastor Diotrephes also required that Brother Sheep only address those two emails—he would not be allowed to respond to the many new accusations that Brother Sheep had never heard of before (for they would also easily have fallen apart if a response had been permitted). Furthermore, Brother Sheep could give a 5-minute opening statement, max. After that, he could only answer questions asked him by the panel of deacons. He could then give a short concluding statement—and concluding statements could only reiterate what had already been discussed, not bring up new evidence or rebut what was said earlier. Thus, Brother Sheep would not be allowed to read his statement of defense, as that would take longer than five minutes. Could Brother Sheep give copies of his opening statement to the panel, since he was forbidden from reading it? No—that also was rejected.

Defense is Not Allowed

How could Brother Sheep respond to all the new accusations, as well as all the accusations that he was supposedly on trial for, in five minutes? While this was impossible, he determined to do the best he could. He would play the audio of the other pastor, unambiguously proving that neither slander nor even any negative statement about the three pastors of BBC had been made to this other pastor. Here also Pastor Diotrephes intervened—playing the audio was forbidden.

Brother Sheep could not read his statement of defense and would not be allowed to provide proof that he was not guilty. Such proof could not reach the ears of the deacons or the assistant pastors if he was to be condemned—as Pastor Diotrephes had determined he must be. Brother Sheep had brought copious written documentation from Pastor Diotrephes proving that he had done exactly what Pastor D. now claimed he had never done. This evidence was also ignored, remaining unread by the panel. Nor was Brother Sheep ever allowed to point out that Matthew 18 was not being followed.

Instead, Pastor Diotrephes held up the letter of transfer request from Brother and Sister Sheep, enclosed within a manila envelope. "This alone is sufficient to show Mr. Sheep is guilty and deserves discipline!" he exclaimed. (He did not mention that the steps of Matthew 18:15-17 were never followed for the alleged sin of writing the letter, nor that the first Brother Sheep had heard about it being a excommunication-worthy sin was when he was given the casting-out document.) "But this letter is not open for examination. Just trust me."

"He's Guilty. Just Trust Me."

Pastor Diotrephes claimed, "A pastor told me that Mr. Sheep has a personal problem with me."

Brother Sheep inquired if they could ask that pastor if it had happened.

"No," Pastor Diotrephes affirmed—"You can trust me on this one."

The deacons piled on. "What problem do you have with Pastor D? What is your problem with him?"

Brother Sheep said he had nothing personal against Pastor D., but he did not appreciate being brought to trial in order to be removed from BBC for something he had never done.

That response was insufficient. (After the meeting Brother Sheep asked this other pastor if he had told Pastor Diotrephes about an alleged personal grudge held against Pastor Diotrephes. The other pastor said he had told Pastor Diotrephes exactly the opposite, and that he did not appreciate being brought into a hearing in this manner without his knowledge or consent. But the assistant pastors and deacons never found out that Pastor Diotrephes had lied—they simply trusted him and never took the time to verify his claims.)

The Assistant Pastors Back Diotrephes

The assistant pastors refused to expose what they knew were lies on the part of Pastor Diotrephes. One of them had previously said, both in person and in writing, that Mr. and Mrs. Sheep's transfer request was *not* a violation of 1 Timothy 5:19. But now he changed, adopting Pastor Diotrephes' position that it was a church-discipline worthy sin for the Sheep family to have sent their letter to the three pastors of their own church asking to quietly be transferred, instead of to Pastor Diotrephes, alone.

"I should never have even read Mr. Sheep's request for a letter of transfer," the assistant said. This assistant pastor said that Brother Sheep's letter was not true "because it was not who Pastor D. is."

Well-documented facts could be set aside without any contrary evidence, because they were not "who Pastor D. is."

On the other hand, Brother Sheep deserved to be delivered to Satan as a scornful, contemptuous, malicious, misleading, hubristic, unrepentant, libelous talebearer, in a persistent pattern of dishonor and disrespect. Why? Undocumented and unproven statements by Pastor Diotrephes—these were enough. This *was* who Brother Sheep is. Not one statement in his request to transfer was shown to be inaccurate—no attempt of that kind was even made. Rather, the transfer request was allegedly false because Pastor Diotrephes must have a good heart and must be right, so there was no need to deal with the actual evidence. This assistant pastor, by saying that Brother Sheep's letter was false, conveyed to the deacons the misleading impression that it contained actual false statements that had been proven false, rather than it was just "not who Pastor D" is and so was "false" despite being completely accurate. The deacons were never allowed to read the letter—they simply needed to trust the assistant pastors.

Pastor Diotrephes claimed that Matthew 18 teaches that one must simply trust whatever two witnesses claim—everyone else needs to just trust two witnesses. Supposedly this was also how trials took place in ancient Israel—if two witnesses could be found for any accusation, it was automatically treated as valid and the accused person was guilty; no successful defense was possible, and no careful investigation was necessary. Since the assistant pastors backed up Pastor Diotrephes, there was no need for the deacons to do any investigation themselves. The assistant pastors should trust Pastor Diotrephes; the deacons should trust the assistant pastors; and the whole congregation should trust the deacons—nobody needed to verify anything objectively. Pastor Diotrephes should be unconditionally followed. (Of course, blind faith in two "witnesses" only applied to those whom Pastor Diotrephes accused of things—such a procedure would absolutely not be followed were anyone to accuse Pastor Diotrephes of any wrongdoing.)

The other assistant pastor said nothing in the entire meeting. Brother Sheep was disappointed to hear one assistant pastor adopt the extremely unbiblical position, advocated by Pastor Diotrephes, that not only regular church members, not only deacons, but even assistant pastors in one's own church should not be allowed to read well-documented and respectful expressions of concern about the conduct of a head pastor. It was disappointing that the other assistant pastor just let all the falsehoods go, without exposing them, saying nothing.

Brother Sheep knew this was all wrong—very wrong. He was disappointed that the assistant pastors, whom he respected, fell in completely behind Pastor Diotrephes' grossly unscriptural position. He knew that this new position, where well-documented, clearly-proven concerns should be rejected out of hand and be turned on the Christian who brought them as a church-discipline worthy offense, would enable a wolf in sheep's clothing to perpetrate all kinds of sin and abuse—and get away with it (at least until Judgment Day—cover-ups would not work then). Brother Sheep knew that this was a change from the former position of the church.

Pastor Diotrephes had changed the Biblical, Baptist church polity of their assembly. From Christ and His Word being preeminent, now it was Pastor Diotrephes' church—whatever Diotrephes said was preeminent and should be received without question. It was no longer a place to faithfully worship the resurrected Lord Jesus. This was not Biblical church discipline (Matthew 18:15-17) but unbiblical casting out (3 John 9-11).

The Predetermined Verdict Reached

Pastor Diotrephes spent almost his entire concluding statement reading from Roy L. Branson's book *Dear Preacher, Please Quit!* Pastor Diotrephes was someone great like Moses—the Lord's Anointed—and Brother Sheep was like Dathan, Korah, and Abiram, rebels against God who deserved to have the ground open beneath them and be taken screaming into hell. The deacons then voted dutifully—Brother Sheep was guilty. The deacon panel, which allegedly constituted the "church," would exclude him, and so he would be forbidden from being present when the "congregation" assembled to hear their decree. The "congregation" would then be required to simply trust what the deacons—"the church"—said. It was not at all clear if Brother Sheep was (supposedly) guilty of what was in Pastor Diotrephes' original accusation or of something else. Since the BBC constitution stated that someone placed under church discipline is entitled to receive in writing what he is found guilty of, Brother Sheep asked if he could get that information; what was he actually said to be guilty of? Like Brother Sheep's other requests, Pastor Diotrephes again ignored BBC's constitution and this request also, rejecting it out of hand.

"Destroy All the Evidence."

Pastor Diotrephes ordered all records of what happened in the meeting destroyed. Brother Sheep's evidence, proving he was not guilty, was destroyed unread, as were the copies of his opening statement, which he never was permitted to share. Only the minutes of the meeting, created by one of the assistant pastors, would stand—and Brother Sheep was forbidden from seeing those or getting a copy.

Forbidding Others From Receiving the Brethren

After casting out Brother Sheep, Pastor Diotrephes got the word out, mainly through third party cut-outs so that he would not have to answer any questions about what happened, that Brother Sheep had been placed under church discipline. What he and his cut-outs told others Brother Sheep was guilty of was quite different from what was contained in the original accusation, but the other pastors needed to just trust that BBC had done the right thing; no documentation would be shared with them.[357] They honored the decisions of the Lord's church, didn't they?

A Biblical Church Impartially Investigates

Brother Sheep sought to join a church that still held to the faith and practice that used to characterize BBC before Pastor Diotrephes had brought Bovine Baptist into bondage. That church reached out to Pastor Diotrephes to hear his side of the story and also asked Brother Sheep to explain his side. The church gave Pastor Diotrephes months to provide proof of guilt, or even reasonable evidence thereof, but he steadfastly refused to do so. First there was one excuse, then a different one, then another, for why he needed more time and could not provide any proof.

Finally, Pastor Diotrephes explained that his word was enough—that was all the other church needed. Brother Sheep deserved to be cast out—"trust me." Pastor Diotrephes explained that he had spoken to other churches about Brother Sheep and they all just believed him, so the church the Sheep family sought to join should similarly just trust Pastor Diotrephes, without evidence.

After giving Pastor Diotrephes around six months to make his case, the pastor of the other congregation led their Biblical Baptist church to examine all the evidence they could acquire. It was overwhelmingly clear that Brother Sheep was unjustly cast out, not justly placed under church discipline. This Biblical

Baptist church received him into their membership, embracing him as their faithful brother in Christ. Sister Sheep was also received into the membership of this Biblical, faithful church.

"Lie, Or We Will Cast You Out, Too."

Part of Pastor Diotrephes' successful plan to cast out Brother and Sister Sheep involved casting them out on separate occasions—it would be hard to claim that their letter of transfer request was "100% lies," and that they deserved to be cast out for writing it, completely ignoring and setting aside its overwhelming documentation, if two witnesses for it were together, right there. Pastor Diotrephes therefore cast out Brother Sheep first, reserving Sister Sheep for later. Brother Sheep, after being cast out, inquired about the status of Sister Sheep's transfer request—his had obviously been rejected, but what about hers?

Pastor Diotrephes explained that, having refused to act on it for months and months, he had finally unilaterally rejected her request to transfer. She needed to start over, validating that what the deacon panel had done was just and that her husband deserved to be cast out—although even she would not be given any written statement of what he allegedly was guilty of. She needed to agree, without any evidence being supplied, that he was a scornful, contemptuous, malicious, misleading, hubristic, unrepentant, libelous talebearer, in a persistent pattern of dishonor and disrespect, based on the most absurdly slender "evidence." She needed to reject her conscience and lie, stating that her husband was guilty of things she knew perfectly well had never happened, or else. Both she and Brother Sheep knew perfectly well that they had discussed how they could bless Pastor D., and had therefore written a kind, 100% positive note to him, accompanied with a gift—yet this note, taken out of context, was "proof" Brother Sheep actually deserved to be cast out. If she would not agree to such egregious falsehoods, she would also be cast out.

Sister Sheep was unwilling to either lie or slander her husband. She would not violate her conscience. Determining instead to bear the wrath and slander that Pastor Diotrephes would pour on her as well, she chose to join the other, Biblical Baptist church with her husband, without a letter of transfer, recognizing that BBC, under Pastor Diotrephes, had departed from the Biblical faith.

Free At Last!

The Sheep family was thankful that, in God's providence, despite their being too slow to recognize it, Pastor Diotrephes had finally and unambiguously revealed himself. That revelation made it clear that they did not need to keep poring over his crushingly harsh and unbiblical advice, as they had done for so long, seeking to please him. Rather, they could recognize that what he had said was the nonsense-speech that characterizes Diotrephes. His oppressive hand was no longer over them, seeking to separate them from each other, forbidding them from having Christian conversation with others, discouraging them from studying Scripture, setting at naught their work for Christ, filling them with fear, doing the slanderous work of Satan in accusing them falsely of one thing after another. Finally, they were free—free to serve Christ, free to love the brethren, free to obey the Word joyfully, free to fit into a Biblical church of Christ and receive godly pastoring instead of wolfish soul-ripping. Hallelujah!

God Knows It Was For Christ's Holy Name

While it generated extremely harsh responses at the time, Brother Sheep also had no regrets about respectfully asking why Pastor D. was using minced oaths in God's pulpit. While bringing harsh condemnation from Pastor D., Brother Sheep drew consolation from 1 Peter 4:14: "If ye be reproached for the name of Christ, happy *are ye*; for the spirit of glory and of God resteth upon you: on their part he is evil spoken of, but on your part he is glorified." It may have brought savage recrimination from Pastor Diotrephes, but asking about it was, quite literally, for the name of Christ.

Reviewing the situation a year later, thankful to be able to worship and serve their Good Shepherd at their new, Biblically faithful Baptist church, Sister Sheep wrote:

> *I do not mark this day with pleasure,*
> *But thank the God who, without measure,*
> *Pours out His grace in darkest woe,*
> *And walks where silent sorrows grow.*
>
> *The snare was set, the truth suppressed,*
> *Yet God stood near and gave us rest.*
> *No justice came by mortal hand,*
> *But still His throne and verdict stand.*

God knows the wrongs still veiled in night—
He'll bring them all into the light.
One year beyond that shadowed day,
One year nearer the dawning day.

"[He] will bring to light the hidden things of darkness ..."
– 1 Corinthians 4:5

Lessons From This Case Study of a Classic Pastor Diotrephes

Understand God's Warning About Diotrephes

Among the many lessons from this case study, a number stand out. First, the Sheep family's lack of familiarity with the Biblical teaching on Diotrephes allowed them to think too highly and too well of Pastor D. for too long. Their striving to take seriously and implement what was simply his "prating," his nonsense-speech (3 John 10), caused serious harm to their family. Only by the grace of God did Sister Sheep not snap mentally under the crushing weight of Pastor Diotrephes' harshness, while Brother Sheep suffered many tearing wounds from Diotrephes' claws. They had been so far from being warned day and night with tears about the possibility of unconverted wolves being able to enter the pastoral office (Acts 20:29-31) that the possibility seemed almost inconceivable to them. Their striving for month after month to take Pastor Diotrephes' plainly unscriptural advice seriously led them into horrible spiritual confusion.

Christ, Not A Man, Must Be Preeminent in Your Mind

Second, the Sheep family should have realized by the way Pastor Diotrephes became dominant in their thoughts that something was not right. Certainly it is appropriate to carefully ponder wise, Biblical counsel from one's pastor and seek to please him out of love and for the glory of God. But Jehovah and His Word alone are to be in one's thoughts morning and evening, day and night, when at home and when away from home (Deuteronomy 6:7). A godly pastor would not want his flock to have as their first thoughts when getting up, their last thoughts before going to bed, their discussion around the dinner table at home, their topic of conversation for hour after hour when on vacation, for week after week, month after month, how they can please him, but how they can please Jesus Christ. When Pastor Diotrephes never counseled the Sheep family that their ceaseless attempts to please and abase themselves before him were unbiblically excessive, and something a cult, not a Biblical Baptist church, would encourage, but instead constantly insisted that their attempts were sinfully insufficient, the Sheep family should have realized that something was wrong; Pastor Diotrephes was demanding a place in their hearts that properly belonged to Jesus Christ alone.

Never Violate Your Conscience

Third, Pastor Diotrephes' counsel that the Sheep family needed to just get over their conscience is extremely dangerous and unbiblical advice. The answer to conscience issues is not to trust leadership against what one thinks Scripture teaches, but to search the Scriptures to see whether those things are so (Acts 17:11). Even if one's conscience has scruples that go beyond what Scripture requires, one must not violate his conscience (Romans 14). Pastor Diotrephes' advice here was Satanic, appropriate for Jesuit casuistry but not for a church that professed to believe in Biblical Baptist distinctives such as soul liberty and the priesthood of the believer.

Accusations Must Be Verified

Fourth, in a church discipline situation, trust without verification is dangerous and unbiblical. Pastor Diotrephes had already clearly violated Scripture when he had earlier cast out another family in the church without trial, before he got to Brother and Sister Sheep. The Sheep family should have seen serious warning signs when this family had written a letter stating their reasons for wanting to leave and asked for a letter of transfer to another Baptist church, but Pastor Diotrephes, having forbidden the church from reading their letter, had required that they be cast out, not transferred, without allowing an examination of the evidence that they (allegedly) deserved to be delivered to Satan. Brother Sheep was wrongly silent[358] when this unbiblical action took place, as he did not recognize its significance as a sign of Diotrephes. Furthermore, when Pastor

Diotrephes initiated procedures to cast out Brother Sheep, the assistant pastors and deacons were too willing to follow without verification. By simply taking Pastor Diotrephes' word on many accusations, and trusting him because he was the head pastor, the assistant pastors and the deacons were deceived into assenting to egregious and easily disproven falsehoods. Lies and slanders that they would never have invented themselves became things that they assented to because they just trusted Pastor Diotrephes' word. There is certainly a place to trust a godly spiritual authority; but in church discipline, Christ requires that "every word ... be established" (Matthew 18:16). The New Testament commands: "I charge *thee* before God, and the Lord Jesus Christ, and the elect angels, that thou observe these things without preferring one before another, doing nothing by partiality" (1 Timothy 5:21). The proceedings at BBC were conducted not only with partiality towards and preferring Pastor Diotrephes before Brother Sheep, but with such partiality that false accusations that would completely collapse under the least impartial examination were allowed to stand, unverified. The assistant pastors were especially responsible for this failure. While they may not have been sons of Diotrephes themselves, they were too open to a Diotrephes-style of leadership. So far were they from requiring obedience to 1 Timothy 5:21 that they encouraged others to violate the verse by their example and advice of blind obedience, and thus contributed to the abomination of condemning the just and justifying the wicked (Proverbs 17:15).

The Hyles / Branson Authoritarian Pastor is Dangerous

Fifth, the Hyles-Branson teaching that the head pastor has special Divine insight by virtue of his office and must be implicitly followed causes tremendous damage. Pastor Diotrephes' torture of the meaning of Scripture and regular and repeated egregious factual distortions could have been justified, in his mind, by the alleged special Divine guidance he was receiving. What need was there to check if he had his facts straight when, simply because he was a pastor, he had special Divine guidance that made him far more likely to be right than anyone else (as Roy Branson affirmed, although the Bible did not)? And what need could there be for anyone else to verify the accuracy of what he said—did they not trust God's special guidance of the pastor? Whether or not Diotrephes convinced himself that his lies represented reality, the assistant pastors' and deacons' assumption that he must be correct and must be trusted contributed to their submitting to his egregious violations of Matthew 18:15-17 and his manipulative lies. Indeed, both Brother and Sister Sheep themselves were damaged by this doctrine of Diotrephes. Both of them were deeply wounded and shaken by his "prating" (3 John 10) because, simply based on his pastoral office, they took extremely seriously his many unbiblical and harsh statements that were not the teaching of Scripture (Isaiah 8:20) and so had no authority from heaven at all.

Classic Diotrephes Prepares the Way for Thieves and Perverts

Sixth, churches that allow a classic Diotrephes to pastor are in great danger of allowing a thieving Diotrephes or a pervert Diotrephes to ravage their congregation. When Pastor Diotrephes has moved a church to a position where any questioning of him or any well-documented concerns must be dismissed out of hand, even by assistant pastors or deacons, and are in fact matters that justify church discipline, terrible danger arises that the greatest kinds of wickedness can run rampant. If sheep in the church must be cast out for privately and respectfully raising well-documented concerns to even the assistant pastors, and, instead, anyone with a concern about the head pastor must speak to him alone, and nobody else, then not just a classic Diotrephes, but even a thieving or pervert Diotrephes can take power and ravage without any fear of exposure. Idolatrous Diotrephes-type preeminence leads to the types of horrifying sin that come from replacing the true God with idols (Romans 1:18-32).

Jesus Christ is the Good Shepherd

Seventh and last, all Christians should be very thankful at how different Christ, their Good Shepherd, is from Pastor Diotrephes. They must learn all the more to model their own opportunities for servant-leadership after Christ. Jesus Christ never quenches the bruised reed nor puts out the smoking flax.

He feeds His flock like a true and good Shepherd and gently leads those with young. Thanks be to God for Jesus Christ!

D.) Diotrephes the Thief and Robber: A Modern Situation Where Diotrephes-type Authority Is Used to Hide Financial Wrongdoing[359]

Joining the Church!

Brother and Sister Lamb moved to Iowa, the town of Lot, to serve the Lord at Enbezel Baptist Church. Brother Lamb was brought in as a ministry assistant, preaching from God's pulpit on a monthly (and sometimes weekly) basis, while working a full-time job, as the congregation was not large enough to support his family financially. Sister Lamb worked as a part-time church secretary. They started a children's Sunday School class and created a curriculum for it that met the needs of the children who came. Brother Lamb ran a bus route on Sundays and led evangelism and visitation every Saturday with Sister Lamb. They ran a midweek Bible Club to which dozens of children from the community came every week, learning about God and His glorious gospel. Brother Lamb also led a "Principles of Christian Growth" class, discipling new converts. Many people (church members and non-church members alike) called him Pastor Lamb; he would always tell them that he was not an ordained minister and not even an assistant pastor. He was thankful that the Lord Jesus allowed him to be well-favored and have great rapport with the saints in the church.

Something is Wrong

Not long after getting settled in and engaging full swing in all church ministries, Brother Lamb sensed that something was wrong. He loved the church's sole pastor, Pastor D.—but Brother Lamb saw that things were not being handled correctly. Brother Lamb would go to Pastor D. about certain issues that arose in the church, and Pastor D. would handle them unwisely and unbiblically. Brother Lamb knew that everyone makes mistakes, but over and over again Pastor D. would handle matters wrongly. Pastor D. and his wife would also gossip to Brother Lamb about certain church members. Brother Lamb understood that, as an assistant, a pastor should be able to tell his right-hand man some things, but Pastor D. went far beyond what was appropriate. Brother Lamb believed that he never needed to know personal details about the church members. He never spoke up to Pastor D. about it, but it always was extremely unsettling.

Money is Missing!

Around six months after they arrived, Sister Lamb told her husband about a conversation that had happened at the church property earlier that week. She had been wrestling with it in her mind and knew she needed to tell him about it. Every Monday morning, Sister Lamb, the church financial secretary, and one of the church trustees counted the tithes and offerings. The financial secretary had nothing to do with the financial decision making; she only counted and recorded where the money went and had no say in where or who got what money. She only did what she was told. (Brother Lamb found out later, from proof supplied by multiple witnesses, that she had replaced a church treasurer whom Pastor D. had run out of the church because he did not like the way the treasurer kept him accountable.) The financial secretary wanted to talk to the trustee about some discrepancies she had made note of over the past couple of months.

She started the conversation with the trustee and Sister Lamb with, "What I'm going to tell you next needs to stay between us." Sister Lamb immediately explained that she never kept anything from her husband, so if they were fine with Brother Lamb knowing, she could continue the conversation. They both agreed and did not oppose Sister Lamb staying and informing Brother Lamb of what happened.

The secretary went on to show a paper trail—receipts turned in for reimbursement—of Pastor D. using the church checking account for numbers of personal purchases that were completely unrelated to what was within his right. She told them that many times she saw things that did not appear to be right, but she looked the other way. On more than one occasion, Pastor D. reminded her and even the church that she was just a "financial secretary" and that her position carried no weight; she was not supposed to ask any questions about any of the money and made no decisions whatsoever. Pastor D. even told Brother Lamb before all of this happened that if the financial secretary had a problem with anything, she was supposed to talk to the Pastor alone—no one else.

The Trustees Informed

Sister Lamb struggled holding on to this information. Knowing what this might do to the church, her heart was heavy with the news. What would Brother Lamb do, now that he had found out? He thought that looking the other way would definitely be the easiest thing to do—but it would not be right.

He reached out to one of the other church trustees. (The three church trustees were upstanding members of the church and in the community who were always at every church service, unless on vacation or at work. They were the "backbone" working-class of the church, pillars in the congregation.) The following Sunday night, Brother Lamb met with one trustee and asked him if he knew what Pastor D. was allowed to spend church funds on. (If the sort of personal spending from the church account was actually something allowed, he wanted to know, so that allegations of impropriety could be set aside.)

The trustee told Brother Lamb, "I have no idea what is allowable for the pastor to spend." He had been in the position of trustee for about six months, but Pastor D. had never given him information on his position or what his responsibilities were. The trustee had asked for the trustee guidelines on more than one occasion, but they were never given to him.

The Pastor Approached

Brother Lamb would have approached a church deacon next, but the church—in line with the recommendations of Roy

L. Branson—did not have deacons. Brother Lamb, realizing that he was completely inexperienced as to what to do next, called his godly father-in-law. Brother Lamb was advised that he would be out of place were he to attempt some sort of investigation. The right thing to do would be to talk to Pastor D. directly. Therefore, the next day, both Brother Lamb and this trustee met with Pastor D., expressing concern over the finances. Pastor D. said he would take care of it. However, he became extremely hostile and defensive.

Over the next several weeks, the three trustees met on several occasions and verified that thousands of dollars had been misappropriated in the previous two years. They then scheduled a meeting with Pastor D. about the matter.

Two of these men went over to Brother Lamb's house the night before to pray with him. The only intention of the group for confronting Pastor D. was their desire for a clean church. They knew it would be wrong to turn a blind eye to everything they knew. They planned to confront Pastor D., request that he tell the church what happened, ask the church for forgiveness, and then together with the men, come up with a plan going forward on how to avoid having something similar happen again. Brother Lamb and these men wept on their knees for hours, crying out to God in humility, asking Him to be merciful and spare their church. They desperately did not want Pastor D. to be removed, nor did they want a church split, nor did they wish to be divisive.

The Pastor Resigns

Sadly, the next day's meeting with Pastor D. went downhill fast. Brother Lamb was called into the meeting by one of the trustees to fact-check something Pastor D. was saying; he had told many lies, but Brother Lamb knew what the truth was and could verify if what was being said was accurate. The meeting ended by Pastor D. standing up, turning in his keys, and resigning.

He said: "I'm done; I quit; I'm not pastoring this anymore. If you guys decide you want me as your pastor, you can let me know." He said that he had resigned—but that was just the beginning.

The "Lord's Anointed" Unresigns, Then Attacks

The next day, Pastor D. called Brother Lamb, stating that he had *not* resigned; his resignation did not count, he claimed, for it had not taken place before the whole church. Pastor D. then went on to assassinate the character of these three men and their families, calling these men, as well as Brother and Sister Lamb, "poisonous asps."

Pastor Diotrephes told Brother Lamb that these men were coming after him with a vendetta; it was "a personal assault against the man of God." The trustees had crossed a line by "touching the Lord's Anointed." Pastor Diotrephes attacked Brother Lamb for allegedly leading the trustees to distrust him because of the lies that Brother Lamb had allegedly spread.

Pastor Diotrephes and his wife then went to one trustee's house unannounced. They were in the middle of a screaming match with the trustee in front of their young children when the trustee's wife called Sister Lamb, bawling, asking the Lambs to come and take her children, so that they did not need to see any of it. Having heard how Pastor Diotrephes handled everything with the first trustee, the other two trustees refused to meet with Pastor Diotrephes at their houses. The trustees called the other men of the church to tell them what had happened and called a men's meeting in three days on Friday night.

Calling the Police to Kick Out the Trustees

Meanwhile, Pastor Diotrephes had other plans. He went to five senior citizens in the church who had no idea what was going on, and led them to sign a petition to remove these three trustees from the church membership—effective immediately—because they had (allegedly) started a coup against the pastor. The steps of Matthew 18:15-17 were completely ignored.

Pastor Diotrephes then went individually to as many other church members as possible, telling them that these men were out to get the pastor and were lying about the money. Disregarding the principle of 1 Corinthians 5, Pastor Diotrephes then went to the state police to bar the church trustees from the church property. They received formal letters of trespass from the state police, at Pastor Diotrephes' instigation. His heart was set on casting them out, and whatever means were necessary to affect that end would be pursued.

The Members Meeting Manipulated

Pastor Diotrephes' actions did not stop the men from showing up to the men's meeting. Pastor Diotrephes called the police when the trustees arrived, but the police officer who responded ended up being a born-again believer from a different but like-minded church. He told Pastor Diotrephes that he could not legally remove voted-in church trustees as trespassers, just as the trustees could not remove Pastor Diotrephes as a trespasser.

That Sunday, there was a members-only church meeting. Pastor Diotrephes, having made his father-in-law moderator of the meeting, started the gathering by saying that the trustees wanted him out of the church and that the church was going to vote that day on his removal. Immediately, the men got up and said that it was unconstitutional to vote the same day that the church members were hearing both sides of the story for the first time, for their church constitution mandated that a vote for removal of the pastor for disciplinary actions could not be held sooner than one week after the membership was made aware of the issue on a regular Sunday morning.

However, Pastor Diotrephes appealed to his father-in-law, the meeting's moderator, obtaining the decision that the vote had to happen that day because he was losing too much sleep over this problem. Some of the members would have been present and voted for the removal of Pastor Diotrephes had they known the vote would have taken place the same day—they had trusted that Pastor Diotrephes would do the right thing and follow their church constitution.

Emotion Or Evidence?

Having survived Pastor Diotrephes' attempt to have the police remove them as trespassers, the trustees had an opportunity to present their side fairly before the church. They gave all the members copies of receipts where the pastor used the church checking account for his own personal purchases, or where the pastor billed the church for his own personal purchases.

Afterwards, Pastor Diotrephes got up and made his case. Instead of refuting the fact that he had embezzled money, he merely argued that he worked up to eighty hours a week most weeks and that his hourly pay came out to basically nothing. (Sister Lamb worked Monday through Thursday at the church property for twenty hours a week and Pastor Diotrephes was at the church property for only five of those hours. Apparently, he worked the other seventy-five hours every night after 5 PM when Sister Lamb went home.)

Pastor Diotrephes displayed no tone of humility, nor did he plead for his church family to reconsider and hear the truth; rather, he displayed a defensive attitude while stating over and over: "I've given my life to this church!" (The church had started a few years earlier because he had unbiblically split it off from the other Baptist church in town.) At the end, Pastor Diotrephes read a tear-jerking letter to the congregation from his nine-year-old daughter that repeated something along the lines of: "My daddy's innocent, he's done nothing wrong, I know it." Pastor Diotrephes made many emotional appeals—but did he refute the charges? Not even close.

Diotrephes Splits The Church

An oral vote—no secret ballot—was then called for, where Pastor Diotrephes from the pulpit very intimidatingly stared down everyone when he gave his vote. According to their church constitution, a supermajority was required to vote him out, but the church vote split around 50/50—not enough to vote him out. (Brother Lamb did not vote because he was conducting a tally in the back; he realized his vote would not determine the outcome, and he desperately tried not to burn bridges with Pastor D.)

After church, Brother Lamb went up to Pastor D. and had a conversation with him. Brother Lamb's heart was absolutely shattered and broken, knowing the church had split right down the middle. Many members had walked out, never to return. While crushed, feeling at his lowest, Pastor Diotrephes smirked smugly at him. Confused, Brother Lamb asked him how he thought that meeting just went.

Pastor Diotrephes proudly responded, "It's all good, I won!" Whether a huge portion of his flock had left, never to return, was not the issue for Pastor Diotrephes.

After the meeting, he texted others, "God blessed, I had a great victory today!" In his mind, his church splitting in half was a great victory—for he still had job security.

"It's Your Fault That I Steal."

Pastor Diotrephes claimed that he used church money to get by, because the church was not taking care of him; however, they had recently given him an 18% raise, helped him with his home bills, gave him money for gas and extra expenses, and provided him a vehicle. When he had attempted to purchase a home, not being able to receive approval for a loan on account of his massive credit card debt, a church trustee had allowed him to borrow a large sum of money and co-signed the note for Pastor Diotrephes' home. (The trustee never received back any money from his loan.) Before that time, another trustee had given Pastor Diotrephes a special deal on a home to rent, but Pastor Diotrephes had repeatedly failed to make his rent payments on time—he had been, by far, the worst tenant the trustee had ever worked with.

More Misdeeds by Diotrephes

During the meeting in which Pastor Diotrephes resigned, and then renounced his resignation, the fact arose that he had been watching "R" rated videos, while seeking to cover up that he was doing it. After he had been caught and could not continue to lie about what he was doing, he stated that "God had worked in his heart about it." The church had given him the benefit of the doubt, overlooking the fact that he had lied about what he was doing; he had only claimed that God had worked in his heart after it was no longer possible to deny the charges.

"The Sheep Are Ignorant, And I'm Keeping It That Way."

Pastor Diotrephes strongly emphasized the "ignorance" of his church men—they were naive when it came to spiritual things, he explained. However, that was just how he liked to keep them. He never prepared them to exegete the Bible for themselves nor taught them to know the Bible well enough to "prove all things." They were never really taught how to think for themselves after the fashion of the Bereans in Acts 17. Furthermore, when they went to him with serious questions that they got from their Bible reading, he too often just dismissed them because he either did not know the answer or he simply liked the fact that, as he declared, "he knew more than they did." He would also accuse them of seeking to catch him off guard with hard questions, and so shut them down. Some people were indeed growing—but mainly because they were searching the Scriptures for themselves at home.

Diotrephes Forces Out The Sheep

Pastor Diotrephes taught that Christians were not to meet or have fellowship with anyone who did not believe the same way—even family. What about the Lord Jesus's interactions with publicans and sinners? The call to be separate "overrode" such interactions with others. It was necessary to cut ties completely with unsaved relatives and neighbors—they were not likeminded. Furthermore, Pastor Diotrephes maintained his preeminence at all costs. While his initial attempts to cast out those who threatened his dominion by manipulating several senior citizens and bringing in the state police failed to accomplish his plan to cast them out, he then created such intolerable circumstances for them that they had to leave—he achieved what he could not do with the police.

The Lambs concluded that Pastor Diotrephes had allowed pride and arrogance to sneak in—everything became "my way or the highway." The Lambs had to leave the church for another one of Biblical faith and practice. They continue to sincerely pray that God would change Pastor Diotrephes' heart, so that his church could still be a lighthouse in their community.

Growth In Grace Through Trial

Looking back, Brother Lamb believes the situation definitely strengthened his walk with the Lord. He regularly asked God to help him to handle things the right way, and God answered his prayer. In one situation when the church men met with Pastor Diotrephes, Brother Lamb had been called in to corroborate the truth; he went in and attacked Pastor Diotrephes, failing to manifest sufficient Christian respect and humility. While Brother Lamb had not said anything inaccurate, he certainly was not Spirit-led in his attitude on that occasion. He asked, and received, forgiveness from Jesus Christ.

Lessons From This Case Study Of A Thief and Robber Pastor Diotrephes

Diotrephes Can Usurp Preeminence by Stealing Christ's Money

A primary lesson from this case study is the reality that a Pastor Diotrephes may usurp Christ's preeminence by stealing money consecrated for the use of the great Head of the church. Christ warned about false pastors who would be thieves and robbers—who would steal, kill, and destroy (John 10:1, 8, 10)—of which the thief Judas was a type (John 12:6). The Lord Jesus spoke of some who made God's holy house a den of thieves (Matthew 21:13). Scripture emphasizes that elders and deacons must not be "greedy of filthy lucre."[360] Christ by His Spirit gave His church so many warnings because throughout the church age there would be a minority of thieving Pastors Diotrephes whose evil deeds would give the large righteous majority a bad name.

Classic Diotrephes Leads To Thieving Diotrephes

Second, a pro-Diotrephes or soft-on-Diotrephes pastoral philosophy provides room for the depredations of a thieving Diotrephes. Not everyone who proclaims himself the Lord's untouchable Anointed is a thief—but those who are thieves greatly encourage a pro-Diotrephes pastoral philosophy. A church that falls prey to pro-Diotrephes ministry practices provides space for a thieving wolf to escape detection while robbing God's sheep.

Safeguard God's Money

Third, as individuals take precautions to prevent the theft of their own funds, so churches should have safeguards to prevent the embezzlement of God's money. Most pastors are godly and sanctified men, but spiritual wolves who seek to steal and destroy are on the prowl. While onerous restrictions that make it difficult for pastors to make even minor financial decisions are not necessary, something is wrong if a pastor opposes transparency and financial accountability. Furthermore, one who is unable to properly rule his own household by avoiding financial traps like massive credit-card debt is not qualified to rule the church of God (1 Timothy 3:5).

Leadership Requires Higher, Not Lower, Standards

Fourth, God's requirements for pastors are higher, not lower, than the standards for all. If a secular company would immediately fire someone for theft, it is a weak-on-Diotrephes mindset that would excuse a pastor's regular lying, watching filthy R-rated movies, and thieving, and hope to have that person continue in the holy pastoral office as long as a few safeguards are installed. Someone who would be removed from the position of a grocery-store cashier has no business holding the office of a bishop.

Diotrephes Has Many Ways To Cast Out Sheep

Fifth, Diotrephes can cast people out of the church in more ways than by simply manipulating and distorting the steps of Matthew 18:15-17, pressing his thumb heavily on the scale of an unequal justice. He can sinfully contact the civil power (1 Corinthians 6:1-11) so that police bar church members from church property. He can simply make church intolerable until a sheep just cannot take it any more and leaves "voluntarily."

Thieving Diotrephes May Win (In This Life)

Sixth, a thieving Pastor Diotrephes may be able to get away with stealing (in this short life) even after being caught red-handed. A congregation that has not been trained both to prize and highly value godly pastors and to detect and remove the sons of Diotrephes may be content to have a thief and a robber over them. Those willing to follow a pastor who is stealing God's money will fail to have him rebuked before all (1 Timothy 5:20), resulting in new members joining a church with a robber-pastor because of the over-docility of the long-time members and former members. The power of the pastoral office is real and can be an instrument of great good in the hands of a Spirit-filled and righteous man—but it can also be an instrument of great evil in the hands of a self-centered and unrighteous one.

The Life-Giving Love of the Good Shepherd

Seventh, the self-sacrificial love of the Good Shepherd, Jesus Christ, appears all the brighter against the black backdrop of a thieving Diotrephes (John 10). While a thieving Diotrephes takes what is not his and destroys the sheep, the Good Shepherd had everything, but sacrificed it all so that he might save the sheep. But this precious One who made Himself of no reputation also rose from the dead, is ascended on high, and will soon come again to rule forever (Philippians 2:5-11). For the Lord's blood-bought beloved people, any depredations from Diotrephes are but for a moment, when compared to the exceedingly great and eternal weight of glory purchased for them by the self-giving love of Jesus Christ. "Worthy is the Lamb that was slain to receive power, and riches, and wisdom, and strength, and honour, and glory, and blessing" (Revelation 5:12). Amen!

E.) Diotrephes the Pervert: A Modern Situation Where Diotrephes-type Authority Is Used to Hide Sexual Immorality

Note: While this author believes that nothing explained in the story below falls beyond the boundaries set forth in Scripture, parents would do well to read it before allowing any young person in their household to do so. Children should not read this account without getting their parents' permission first.

Joining the Church!

"What a great ministry opportunity!" thought Brother Hogget.[361] "Why would he have thought of me, when I have so little training for the ministry!" Dr. D., an older man and pastor of the First Baptist Church in Coversynn, a small town in the upper peninsula of Michigan, had asked young Brother Hogget to become his assistant at First Baptist Church. Dr. D. had left a large church with a significant Christian school to pastor this small work in Coversynn, MI. He was a famous preacher. He had been on the executive board of a well-known missions agency and had received an honorary doctorate from an influential Baptist college. And now he had called Brother Hogget—a young single man who had not been to Bible college and had been preaching for less than a year—and offered to make him assistant and youth pastor. What an opportunity! After getting counsel from some godly people and much prayer, young Brother Hogget moved to Coversynn, U.P. to take the position.

Graphic Talk

Not long after his arrival, Bro Hogget began to sense that something was not right. It was ingrained in Brother Hogget to trust and follow the pastor—God's man. So when Dr. D. did something inappropriate, Bro Hogget wrote it off as his own fault—he must simply be overly prudish and have been too sheltered in his upbringing. Dr. D. would talk with Bro Hogget about people he had counseled, getting into details about their love life. He would discuss intimate details about his own wife and marriage. Dr. D. said it was pastoral training—and this seemed logical, to a degree. At first, Bro Hogget was extremely uncomfortable when Dr. D. would discuss these things, but he was always afraid to cross the line of rebuking or correcting the pastor. Bro Hogget just assumed he was too uptight, and Dr. D. was right. He lowered the standards of his conscience. Over time, Bro Hogget grew more and more accustomed to what he had earlier considered serious impropriety. While he never enjoyed it, he got to the place where he figured that this was just how Dr. D. did things; Bro Hogget went along with it.

"How Big Are Your Private Parts?"

Dr. D., however, had just gotten started. One day, as they were driving somewhere together, he asked Bro Hogget if he knew his shoe size; Bro Hogget told him. Then he asked about Bro Hogget's shirt size; he told him. Pant size? He told him. Then Dr. D. asked him about the size of his private parts. Dumbfounded, Bro Hogget blinked and looked away. Dr. D. then told him how wrong it was to know so little about his own body, and how he was wrong to be ashamed to talk about it. Bro Hogget was shell-shocked. His pastor—his boss—the man of God—was asking him to describe his private parts to him? Was this normal? Just how sheltered had he been, growing up? Dr. D. dropped the subject—for the time being.

Dr. D. Sets A Snare

On another occasion, they were in a car, and Dr. D. pulled over into a parking lot. He reached into his Bible and pulled out a letter and a photograph. He handed the letter to Bro Hogget and asked him to read it. Brother Hogget was shocked—it accused him of being a pervert and immoral, and said that he had no place in the ministry! The letter closed by declaring that along with it, proof had been enclosed that Bro Hogget was the kind of immoral person described.

Bro Hogget looked up from the letter with a feeling of disgust and great anxiety. Who had written this? The letter was obviously a pack of lies, but how could he prove it? Finally he spoke up: "I have no idea what this is, but none of this is true."

Dr. D. looked at him for a long time. Finally, he spoke: "Well, they have the proof right here." He pulled the photo out of the envelope, but hid it from Bro Hogget.

"Proof?" There's no way they have any proof, because there is not a shred of truth to anything in this letter!"

"They have the proof, and it is very bad."

Again Bro Hogget spoke, this time getting angry. "There's no way they can have any proof because I've never done those things! Here, let me see it."

"Are you sure you want to see this? It is very convincing."

"Give it here."

Bro Hogget took the picture out of Dr. D's hand. He took one glance at it and quickly handed it back to him. It was a snapshot of a naked man, but his head was not in the picture. Bro Hogget had no idea who it was or where it was taken, but if this was the "proof" of the anonymous letter, it was without a doubt the worst "proof" ever. Relief flooded Bro Hogget's soul.

"That's not me. Trust me. That's not me. I have no idea who that is or where that was taken, but trust me; that is not me, and I have never been in the house that is in the background of that picture."

Dr. D. stared at the picture for a while before speaking. "How do I know that is not you?"

Bro Hogget stared at him in disbelief. "Because I'm telling you that is not me."

"Prove it."

There it was. This was what the whole thing was about.

"Prove it? What do you mean prove it? How am I supposed to prove that is not me in the picture?"

"There's only one way you can prove it is not you. It won't take you but ten seconds to prove this is not you in this picture."

Bro Hogget stared at Dr. D. in shock. Was he for real? Oh yes. He was for real. Bro Hogget laughed nervously and shook his head.

"Well, you can forget it. I don't have to prove anything. Just take my word for it; that is not me. I don't know who sent you this letter, or who that is in the picture, but it is not me."

Dr. D. was disappointed. For weeks he hounded Bro Hogget to prove that the headless model in the snapshot was not him. Bro Hogget always told him to just forget it. At one point Bro

Hogget told Dr. D. that if he thought that letter was true, he should just fire him. Dr. D. did not want to do that.

Bro Hogget spent days trying to figure out who had sent Dr. D. that letter. Why would someone do that to him? Who could hate him so badly that he would make up such terrible lies? He racked his brain for the longest time trying to figure it out. It never occurred to him that the entire thing was fabricated by Dr. Diotrephes.

Looking back upon the situation years later, Brother Hogget realized that this situation should have told him everything he needed to know about Dr. Diotrephes. A real letter like that one would have required immediate and serious attention, but not in the way Dr. Diotrephes handled it. If the letter had been real, why had not Dr. Diotrephes confronted Brother Hogget in the church office, with a witness or witnesses to verify their interaction? If he really thought it possible that his youth pastor was a sexual pervert, why approach him about it alone, in a car? What was Dr. Diotrephes' plan had Brother Hogget confessed to the accusations? There would not have been any witnesses. Would he have attempted blackmail? Dr. Diotrephes had orchestrated a pretty convincing act. How many other young men in Bro Hogget's situation would have felt that they had no other choice to clear their name but to unclothe themselves? It would have only taken a few seconds. Dr. Diotrephes did not win the war in this battle, but it still contributed to the process of wearing down Brother Hogget's defenses, working to groom and ensnare him, chipping at his conscience.

Breaking Down The Conscience

Dr. D. continued working relentlessly at breaking down Bro Hogget's barriers. But Brother Hogget always felt like it was his fault. He was too sheltered. He was reading too much into it. He was guilty of thinking Dr. D. was doing something wrong, when there was *no way* he could be doing something wrong. He was the pastor. He was God's man. He had thirty years in the ministry. A man of his stature and position could not be in the wrong. Brother Hogget chided himself for being so critical of Dr. D. Dr. D. had extended an amazing ministry opportunity to him—an untrained, untested single youth—and his unthankful response was to think the great Dr. D. was some kind of weirdo? It could not be. Bro Hogget kept telling himself he just needed to grow up; loosen up; stop being so uptight in his conscience about everything and get with the program. He did not want to fail in this new endeavor as a staff member. He had so much to learn. He was so grateful for the opportunity to be mentored by such an experienced and well-seasoned pastor as Dr. D. Brother Hogget worked very hard to please him. If the godly people at a leading Baptist Bible college had given Dr. D. an honorary doctorate, who was Bro Hogget to judge him?

Gifts Prepare The Way

On Christmas that year Dr. D. gave Bro Hogget crazily generous presents—so much, and so many, that Brother Hogget could hardly keep track. The gifts were so numerous that when Brother Hogget told a friend, that person was astounded. Brother Hogget himself was beyond embarrassed; he was both mortified and confused. Was this normal? Each gift was wrapped in the nicest paper. Every gift was extravagant and very personal. Bro Hogget had no idea how to respond. There was no telling how much money Dr. Diotrephes had spent on him that year. Brother Hogget felt like a fool for not doing more for Dr. Diotrephes, and said so. Dr. D. assured him that it was fine—he just wanted Bro Hogget to know how much he meant to him.

The "Prayer and Fasting" Retreat

Not many days later, early in the new year, Dr. D. approached Bro Hogget about a prayer and fasting retreat. He asked if Bro Hogget thought it would be good to get away for a couple of days and spend time praying, fasting, and planning church events. It sounded like a good idea. He recommended a cabin up in the mountains. Who would turn that down?

At first, it was going to be Dr. D., his wife, and maybe another person or two. But when the day of the retreat came, Dr. D said that his wife was not going to be able to go—she was sick. Also, the others weren't going to make it either—it was going to be just the two of them. Bro Hogget was fine with it. They were going to be praying and fasting, and he did not care who came along.

Two Men In a Hotel Room

When it came time to pick him up for the retreat, Dr. D. called Brother Hogget. The retreat accommodations had fallen through—they would not be able to go to the place they had booked. It did not make sense to drive for a few hours to a place in the mountains when they could just get a nice hotel room in town and fast and pray and plan there. That made sense to Bro Hogget. They drove their cars to the hotel and checked in. Bro Hogget felt weird standing next to another man in a hotel lobby, checking into a hotel room, when they only lived fifteen minutes away. They went to the room and unpacked. Dr. D. sat down on his bed and started reading his Bible. Bro Hogget started reading his Bible as well. They talked a little bit, but not much; they mainly just read and marked things in their Bibles. So far the staff retreat was off to a great start!

Washing Up

Dr. D. eventually mumbled something about needing a shower and headed toward the bathroom. After his shower he came out in his bathrobe and sat down on his bed and went back to reading his Bible. It felt a bit awkward, but Bro Hogget squelched any ideas of impropriety. He had never stayed in a hotel room with another man before, so maybe this was normal.

Pervert Diotrephes Propositions!

After a while, Dr. D. started talking to Bro Hogget about needing to share a very important prayer request. He went into an elaborate explanation of a very personal health problem; he had been to many doctors, he claimed, and none of them could help him. Bro Hogget had difficulty following Dr. D's convoluted explanation. He rambled on and on; Brother Hogget was lost in the sea of words. However, he wrapped up his long health history with a very plain and specific request. Dr. Diotrephes asked if he could perform a sexual act with Brother Hogget!

Diotrephes' request startled Brother Hogget back to reality. He was floored, completely caught off guard. So that is what this whole "prayer request" monologue was about? He was dumbfounded.

For the next two minutes, Brother Hogget stared at Dr. Diotrephes in disbelief. Did he just ask him to do that? There was no way Brother Hogget could have heard him correctly. This could not be happening. His mind must have wandered off. He had to be daydreaming. But no! Who daydreams about what Dr. Diotrephes had just said? Brother Hogget certainly did not! He looked over at Dr. Diotrephes with a blank, stupid look.

"So will you do it?" asked Dr. Diotrephes.

Dr. Diotrephes turned from leaning against the headboard of the bed and faced him. Brother Hogget looked at him disbelievingly. He felt like he was in a time warp.

"You've got to be kidding me!? There is no way I'm doing that!" Bro Hogget was flabbergasted.

Dr. Diotrephes' response took the cake. He looked at Bro Hogget, almost pitifully, and said, "Well, I was hoping you would at least pray about it."

Brother Hogget was numb and speechless. His pastor had just asked him if he could sodomize him, and having refused, his pastor wanted him to pray about it?

Brother Hogget's entire world exploded in that moment. His life, his ministry, his job, his reputation, his name, his call to preach—everything became one huge question mark. What would his parents think? What would the church think? What would the girl he was interested in marrying think? He had not the foggiest idea what they would think because he did not even know what to think. His mind was racing to absorb the insanity of the moment. How had he gotten here?

The Sodomite Predator Pastor

In that moment, everything began to make sense. The isolated comments, the random innuendos, the disjointed remarks and months of red flags all came together to form a clear picture. His pastor—the highly respected, white-haired Dr. D.—was a sodomite. He was a pervert Diotrephes. And not just a sodomite, but a homosexual predator who had no problem wielding his power over the people under him to get what he wanted. He was a con-artist, and a very experienced and calculating one at that. He was a patient, methodical, and diabolical man.

It became clear to Brother Hogget that his being in that hotel room was no accident. The last six months of his life had been one long con game, and he was the mark. This had been Dr. Diotrephes' plan from day one. Now it all made sense.

Just Say "No!"

The pervert Dr. Diotrephes stood up and walked toward his clothes hanging on the rack. He looked old and tired in his bathrobe. His shoulders were slumped over dejectedly. His plan had failed. His months of ensnaring, of grooming, had been for naught.

Brother Hogget had said "No."

That is the last thing a predator, pervert Diotrephes wants to hear.

"No."

Two letters. One small word. But a huge word to a pervert.

"No" is his worst nightmare. "No" means he failed. "No" means he picked the wrong mark. "No" means he has to start all over with someone else. "No" means all his plans, his fantasies, and his efforts were in vain.

And Brother Hogget had said, "No."

Dr. Diotrephes got dressed and mumbled something about how he was just going to go home. He told Bro Hogget that since the room was already paid for, he might as well just stay the night. Dr. Diotrephes packed and left him there. Bro Hogget just sat on the bed in shock, alone—and scared out of his mind.

"What Do I Do Now?"

He grappled with how this was going to play out. He could not believe what had just happened. How would anybody else believe it? He did not even want anyone else to know about it.

He spent an agonizing night at the hotel, trying to figure out what to do. If he called his dad, his father would insist that he come home. But he could not just skip town with this disaster unresolved. If he ran from this, there would be a cloud over him forever. How could he tell his home church and home pastor that it was God's will for him to move up to Coversynn, U.P., but then come running back home six months later without a reason?

Fervent Prayer

He prayed fervently that night—more fervently than he had ever done in his life. He confessed his utter ignorance to God and begged his forgiveness for ignoring the months of red flags. He begged God to forgive him for anything he might have said or done that could have made this sodomite think that he could succeed in committing an abomination with him. He begged for wisdom, direction, boldness, courage, and for his name to be cleared and his ministry not ruined before it had even gotten started.

Faking And Questioning

He tried to act like the retreat was cut short for some reason or another. To say things were weird at church the next service would be an understatement. Bro Hogget could not believe he was still there. He could not believe Dr. Diotrephes was still there. Dr. Diotrephes could not believe Bro Hogget was still there. Neither of them knew what to do. They could not decide what they were going to do until the other one made a move. Bro Hogget could not involve the law, for Dr. Diotrephes had done nothing illegal. Even if Brother Hogget had called the sheriff, where was his proof?

Brother Hogget became withdrawn and conflicted. His whole world had been shattered. He felt like he could not tell a soul. He started questioning everything he had ever been taught. He questioned the Bible. He questioned God. He questioned his upbringing. He questioned the ministry. He grappled with basic ministry philosophies. He questioned literally every single aspect of everything he had ever been told or taught.

If this was what the ministry consisted of, what had he gotten himself into? If Dr. Diotrephes could rise to the top, being a sexual pervert and predator, why was Brother Hogget even thinking about being in the ministry? This was not what he had signed up for. Not at all!

Brother Hogget waited a few weeks. He was on auto-pilot. Life was a blur. His time with Dr. Diotrephes was almost like an out-of-body experience. He did not want to be there. He went soulwinning with Dr. Diotrephes. He went to church with him. He went out to eat with him. He went to visit people in the hospital with him. He listened to Dr. Diotrephes preach. But Brother Hogget was a hollow and lifeless machine. For the last six months he had worked to please Dr. Diotrephes. Now he just wanted to please the Lord Jesus Christ. But Bro Hogget kept the nightmare he was living a secret.

"I'm Not Alone!"

Around a month after he realized in that hotel room that Dr. Diotrephes was a pervert, Bro Hogget was listening to a preaching tape. The preacher was talking about sin in the ministry. He gave an illustration of a pastor in Texas who had been caught engaging in illicit activity with his male staff members. As the preacher recounted the story, he made the statement that after the scandal broke, the pastor's wife confessed that her husband had not touched her in years. Their marriage was a sham, but nobody had suspected a thing.

It was during that message that Bro Hogget realized that what had happened to him had also happened to others. He was not the first. This was not an isolated incident. As unbelievable as it had seemed to him, there was someone, somewhere who would believe him, because this had happened before. God flooded his soul with peace and the promise that He would vindicate him through that nightmare. Bro Hogget purposed to confront Dr. Diotrephes about his sin that Monday.

Preparing to Confront the Pervert

God helped Bro Hogget not to be motivated by vengeance. He had been very angry at first, but his anger had been reduced to a low smolder. That was the only way he could function. But he was concerned for the welfare of the church. The precious saints at First Baptist Church in Coversynn, U.P., had no idea that the man they listened to every service was a sexual predator. They had no clue that the wolf they called "Pastor" was trying to seduce the youth pastor. They did not know that their "man of God" was a cold, calculating sodomite with a wicked personal agenda that was an affront to God, the Bible, the church, and everything God and godly people stood for. Diotrephes had to be confronted. His true colors needed to be revealed.

Bro Hogget's second concern was to stop Dr. Diotrephes from ever targeting someone again. It was a distasteful task; a thankless job; but somebody had to do it and, for the moment, that lot fell to him. He was the one who had been targeted and groomed. He was the one who had witnessed those despicable conversations and been manipulated into that hotel room under false pretenses. He was the one who had been propositioned. Nobody else could do what had to be done. It was up to him—and he knew he could not do it alone. He was in way over his head—and he knew it. He called on God for aid; and, just as His Word promised, God came through.

Confronting Diotrephes Alone

Brother Hogget called another pastor and, without revealing any specifics about the parties involved, asked him what to do. He was advised to set up a meeting with Dr. Diotrephes. They met in the church auditorium. "What is this about?" asked Dr. Diotrephes.

Brother Hogget told him, "The only reason you brought me here was to break me down and take advantage of me to satisfy your filthy, rotten lusts. Now either you can tell the church what you are, or I will. It does not make any difference to me; but one way or the other, you are done. You're finished!"

Dr. Diotrephes did not flinch. He did not blink. He did not move a muscle. He just looked at Bro Hogget. After a moment, he spoke.

"Well, if I tell you I'm sorry, then you have to forgive me. And you have to forgive and forget."

Bro Hogget shook his head in disbelief at the gall. "The church will know what you are. Now do you want to tell them, or do you want me to tell them?"

"I'm not telling them," said Dr. Diotrephes.

"So you want me to do it?" asked Brother Hogget.

"No. I want you to forgive me like the Bible says you're supposed to do and let's just forget about it," said Dr. Diotrephes.

"Wrong answer. Looks like it is my move. I'll keep you posted." Bro Hogget walked past Dr. Diotrephes and out the back door.

Brother Hogget got a notebook and wrote down every detail he could recall. Every conversation; every single inappropriate comment or incident. He felt very vulnerable. He had just confronted the senior pastor and threatened to expose him to the whole church. He moved his things out of the place where he was staying and moved home. He was aware of the fact that a man with a thirty-year track record in the ministry, and, as it seemed, an impeccable reputation, was being accused by a kid that nobody knew.

Confronting Diotrephes With the Deacons

A meeting with the deacons of First Baptist Church was arranged. Bro Hogget knew it would be a showdown between a veteran pastor with an honorary doctorate and a rookie preacher boy who was not even qualified to be on staff in the first place. Bro Hogget poured out his heart to God. He begged Him to protect him in this scandal, that he might come through victorious and unscathed. He prayed, as Paul did, to deliver him from every evil work, and to preserve him; that by him, the preaching of Christ might be fully known. He begged God's forgiveness for doubting Him, for doubting His Word, for doubting the truth he had been exposed to and taught his whole life. He asked God not to let a few bad apples in the ministry turn his heart away from the highest calling in the world—to preach the gospel to lost and dying souls. He begged God to give him power, courage, integrity, stamina, and will to stand and fight. He begged God to help him never to become a hireling, a fake, or a phony. Bro Hogget asked God to make him a truly godly man—not just with a title, but with spiritual reality. And God met Bro Hogget, blessed him, and empowered him! Never again would he be a victim. He was a sheepdog now. The wolves had better beware!

The next night, Bro Hogget and his father, as well as the deacons and trustees from First Baptist of Coversynn met together with Dr. Diotrephes. At first Dr. D. had refused to come, but somehow the men of First Baptist had persuaded him to attend. Bro Hogget was surprised; he had never expected Diotrephes to show up and face his accuser. Men in his position rarely do. They protest from a distance and insist on their innocence but do not have the gall to face the charges. The fact that he came caught Bro Hogget slightly off guard, but he was glad.

Dr. Diotrephes was asked if he had anything he wanted to say. He sarcastically answered that he had come to listen to Bro Hogget. He said that since Bro Hogget had so much to say, he should go first.

That was a mistake by the pervert, Dr. Diotrephes. Bro Hogget was glad that he had written down everything that had happened. He had a list of pages of inappropriate comments and incidents. Bro Hogget started down the list with the question:

"Do you deny saying ... ?" He rattled off one of the inappropriate comments he had made.

"No," said Dr. Diotrephes.

Bro Hogget was taken aback. He was not ready for that answer. He continued.

"Do you deny making this comment ... ?"

"No."

"Do you deny going into detail with me about you and your wife and your intimate relationship?"

"No."

Bro Hogget went down that list systematically. His answer was the same. He did not deny a single accusation that Bro Hogget had written down. Not one! Bro Hogget was amazed at God's glorious intervention. God was directing this meeting! Brother Hogget had never imagined that Dr. Diotrephes would admit to being a sexual predator in a room filled with his church's leadership. He could not believe what was happening!

The more Bro Hogget questioned, and the more Dr. Diotrephes admitted, the more one could feel the air being sucked out of the room. Bro Hogget noticed the deacon sitting beside Dr. Diotrephes started shifting in his chair.

"Do you deny propositioning me the other night in that hotel room?"

"No."

There it was. A full and unmistakable confession. By the time Bro Hogget had finished with the list, the deacon had turned in his chair with his back completely to Pastor Diotrephes.

Diotrephes' Defense

But Dr. Diotrephes had a defense. "I brought Bro Hogget to work with our young people. He was inexperienced and he was untested. I wanted to make sure that he was the right man for the job and that he had the character to be in that position. I said and did those things as a test to see what he would do."

Bro Hogget glared at Dr. Diotrephes. Did he say "test"? That was the best he could come up with? "A test? All of this was just a test?" Bro Hogget's blood pressure was rising. Fast. "Seriously? Well, answer me this. Did I pass the test?"

"Yes. You did. You handled yourself correctly and you passed the test," answered Dr. Diotrephes.

"The only reason you called me and asked me to come on staff was because you thought I would be vulnerable and easy. You thought I would not be able to say 'no.' Well, I did! I said 'no'!"

Dr. Diotrephes just sat there. Bro Hogget turned to the deacons. They still had their faces turned away from him. He felt sorry for them. They were extremely uncomfortable.

Diotrephes With the Deacons

Bro Hogget said, "Dr. Diotrephes hired me, and I am resigning. I'm gone. I'm out of here. I'm going back home. Now you have a decision to make about what to do with Dr. Diotrephes. Either way, I will not be there to see it."

Bro Hogget left the meeting, as did his father and one other person. He was jubilant. The pervert Dr. Diotrephes had been exposed! The deacons stayed behind with Dr. Diotrephes.

The Pervert Pastor Escapes Exposure

Unfortunately, the story did not end well. Dr. Diotrephes was able to manipulate the deacons into a sinful exit strategy. He made three very specific demands:

1.) Three months' severance pay.
2.) A letter of recommendation to another ministry.
3.) To never refer to him as a homosexual.

The deacons agreed to all of Dr. Diotrephes' conditions. He left town, and the sheep at First Baptist in Coversynn, U.P., never really knew what happened. People whispered, but there was no official statement to inform the church why Dr. Diotrephes left—or why Brother Hogget left.

Brother Hogget received no severance pay, nor a letter of recommendation.

Dr. Diotrephes was removed from his position on the Baptist mission board. The reasons were kept under wraps. He moved to Broad Road Baptist Church in Gateway, Missouri, where he became the administrator of the Christian school. Dr. Diotrephes had gone to church there as a teen. Brother Hogget could not believe it. With some witnesses to Dr. Diotrephes' confession of sin, he informed the pastor of Broad Road Baptist about what had happened, handing him a list of every man who was in the meeting the night of Dr. Diotrephes' confession. Sadly, the pastor kept Dr. Diotrephes on staff—he allowed a proven pervert and Diotrephes to run his Christian school, setting aside the verified accusations.

Brother Hogget began to get calls from people who had worked with Dr. Diotrephes over his thirty years in the ministry. Men told Bro Hogget horrifying stories of how Dr. Diotrephes had abused them. Dr. Diotrephes had used his position of power to manipulate, intimidate, abuse, and violate. Brother Hogget would have found the stories impossible to believe—except that he had experienced similar things himself. The men thanked Bro Hogget for standing up to Dr. Diotrephes and his perversion. None of them had confronted Dr. Diotrephes publicly.

The Pervert Escapes Punishment On Earth: The Pervert Receives Eternal Punishment In Hell

But Dr. Diotrephes remained secure in his new position as Christian school administrator. No evidence exists that he stopped the serial abuse he had been guilty of for decades previously. No evidence exists that he ever experienced repentance unto life. He later went on to start a church, giving it the same name as the congregation where he had sought to ensnare Bro Hogget. Dr. Diotrephes pastored that church until he died and—as far as the evidence points—went to hell, joining the rest of the damned in being tormented day and night, for ever and ever.[362]

Lessons From This Case Study of a Pervert Pastor Diotrephes

Know What Scripture Says About Pervert Pastors

Brother Hogget's encounter with a pervert Pastor Diotrephes supplies many important lessons.[363] First, as with the classic and thieving Diotrephes examples, here again a saint was completely ignorant of the possibility that a pervert Pastor Diotrephes could exist. Had Bro Hogget been warned day and night with tears about such a possibility (Acts 20:29-31), had he recognized that Scripture itself mentions leaders in churches who seek to seduce God's servants to commit fornication (Revelation 2:20), had he meditated upon the fact that Scripture mentions "sodomites" who liked to spend time "by the house of the LORD" and needed to be driven away (1 Kings 22:46-47), he would have seen the warning signs of a pervert Pastor Diotrephes far earlier. The snares, the grooming, of this pervert Pastor Diotrephes would have been recognized much sooner had Brother Hogget not been taught the naïve and unbiblical view that such ensnaring wolves could not exist. Brother Hogget did not even ask his godly parents for counsel when this pervert Pastor Diotrephes was doing all kinds of wildly inappropriate things—so strongly had the unbiblical idea been implanted in him that the pastor must always be right and must always be followed, with no consideration of the possibility of a pervert Pastor Diotrephes. Furthermore, he waited a long time, confused, before doing anything to expose Diotrephes, his wait only coming to an end when, through hearing a preaching tape, his illusion was shattered that there could be no such perverted Pastors Diotrephes in the ministry. While this son of Belial ultimately failed to commit abomination with Brother Hogget, Dr. Diotrephes did successfully and dangerously break down Brother Hogget's conscience over time. After spending months with Diotrephes, his conscience was no longer warning about improper words and deeds it had previously warned about loudly. This extremely dangerous progressive breakdown of the conscience would not have been possible had Brother Hogget been more alert to the possibility of wolves like a pervert Diotrephes. Nor would Bro Hogget have been in utter shock, and have questioned everything he believed, when he finally realized he was interacting with a sodomite. God's Word provides the Biblical balance that, as with Christ's first apostles, the large majority of pastors today are righteous men, but a small minority are anti-Christs and wolves like Judas. Acts 20, 3 John, and other texts specifically indicate that this sort of evil man can and will find his way into a pastorate on occasion. Confronting a Judas was no reason to doubt the reality of the righteous majority. But Brother Hogget had the mistaken idea that there were no sons of Judas and Diotrephes, no antichrists that could creep in secretly, and so when he discovered one, he (at first) questioned everything (until God restored him by His glorious grace) when what he had just experienced was exactly what Scripture should have led him to expect in the first place, and be on guard against.

Know What Scripture Says About All Manifestations of Diotrephes

The weakness toward Diotrephes in the circles of churches in which Brother Hogget was raised allowed this pervert Pastor Diotrephes to continue to prey on unsuspecting sheep. Dr. Diotrephes should have been exposed publicly after his first attempt to consume a sheep, rather than having his sin covered for year after year, upon victim after victim. He should have been excommunicated and publicly rebuked before all far earlier, and if he did not just break God's law but also broke man's law, he should have been investigated, prosecuted, and locked up with the active encouragement and support from the churches. However, this Biblical mindset was severely lacking in the congregations among whom Pastor Diotrephes hunted.

Exposure—Not Coverup—Required

How deeply ingrained the cover-up mentality was appears in Bro Hogget's initial reaction after Dr. Diotrephes asked him to engage in sodomy: "He did not even want anyone else to know about it." He then waited around a month—going to church with this sodomite, eating meals with this sodomite, listening to this sodomite preach—before doing anything. During this time, Diotrephes could have done even more damage. Scripture indicates that such wicked men should be exposed publicly, by name (3 John 9-11; Revelation 2:20). This should have happened immediately.[364]

The complete unpreparedness for a pervert Pastor Diotrephes was also evident in the willingness of the church deacons to cover up Dr. Diotrephes' sin, give him several months pay, a letter of recommendation, and a promise never to expose him as a homosexual. Diotrephes should have been immediately placed under church discipline and publicly exposed, so that he could never prey on another young man. Indeed, as the assistant and youth pastor, Bro Hogget was especially accountable to have Dr. Diotrephes placed under church discipline. Bro Hogget deserves high commendation for exposing this sodomite—something, it seems, none of those Diotrephes had previously victimized or attempted to prey upon had done. However, he should not have left immediately after Diotrephes was exposed before the deacons. As both the primary witness and a pastor, equal in office to the wicked head pastor if far from equal in years of life, he should have taken the lead in having Dr. Diotrephes placed under church discipline (Deuteronomy 17:7; Matthew 18:15-17). He should not have resigned, leaving the deacons and the congregation with Diotrephes as their sole elder. He should not have left until Diotrephes was gone, under discipline and publicly exposed. It was very good that Bro Hogget cried "Wolf!" for a wolf there was—but after (rightly) crying out to expose the wolf, as a shepherd, he should have stayed and fought the wolf to the death for the sake of the sheep, instead of resigning immediately. The deacons obviously did not know what to do next, so Diotrephes manipulated them into allowing him to escape. Furthermore, when the deacons refused to tell the whole church what had happened, Bro Hogget, as the other pastor, could have written letters to or gone personally to the home of every church member with the evidence, the names, and the phone numbers of those who had witnessed Diotrephes' confession. What if Dr. Diotrephes had not only attempted to seduce Bro Hogget, but had also plied his filthy trade on others in the congregation? First Timothy 5:20 is not optional, but a command: "Them that sin rebuke before all, that others also may fear."

The Young Are Weak

Why do pervert Pastors Diotrephes seek to prey on youth, and too often succeed? They know that the "children of Belial" are apt to succeed in their aims when they are dealing with those who are "young and tenderhearted, and [often] [can]not withstand them" (2 Chronicles 13:7). Parents need to keep in mind that a feature of youth is weakness in standing against the wicked that must, through godly training, be extirpated so that their boys become strong men. Godly young people must keep it in mind themselves, and watch against it as their weakness, for both the devil and pervert Pastors Diotrephes are already well aware of it, and ready to exploit it.

The Pure Versus The Seared Conscience

Dr. Diotrephes' asking Brother Hogget to pray about committing sodomy with him, his twisting the Biblical doctrine of forgiveness into a plea that Bro Hogget needed to just forgive and forget, and many other episodes in their interaction, demonstrate that Dr. Diotrephes had truly seared his conscience. After years of sinning, he was not bothered at all by manipulating Scripture, manipulating others, hypocritically lisping the name of God to worship his idol lusts, and employing power and deceit to abuse religion, prayer, fasting, and anything else holy, pure, and good for his abominable ends. He had been given up to uncleanness (Romans 1:24). He had overcome his conscience, and he knew it was crucial—in order to obtain his ends—to have the objects of his desire overcome their consciences as well. The tremendous importance Scripture places upon maintaining a "pure conscience" (1 Timothy 3:9) is again clearly manifest. Furthermore, when dealing with Diotrephes, one cannot and must not just trust him to do the right thing, or to refrain from doing things that would utterly shock one's own conscience. He may, like Judas, be demon possessed, and care for conscience as much as do the devils. Diotrephes may be as willing to violate what is right to achieve what he wants as is Satan or the Antichrist.

Watch Out!

Proverbs 11:9 states: "An hypocrite with *his* mouth destroyeth his neighbour: but through knowledge shall the just be delivered." In all three case studies above—the classic, the thieving, and the pervert Diotrephes—the wolf either completely or largely succeeded in devouring his prey and getting away with it. Why? In each case the godly were unprepared for and unaware of the tactics of Diotrephes. Had they been properly on guard against Diotrephes and his wiles (Acts 20:29-31; 3 John 9-11), reproach to the name of Christ and deep wounds to many sheep could have been avoided (Proverbs 11:8) through the knowledge of the just (Proverbs 11:9).

The Power of the Word and Spirit

The power of God's Word and His Spirit is also clearly evident in Bro Hogget's trial with a pervert Pastor Diotrephes. Despite coming from an environment that was far too unaware of Diotrephes, Bro Hogget did not get swallowed up, but fought back. Why? The Holy Ghost showed him what to do in the Word of God, and God providentially guided and protected him, despite his youth and inexperience. Glory to God for His powerful Word, and for the illuminating power of His Almighty Spirit!

Exalt Jesus Christ And Watch For Classic, Thieving, And Pervert Diotrephes

It is absolutely imperative to prepare God's people for Diotrephes in all his forms. A pervert Diotrephes cannot thrive and destroy one life after another in a godly church environment that follows Biblical, Baptist, Christ-exalting, manabasing ecclesiology. If you do not want your little son or daughter abused by a pervert Diotrephes, you must be sure your church is prepared to keep out not just a pervert, not just a thieving, but also a classic Diotrephes, detect him if gets in, and then immediately remove and expose him, for the glory of Jesus Christ, the sole Head of His true church.

XIII.) BIBLIOGRAPHY

Aland, Kurt, Barbara Aland, Johannes Karavidopoulos, Carlo M. Martini, and Bruce M. Metzger, eds. *Novum Testamentum Graece*. 28th Edition. Stuttgart: Deutsche Bibelgesellschaft, 2012.

Aland, Barbara, Kurt Aland, Johannes Karavidopoulos, Carlo M. Martini & Bruce Metzger, eds. *The Greek New Testament: Apparatus*. 5th rev. ed. Deutsche Bibelgesellschaft; American Bible Society; United Bible Societies, 2014.

Ambrosiaster. *Commentaries on Romans and 1-2 Corinthians*. Eds. Thomas C. Oden & Gerald L. Bray. Ancient Christian Texts. Downers Grove, IL: IVP Academic, 2009.

Aristotle. *Politics*. Trans. H. Rackham. The Loeb Classical Library. Cambridge: Harvard University Press, 1932.

Aristotle. *The Works of Aristotle*. Ed. W. D. Ross, trans. Benjamin Jowett, E. S. Forster, and Frederic G. Kenyon, vol. 10. Oxford: The Clarendon Press, 1921.

Arndt, William, Frederick W. Danker, Walter Bauer, and F. Wilbur Gingrich. *A Greek-English Lexicon of the New Testament and Other Early Christian Literature*. (BDAG) Chicago: University of Chicago Press, 2000.

Ascol, Thomas Ascol, "Southern Baptists at the Crossroads: Returning to the Old Paths." *The Founders Journal: Southern Baptists at the Crossroads: Returning to the Old Paths, Winter/Spring* 19/20 (1995): 5-10.

Athanasius of Alexandria. *On the Incarnation: Greek Text.* Ed. John Behr, Popular Patristics Series. St. Vladimir's Seminary Press, 2011.

Athanasius of Alexandria. *Select Treatises of S. Athanasius, Archbishop of Alexandria, in Controversy with the Arians, Translated, with Notes and Indices, Parts 1 & 2*. Vol. VIII of *A Library of Fathers of the Holy Catholic Church, Anterior to the Division of the East and West*. Oxford: John Henry Parker, 1842–1844.

Athanasius of Alexandria. *St. Athanasius: Select Works and Letters*, ed. Philip Schaff and Henry Wace, trans. Archibald T. Robertson, vol. 4, A Select Library of the Nicene and Post-Nicene Fathers of the Christian Church, Second Series. New York: Christian Literature Company, 1892.

Athanasius of Alexandria. *The Orations of S. Athanasius against the Arians*. London: Griffith, Farran, Okeden, & Welsh, 1893.

Athanasius & Didymus. *Works on the Spirit: Athanasius's Letters to Serapion on the Holy Spirit, And, Didymus's on the Holy Spirit*. Ed. John Behr, trans. Mark DelCogliano, Andrew Radde-Gallwitz, and Lewis Ayres. Vol. 43 of *Popular Patristics Series*. Yonkers, NY: St Vladimir's Seminary Press, 2011.

Augustine of Hippo. *On Baptism, against the Donatists*. In *St. Augustin: The Writings against the Manichaeans and against the Donatists*, ed. Philip Schaff, trans. J. R. King, vol. 4, A Select Library of the Nicene and Post-Nicene Fathers of the Christian Church, First Series. Buffalo, NY: Christian Literature Company, 1887.

Baker, Don. *Beyond Forgivness: The Healing Touch of Church Discipline.* Portland, OR: Multnomah Press, 1984.

Barnes, Albert. *Notes on the New Testament*, ed. Robert Frew. London: Blackie & Son, 1884–1885.

Barton, Bruce B. & Grant R. Osborne. *1, 2 & 3 John*, Life Application Bible Commentary. Wheaton, IL: Tyndale House, 1998.

Bauder, Kevin T., et al., *Four Views on the Spectrum of Evangelicalism*. Zondervan Counterpoints Collection. Grand Rapids, MI: Zondervan, 2011.

Bavinck, Herman. *Reformed Dogmatics*. Ed. John Bolt, trans. John Vriend. Grand Rapids, MI: Baker Academic, 2006.

Biblia Sacra Juxta Vulgatam Clementinam. Ed. electronica. Bellingham, WA: Logos Bible Software, 2005.

Birch, Ian. *The Ecclesial Polity of the English Calvinistic Baptists, 1640-1660*. Ph. D. Dissertation, University of St. Andrews, 2014. Elec. acc. http://hdl.handle.net/10023/6362.

Bridges, Charles, *An Exposition of the Book of Proverbs*. New York: Robert Carter & Brothers, 1865.

Boston, Thomas. *The Whole Works of Thomas Boston: A Soliloquy on the Art of Man-Fishing*, ed. Samuel M'Millan, vol. 5. Aberdeen: George and Robert King, 1849.

Branson, Roy L. Jr. *Church Split.* 2nd ed. Bristol, TN: Landmark Publications, 1992.

Branson, Roy L. Jr. *Dear Abner: I Love You, Joab*. 2nd ed. Bristol, TN: Landmark Publications, 1996.

Branson, Roy L., Jr. *Dear Preacher, Please Quit!* Bristol, TN: Landmark Publications, 1996.

Brenton, Lancelot Charles Lee. *The Septuagint Version of the Old Testament: English Translation*. London: Samuel Bagster and Sons, 1870.

Bruce, Frederick F. *The Epistles of John: Introduction, Exposition and Notes*. Nashville, TN: Kingsley Books, 2018.

Burghardt, John H. Dillon and Thomas Comerford Lawler, eds. *Ancient Christian Writers*. Mahwah, NJ: The Newman Press, 1992.

Calvin, John. *Institutes of the Christian Religion*, ed. John T. McNeill, trans. Ford Lewis Battles, vol. 1 & 2, The Library of Christian Classics. Louisville, KY: Westminster John Knox Press, 2011.

Cambridge Paragraph Bible: Authorized English Version. Cambridge: Cambridge University Press, 1873.

Carroll, Benajah Harvey. *Ecclesia: The Church*. Elec. acc. https://faithsaves.net/ecclesiology/.

Catechism of the Catholic Church, 2nd ed. Washington, DC: United States Catholic Conference, 2000.

Cathcart, William, ed. *The Baptist Encyclopedia*. Philadelphia: Louis H. Everts, 1881.

Charles, Robert Henry, ed. *Pseudepigrapha of the Old Testament*. Oxford: Clarendon Press, 1913.

Charlesworth, James H. *The Old Testament Pseudepigrapha*, 2 vol. New York: Yale University Press, 1983.

Chayyim, Jacob Ben, ed. *Biblia Rabbinica,* with Targums, Massorah, and Rabbinic commentaries (1524-1525). Good Books, 2456 Devonshire Road, Springfield, IL, 62703.

Charles, Robert Henry, ed. *Apocrypha of the Old Testament*. Oxford: Clarendon Press, 1913.

Charles, Robert Henry, ed., *Pseudepigrapha of the Old Testament*, 2 vol. Oxford: Clarendon Press, 1913.

Chitwood, Paul Harrison. *The Sinners Prayer: A Historical and Theological Analysis*. Ph. D. Dissertation, Southern Baptist

Theological Seminary, 2001. Elec. acc. https://faithsaves.net/the-sinners-prayer/.

Church of Scotland. *The Confessions of Faith and the Books of Discipline of the Church of Scotland*. London: Baldwin and Cradock, 1831.

Clement of Alexandria, *Stromateis, Books One to Three*. Ed. Thomas P. Halton, trans. John Ferguson. Vol. 85, The Fathers of the Church. Washington, DC: The Catholic University of America Press, 1991.

Cloud, David. "Another Warning About Unquestioning Loyalty to Church Leaders." Elec. acc. https://www.wayoflife.org/database/another_warning_about_unquestioning_loyalty.html/.

Cloud, David. "Ignoring the Sin of First Baptist of Hammond." Elec. acc. https://www.wayoflife.org/reports/ignoring_sin_first_baptist_hammond.html.

Cloud, David. "Pentecost vs. Hylescost." Elec. acc. https://www.wayoflife.org/database/hylescost.html.

Cloud, David. *The Hyles Effect: A Spreading Blight*. Port Huron, MI: Way of Life Literature, 2012.

Cloud, David. "The Jack Hyles Philosophy." Elec. acc. https://www.wayoflife.org/reports/jack_hyles_philosophy.html.

Cloud, David. "The Women Who Knew Jack Hyles." Elec. acc. https://www.wayoflife.org/reports/the_women_who_knew_jack_hyles.php/.

Cloud, David. "Unquestioning Loyalty to Pastoral Leadership the Mark of a Cult." Elec. acc. https://www.wayoflife.org/database/unquestioningloyalty.html/.

Crosby, Thomas. *The History of the English Baptists*. 4 vol. Bellingham, WA: Logos Bible Software, 2011.

Dever, Mark, ed. *Polity: A Collection of Historic Baptist Documents: Biblical Arguments on How to Conduct Church Life.* Michigan: Sheridan Books, 2001.

Dike, Charles C. "Pathological Lying: Symptom or Disease? *Psychiatric Times* (June 2008) 67-73.

Downen, Robert, Lise Olsen & John Tedesco. "20 years, 700 victims: Southern Baptist Sexual Abuse Spreads as Leaders Resist Reforms." *Houston Chronicle* 2/10/2019. Elec. acc. https://www.houstonchronicle.com/news/investigations/article/Southern-Baptist-sexual-abuse-spreads-as-leaders-13588038.php.

Dunn, James D. G. *Unity and Diversity in the New Testament: An Inquiry into the Character of Earliest Christianity*, 3rd ed. London: SCM Press, 2006.

Elliger, K., W. Rudolph, & Gerard E. Weil. *Biblia Hebraica Stuttgartensia*. Electronic ed. Stuttgart: German Bible Society, 2003.

Epictetus. *All The Works of Epictetus*. Ed. Rex a Kovisto, trans. Elizabeth Carter. Port Orange, FL: Oak Tree Software, 2016.

Epictetus. "Epicteti Dissertationes Ab Arriano Digestae." Medford, MA: B. G. Teubner, 1916.

Epictetus. *The Discourses of Epictetus, with the Encheridion and Fragments*. Ed. George Long. Medford, MA: George Bell and Sons, 1890.

Epictetus. *The Works of Epictetus: His Discourses, in Four Books, the Enchiridion, and Fragments*. Ed. Thomas Wentworth Higginson. Medford, MA: Thomas Nelson and Sons, 1890.

Epictetus. *Discourses*, tagged Greek text ed. Rex A. Koivosto. Port Orange, FL: Oak Tree Software, 2016.

Epiphanius. *The Panarion of Epiphanius of Salamis, Book 1 (Sects 1-46)*. 2nd rev. & exp. ed. Trans. Frank Williams. *Nag Hammadi and Manichaean Studies* 63. Brill: Leiden, 2009.

Eusebius. *The Ecclesiastical History*. Ed. T. E. Page, E. Capps, W. H. D. Rouse, L. A. Post, & E. H. Warmington. Vol. 1 of *The Loeb Classical Library*. Cambridge, MA: Harvard University Press, 1926–1932.

Evans, Craig, ed. *Old Testament Pseudepigrapha*. Grand Rapids, MI: Eerdmans, 2015.

Garrett, James Leo, Jr. *Baptist Church Discipline*. Rev. ed. Paris, AK: Baptist Standard Bearer, 2004.

Garrett, James Leo, Jr., "Church Discipline: Lost, but Recoverable." *The Founders Journal: Systematic Theology and Preaching* 4 (1991) 26-27.

Garrett, James Leo, Jr. *Systematic Theology: Biblical, Historical, and Evangelical*, Second Edition, 2 vol. Eugene, OR: Wipf & Stock, 2014.

Gill, John. *An Exposition of the Old Testament*. London: Mathews and Leigh, 1810.

Glare, P. G. W., ed. *Oxford Latin Dictionary*. Oxford: Oxford University Press, 2012.

Glimm, Francis X., Joseph M.-F. Marique, and Gerald G. Walsh, trans. *The Apostolic Fathers*. Vol. 1 of *The Fathers of the Church*. Washington, DC: The Catholic University of America Press, 1947.

Henry, Matthew. *Matthew Henry's Commentary on the Whole Bible: Complete and Unabridged in One Volume*. Peabody: Hendrickson, 1994.

Hiscox, Edward. *Standard Manual for Baptist Churches*. Philadelphia, PA: American Baptist Publication Society, 1890.

Hiscox, Edward T. *The New Directory For Baptist Churches.* Philadelphia: American Baptist Publication Society, 1902.

Hiscox, Edward Thurston, and Frank T. Hoadley. *The Star Book for Ministers*. 2nd rev. ed. Willow Grove, PA: Woodlawn Electronic Publishing, 1995.

Hitchcock, F. R. Montgomery. *Irenaeus of Lugdunum: A Study of His Teaching*. Cambridge: Cambridge at the University Press, 1914.

Hodges, Zane Clark, Arthur L. Farstad, and William C. Dunkin. *The Greek New Testament according to the Majority Text*. 2nd ed. Nashville: T. Nelson Publishers, 1985.

Holmes, Michael William. *The Apostolic Fathers: Greek Texts and English Translations*. Updated ed. Grand Rapids, MI: Baker Books, 1999.

Holy Bible: King James Version. Elec. ed. of the 1900 Authorized Version. Bellingham, WA: Logos Research Systems, Inc., 2009.

Hutson, Curtis. "Sumner's Slander, Slant, and Slop." *The Sword of the Lord* 55:11 (May 26, 1989) 1-6.

Hutson, Curtis. "As Many As Received Him." Elec. acc. https://cavaliersonly.com/christian_articles_and_messages/as_many_as_received_him_by_curtis_hutson.

Hyles, Jack. *Enemies of Soulwinning*. Hammond, IN: Hyles-Anderson Publishers, 1993. Elec. acc. https://www.soulwinning.info/books/jack_hyles/enemies_of_soulwinning/misunderstood_repentance.htm.

Hyles, Jack. *Exploring Prayer With Jack Hyles*. Hammond, IN: Hyles-Anderson Publishers, 1983. Elec. acc. https://www.jackhyles.com/exploringprayer.htm.

Hyles, Jack. *From Vapor to Floods.* Hammond, IN: Hyles-Anderson Publishers, 1974.

Hyles, Jack. *Jack Hyles Speaks on Biblical Separation*. Hammond, IN: Hyles-Anderson Publishers, 1984.

Hyles, Jack. *Jack Hyles on Justice*. Elec. acc. https://nashpublications.com/wp-content/uploads/2013/10/Great_Books/Hyles_PDF/Jack-Hyles-on-Justice-Dr.-Jack-Hyles.pdf.

Hymers, R. L. Jr. "Dr Hymers Answers the Critics." Elec. acc. http://www.drrlhymersjranswershiscritics.com/.

Hymers, R. L. Jr. "Has America Been Given Up By God?" 2/21/2021, Baptist Tabernacle of Los Angeles. Elec. acc. https://www.rlhymersjr.com/Online_Sermons/2021/022121PM_HasAmericaBeenGivenUpByGod.html.

Hymers, R. L. Jr. "Lessons From Dr. Roy Branson." 8/2/2020, Baptist Tabernacle of Los Angeles. Elec. acc. https://www.rlhymersjr.com/Online_Sermons/2020/080220PM_LessonsFromDrRoyBranson.html.

Hymers, R. L. Jr. "More Lessons From Dr. Roy Branson." 8/9/2020, Baptist Tabernacle of Los Angeles. Elec. acc. https://www.rlhymersjr.com/Online_Sermons/2020/080920PM_MoreLessonsFromDrRoyBranson.html.

Hymers, R. L. Jr., & Christopher Cagan. *Preaching to A Dying Nation.* Los Angeles: Fundamental Baptist Tabernacle, 1999. Elec. acc. https://faithsaves.net/soteriology/.

Hymers, R. L. Jr., & Christopher Cagan. *Today's Apostasy: How Decisionism is Destroying our Churches*, 2nd ed. Oklahoma City, OK: Hearthstone, 2001. Elec. acc. https://faithsaves.net/soteriology/.

Ignatius of Loyola. *Ignatius of Loyola: Letters and Instructions*, ed. John W. Padberg, et al. St. Louis, MO: Institute of Jesuit Sources, 1996.

Irenaeus of Lyons. *Five Books of S. Irenaeus against Heresies*. Trans. John Keble. A Library of Fathers of the Holy Catholic Church. Oxford: James Parker and Co, 1872.

Irenaeus of Lyons. *St. Irenaeus of Lyons: Against the Heresies, Book 1*. Ed. Walter J. Burghardt, John J. Dillon, & Thomas Comerford Lawler. 55th ed. Vol. I of *Ancient Christian Writers*. Mahwah, NJ; New York: The Newman Press, 1992.

Irenaeus of Lyons. *The Writings of Irenaeus*. Ed. Alexander Roberts & James Donaldson. Vol. 1 & 2 of *Ante-Nicene Christian Library*. Edinburgh: T. & T. Clark, 1868–1869.

Ironside, H. A. *Addresses on the Epistles of John*. Neptune, NJ: Loizeaux Brothers, 1931.

Jerome. *Select Letters of St. Jerome*. Eds. T. E. Page, E. Capps, and W. H. D. Rouse. Trans. F. A. Wright. The Loeb Classical Library (London: William Heinemann, 1933.

Josephus. *The Life, Against Apion*, English and Greek text. Edited by T. E. Page, E. Capps, W. H. D. Rouse, L. A. Post, and E. H. Warmington. Translated by H. J. Thackeray. Vol. I of The Loeb Classical Library. Cambridge, MA: Harvard University Press, 1966.

Josephus. *The Jewish War: Books 1–7*. English and Greek text. Edited by Jeffrey Henderson, T. E. Page, E. Capps, and W. H. D. Rouse. Translated by H. St. J. Thackeray. Vol. 3 of *Loeb Classical Library*. Cambridge, MA: Harvard University Press, 1927–1928.

Josephus, Flavius, and William Whiston. *The Works of Josephus: Complete and Unabridged*. Peabody: Hendrickson, 1987.

Kittel, Gerhard, Geoffrey W. Bromiley, and Gerhard Friedrich, eds. *Theological Dictionary of the New Testament* (TDNT). Grand Rapids, MI: Eerdmans, 1964.

Laertius, Diogenes. *Lives of Eminent Philosophers*, ed. R. D. Hicks. Kansas City: Harvard University Press, 2005.

Lampe, G. W. H., ed. *A Patristic Greek Lexicon* (PGL). Oxford: At The Clarendon Press, 1961.

Liddell, Henry George, Robert Scott, Henry Stuart Jones, and Roderick McKenzie. *A Greek-English Lexicon* (LSJ). Oxford: Clarendon Press, 1996.

Lightfoot, J. B., ed. *The Apostolic Fathers*. 2nd ed. London: Macmillan, 1889.

Lilienfeld, Scott O., John Ruscio, and Steven Jay Lynn. *Navigating the Mindfield: A Guide to Separating Science from Pseudoscience in Mental Health.* Amherst, NY: Prometheus Books, 2008.

Lockett, Darian R. *Letters for the Church: Reading James, 1-2 Peter, 1-3 John, and Jude as Canon*. Downers Grove, IL: InterVarsity Press, 2021.

Lorencin, Igor. "Hospitality versus Patronage: An Investigation of Social Dynamics in the Third Epistle of John." *Andrews University Seminary Studies* 46 (2008) 165–74.

Louw, Johannes P., and Eugene Albert Nida. *Greek-English Lexicon of the New Testament: Based on Semantic Domains* (LN). New York: United Bible Societies, 1996.

Lust, Johan, Erik Eynikel, and Katrin Hauspie. *A Greek-English Lexicon of the Septuagint: Revised Edition*. Deutsche Bibelgesellschaft: Stuttgart, 2003.

MacArthur, John F. Jr. *John MacArthur Sermon Archive*. Panorama City, CA: Grace to You, 2014.

Martin, Steven, ed. *Biblical Shepherding of God's Sheep: The Use and Abuse of Authority by Church Officers*. Ministry Mission. Leominster: Day One, 2010.

McBeth, H. Leon, *The Baptist Heritage*. Nashville, TN: Broadman & Holman Publishers, 1987.

McGlothlin, W. J. *Baptist Confessions of Faith*. Philadelphia: American Baptist Publication Society, 1911.

Migne, J. P. *Patrologia Cursus Completus*. Paris: J. P. Migne, 1857.

Montanari, Franco, et. al. *Brill Dictionary of Ancient Greek* (BrDAG). Boston: Brill, 2015.

Olsen, Lise, Robert Downen and John Tedesco. "More than 100 Southern Baptist youth pastors convicted or charged in sex crimes." *Houston Chronicle* 2/13/2019. Elec. acc. https://www.houstonchronicle.com/news/investigations/article/All-too-often-Southern-Baptist-youth-pastors-13588292.php.

Olsen, Lise and Sarah Smith. "Abuse of Faith: Missionaries left trail of abuse, but leaders stayed quiet." *Houston Chronicle* 5/31/2019. Elec. acc.
https://www.houstonchronicle.com/news/investigations/article/Abuse-of-Faith-Missionaries-left-trail-of-abuse-13904418.php.

Owen, John. *An Exposition of the Epistle to the Hebrews*, ed. W. H. Goold. Vol. 18-24 of *Works of John Owen*. Edinburgh: Johnstone and Hunter, 1854.

Oxford English Dictionary. Elec. acc. https://oed.com.

Palmer, Earl F., & Lloyd J. Ogilvie. *1, 2 & 3 John / Revelation*. Vol. 35 of *The Preacher's Commentary Series*. Nashville, TN: Thomas Nelson Inc, 1982.

Pendleton, J. M. *Church Manual: Designed for the Use of Baptist Churches*. Philadelphia: Judson Press, 1846. Elec. acc. https://www.reformedreader.org/rbb/pendleton/churchmanual/bcmtitlepage.htm.

Penner, Ken, and Michael S. Heiser. *Old Testament Greek Pseudepigrapha with Morphology*. Bellingham, WA: Lexham Press, 2008.

Philo. *The Works of Philo: Complete and Unabridged*. Trans. Charles Duke Yonge. Peabody, MA: Hendrickson, 1995.

Pickering, Wilbur N., ed. *The Greek New Testament According to Family 35*. 3rd ed. Pickering: 2020.

Pietersma, Albert, and Benjamin G. Wright, eds. *A New English Translation of the Septuagint*. Oxford: Oxford University Press, 2007.

Plato, *Laws*. English and Greek text. Ed. T. E. Page, E. Capps, W. H. D. Rouse, L. A. Post, and E. H. Warmington. Trans. R. G. Bury. Vol. 2 of The Loeb Classical Library. Cambridge, MA: Harvard University Press, 1926.

Pseudo-Tertullian. *Against All Heresies*, in *Latin Christianity: Its Founder, Tertullian*. Eds. Alexander Roberts, James Donaldson, and A. Cleveland Coxe, trans. S. Thelwell, vol. 3, The Ante-Nicene Fathers. Buffalo, NY: Christian Literature Company, 1885.

Rahlfs, Alfred, and Robert Hanhart, eds. *Septuaginta*. Stuttgart: Deutsche Bibelgesellschaft, 2006.

Reisinger, Ernest C. "The Carnal Christian." Elec. acc. https://www.reformedreader.org/rbb/reisinger/tcc.htm.

Richardson, Wyman Lewis. *On Earth as It Is in Heaven: Reclaiming Regenerate Church Membership*. Cape Coral, FL: Founders Press, 2011.

Roberts, Alexander, James Donaldson, & A. Cleveland Coxe, eds. *The Ante-Nicene Fathers*. Buffalo, NY: Christian Literature Company, 1886.

Robertson, Archibald Thomas. *Types of Preachers in the New Testament*. New York: George H. Doran Company, 1922.

Robinson, Maurice. *Elzevir Textus Receptus (1624): With Morphology*. Bellingham, WA: Logos Bible Software, 2002.

Rodgers, Adrian. *Adrian Rogers Sermon Archive*. Signal Hill, CA: Rogers Family Trust, 2017.

Rogers, Cleon L., Jr. & Cleon L. Rogers III. *The New Linguistic and Exegetical Key to the Greek New Testament*. Accordance electronic ed. Grand Rapids: Zondervan, 1998.

Ross, Thomas. "An Exegesis and Application of Romans 10:9-14 for Soulwinning Churches and Christians in Relation to the Question of the "Sinner's Prayer." Elec. acc. https://faithsaves.net/romans-10-sinners-prayer/.

Ross, Thomas. "Assurance of Salvation in 1 John: The Tests of Life." Elec. acc. https://faithsaves.net/assurance-john/.

Ross, Thomas. "Ecclesiology: The Doctrine of the Church." Elec. acc. https://faithsaves.net/ecclesiology/.

Ross, Thomas, "Four Views On the Spectrum of Evangelicalism: A Book Review." Elec. acc. https://kentbrandenburg.com/2023/05/05/four-views-on-the-spectrum-of-evangelicalism-a-book-review/.

Ross, Thomas. "Hyles-Anderson College & First Baptist of Hammond: Do They Now Please God?" Elec. acc. https://kentbrandenburg.blogspot.com/2020/02/hyles-anderson-college-first-baptist-of.html/.

Ross, Thomas. "Quotations from Three Books by Roy L. Branson: *Dear Preacher, Please Quit! & Church Split & Dear Abner: I Love You, Joab*." Elec. acc. https://faithsaves.net/roy-branson/.

Ross, Thomas. "Repentance Defended Against Antinomian Heresy—A Brief Defense of the Indubitable Biblical Fact that Repentance is a Change of Mind that Always Results in a Change of Action." Elec. acc. https://faithsaves.net/repentance/.

Ross, Thomas. "Resources for Catholics." Elec. acc. https://faithsaves.net/catholic/.

Ross, Thomas. "Southern Baptist Evangelism and Unregenerate Evangelicals." Elec. acc. https://kentbrandenburg.blogspot.com/2016/01/southern-baptist-evangelism-and.html.

Ross, Thomas. "Will I Be Saved if I Ask Jesus to Come into my Heart or Repeat the Sinners Prayer?" Elec. acc. https://faithsaves.net/sinners-prayer/.

Ruckman, Peter. "'Humanism' and 'Love' Are Major Problems Among Baptists." *Bible Believers Bulletin,* August 1993. Elec. acc. https://solascriptura-tt.org/SeparacaoEclesiastFundament/HumanismAndLoveMajorProblemsAmongBaptists-Ruckman.htm.

Sawtelle, Henry A. *Commentary on the Epistles of John*. Edited by Alvah Hovey. An American Commentary on the New Testament. Philadelphia: American Baptist Publication Society, 1888.

Schaff, Philip, and Henry Wace. *A Select Library of the Nicene and Post-Nicene Fathers of the Christian Church, Second Series*. New York: Christian Literature Company, 1892-1900.

Scrivener, F. H. A. *The New Testament in Greek*. Cambridge: Cambridge University Press, 1881.

Shelton, W. Brian. *Quest for the Historical Apostles: Tracing Their Lives and Legacies*. Grand Rapids, MI: Baker Academic, 2018.

Shiflett, Michael Stacey. *Wolves Among Lambs: My Story of Sexual Abuse & Cover-Ups in the Church*. Dundalk, MD: SureWord, 2019.

Shutt, R. J. H., trans. & ed. *The Old Testament Pseudepigrapha*. New Haven: Yale University Press, 1985.

Soanes, Catherine & Angus Stevenson, eds., *Concise Oxford English Dictionary*. Oxford: Oxford University Press, 2004.

Sophocles, E. A. *Greek Lexicon of the Roman and Byzantine Periods (From B. C. 146 to A. D. 1100)*. New York: Charles Scribner's Sons, 1900.

Stephen's 1550 Textus Receptus: With Morphology. Bellingham, WA: Logos Bible Software, 2002.

Sumner, Robert. *Fights I Didn't Start: And Some I Did.* Raleigh, NC: Biblical Evangelism, 2009.

Sumner, Robert. "History of Jack Hyles Exposé." Elec. acc. https://www.biblicalevangelist.org/jack_hyles_story.php.

Sumner, Robert L. "The Hyles Reply!" *The Biblical Evangelist* 23:8, August 1, 1989.

Sumner, Robert L. "The Saddest Story We Ever Published!" *The Biblical Evangelist* 23:5, May 1, 1989.

Sumner, Robert L. "One of the Blights of Bigness!" *The Biblical Evangelist* 22:10, October 1, 1988.

Swete, Henry Barclay. *The Old Testament in Greek: According to the Septuagint*. Cambridge, UK: Cambridge University Press, 1909.

Tabb, Brian J., Andrew M. King, and Stanley N. Gundry, eds. *Five Views of Christ in the Old Testament: Genre, Authorial Intent, and the Nature of Scripture*. Grand Rapids, MI: Zondervan Academic, 2022.

Tanner, Beth & Rolf A. Jacobson, *The Book of Psalms*, ed. E. J. Young, R. K. Harrison, and Robert L. Hubbard Jr., The New International Commentary on the Old Testament. Grand Rapids, MI: Eerdmans, 2014.

Tedesco, John. "Abuse of Faith: Southern Baptist churches harbored sex offenders." *Houston Chronicle* 6/3/2019. Elec. acc. https://www.houstonchronicle.com/news/houston-texas/houston/article/Abuse-of-Faith-Southern-Baptist-churches-13912529.php.

Tedesco, John, Robert Downen & Lise Olsen. *Houston Chronicle* 2/12/2019. "Southern Baptist churches hired dozens of leaders previously accused of sex offenses." Elec. acc. https://www.houstonchronicle.com/news/investigations/article/Southern-Baptist-churches-hired-ministers-accused-13588233.php.

Tedesco, John, Lise Olsen & Robert Downen, *Houston Chronicle* 6/6/2019. "Abuse of Faith: Survivors of Baptist sexual abuse come forward to help others." Elec. acc. https://www.houstonchronicle.com/news/houston-texas/houston/article/Abuse-of-Faith-Survivors-of-Baptist-sexual-abuse-13938643.php.

Tennent, Gilbert Tennent. *The Danger of an Unconverted Ministry, Considered in a Sermon on Mark VI.34. Preached at Nottingham, in Pennsylvania, March 8. Anno 1739-40*, Early American Imprints, 1639-1800; No. 4610. Philadelphia: Benjamin Franklin, in Market-Street, 1740.

Thayer, Joseph Henry. *A Greek-English Lexicon of the New Testament: Being Grimm's Wilke's Clavis Novi Testamenti*. New York: Harper & Brothers, 1889.

The Cambridge Paragraph Bible: Of the Authorized English Version. Cambridge: Cambridge University Press, 1873.

The Holy Bible: King James Version. Electronic Edition of the 1900 Authorized Version. Bellingham, WA: Logos Research Systems, Inc., 2009.

The Holy Scriptures in the Original Languages: תורה נביאים כתובים. 1894/1998, Bomberg/Ginsburg ed. *Η ΚΑΙΝΗ ΔΙΑΘΗΚΗ*, Beza/Scrivener, 1894. London, England: Tyndale House/Trinitarian Bible Society, 1894/1998.

The New King James Version. Nashville: Thomas Nelson, 1982.

Trench, Richard Chenevix. *Synonyms of the New Testament*. London: Macmillan, 1880.

Tyndale, William. *The Obedience of the Christian Man*. Elec. acc. http://www.onthewing.org/user/Tyndale%20%20Obedience%20of%20a%20Christian%20Man%20-%20Modern.pdf.
Vincent, Marvin Richardson. *Word Studies in the New Testament*. New York: Charles Scribner's Sons, 1887.

Waltke, Bruce K. *The Book of Proverbs, Chapters 1–15*. The New International Commentary on the Old Testament. Grand Rapids, MI: Eerdmans, 2004.

Waltke, Bruce K. *The Book of Proverbs, Chapters 15–31*. The New International Commentary on the Old Testament. Grand Rapids, MI: Eerdmans, 2005.

Weber, Robertus, and R. Gryson. *Biblia Sacra Iuxta Vulgatam Versionem*. 5th revised edition. Stuttgart: Deutsche Bibelgesellschaft, 1969.

Weil, Gerard E., K. Elliger, and W. Rudolph, Deutsche Bibelgesellschaft. *Biblia Hebraica Stuttgartensia*. 5. Aufl., rev. Stuttgart: Deutsche Bibelgesellschaft, 1997.

Willis, Gregory A. *Freedom, Authority, and Church Discipline in the Baptist South, 1785-1900*. Oxford: Oxford University Press, 1997.

Willis, Gregory A. "Was Dagg Right?" *9Marks Journal* 6:5 (2009), 18-19.

Willis, Gregory A. "Who Are the True Baptists? The Conservative Resurgence and the Influence of Moderate Views of Baptist Identity." *Southern Baptist Journal of Theology* 9:1 (2005), 17-33.

Zahn, Theodor. *Introduction to the New Testament*, trans. Melancthon Williams Jacobus, 3 vol. Edinburgh: T&T Clark, 1909.

XIV.) ABOUT THE AUTHOR

Thomas Ross is a miserable sinner saved by the free mercy of Jesus Christ during his freshman year in college. After graduating from the University of California at Berkeley with a B. A., he received an M. A. from Fairhaven Baptist College, an M. Div. from Great Plains Baptist Divinity School, and a Th. M. from Anchor Baptist Theological Seminary. He has completed graduate-level education at Baptist Bible Seminary, Calvary Baptist Theological Seminary, and Westminster Seminary, among other institutions of higher learning. He serves his risen Lord with his family at Grace and Truth Baptist Church in San Francisco, California.

Many of his Christian resources are available at faithsaves.net, on the KJB1611 YouTube channel, and on the KJBIBLE1611 Rumble channel.

ENDNOTES

---

1 The main points in this composition are contained in the main body of the text. Endnotes provide supplementary material that may not be necessary for all readers. While the endnotes contain valuable and edifying information, readers should not lose the flow of the study. It may be best to read the text paragraph by paragraph and then go back through the endnotes if one wishes to read them, as well.

Furthermore, Greek and Hebrew appears only in the endnotes, not in the main body of the text. Readers who understand the Biblical languages will likely appreciate the points established utilizing them. Readers who only know English should not be discouraged from reading and getting the most that they can from the endnotes, but they should be careful not lose the flow of the main body of the text.

2 This study is not, and does not intend to be, a comprehensive exposition and analysis of all that is involved in Biblical pastoring. It is specifically a study and theological exposition, with appropriate application, of 3 John 9-11, explaining and applying Scripture's lessons from Diotrephes in the light of the complete canon. While godly pastors, and all Christians, should be aware of what Scripture teaches about wolves that corrupt and abuse the pastoral office, they should not *only* be aware of what the Bible teaches about the wolves; a Biblical balance between understanding what Scripture positively teaches about the good and negatively warns about the bad must be maintained.

3 This author believes that the congregational polity practiced in independent Baptist churches represents the model of church government found in the New Testament.

4 Acts 6:5; Revelation 2:6, 15. It is interesting that, as the traitor Judas is always mentioned last in lists of the twelve apostles (Matthew 10:4; Mark 3:19; Luke 6:16), so Nicolas' name appears last in the list of

the deacons. Irenaeus notes: "The Nicolaitanes are the followers of that Nicolas who was one of the seven first ordained to the diaconate by the apostles. They lead lives of unrestrained indulgence" (*Against Heresies* 1:26:3; Irenaeus of Lyons, *The Writings of Irenæus*, ed. Alexander Roberts and James Donaldson, trans. Alexander Roberts and W. H. Rambaut, vol. 1, Ante-Nicene Christian Library [Edinburgh: T. & T. Clark, 1868–1869], 97–98). Another writer agrees: "A ... heretic emerged in Nicolaus. He was one of the seven deacons who were appointed in the Acts of the Apostles" (Pseudo-Tertullian, *Against All Heresies* 1; *Latin Christianity: Its Founder, Tertullian*, ed. Alexander Roberts, James Donaldson, and A. Cleveland Coxe, trans. S. Thelwell, vol. 3, The Ante-Nicene Fathers [Buffalo, NY: Christian Literature Company, 1885], 650). See also Hippolytus, *The Refutation of All Heresies* 8:24; Eusebius, *Ecclesiastical History* 3:29:1; Epiphanius, *Panarion* 1:20 & 1:25; Augustine, *Concerning Baptism* 4:10:16; but see also Clement of Alexandria, *Stromata* 2:118:3.

5 Jerome, *Select Letters of St. Jerome*, ed. T. E. Page, E. Capps, and W. H. D. Rouse, trans. F. A. Wright, The Loeb Classical Library (London: William Heinemann, 1933), 47. The Ophites were a Gnostic sect.

6 The church at Ephesus took Paul's warning seriously, successfully detected, and was therefore protected from such spiritual wolves: "I know thy works, and thy labour, and thy patience, and how thou canst not bear them which are evil: and thou hast tried them which say they are apostles, and are not, and hast found them liars" (Revelation 2:2). Paul kept the wolves out while he was at Ephesus (Acts 20:29-31) and the church successfully overcame them after the apostle left.

7 In 3 John 9-11, Diotrephes must be a head pastor. A regular church member, or a deacon, would not have the ability to prevent the entire congregation from hearing the letter of John the Apostle (3 John 9). Nor would a non-pastor have the ability to cast people out of the church on his own authority (3 John 10). Zahn notes:

> *The description of the conduct of Diotrephes, especially* the ἐκ τῆς ἐκκλησίας ἐκβάλλει, *presupposes that he occupies an official position, formally recognized even by those who do not*

> *agree with him, and one which even the author is bound to consider, and which enables him successfully to play the autocrat. ... Diotrephes ... [holds] the position of autocratic bishop ... he employs it in an imperious and ruinous manner ... he is an ambitious hierarch who does not follow the precept of Jesus (Mark 10:44) and the example and exhortation of the apostles (1 Pet. 5:3; 2 Cor. 1:24), being in addition an opponent of the author and of the other disciples of Jesus in that Church circle. ... The leader of this congregation is an enemy of the [Apostle John] and of his companions[.] (Theodor Zahn,* Introduction to the New Testament, *trans. Melancthon Williams Jacobus, vol. 3 [Edinburgh: T&T Clark, 1909], 376–377)*

Dunn correctly explains:

> *Diotrephes was clearly in control of this church at least: not only was he able to refuse a welcome to visiting Christians, but he also "expels from the church" those who crossed him. Diotrephes, in other words, was acting with the authority of a monarchical bishop (cf. Ignatius, Eph., 6.1; Trall., 7.2; Smyrn., 8.1f.), and it was against this lust for ecclesiastical prominence and power (philoprōteuōn) that "the elder" wrote. ... III John ... is best seen as ... protesting against the increasing influence of early catholicism. (James D. G. Dunn,* Unity and Diversity in the New Testament: An Inquiry into the Character of Earliest Christianity, *3rd ed. [London: SCM Press, 2006], 392)*

While Diotrephes was certainly a head pastor, application to others who follow his wicked ways is unquestionably appropriate.

8 Second Corinthians 11:26 & Galatians 2:4, ψευδάδελφος. The post-apostolic writers continued to testify to such (*Polycarp to the Philippians* 6:3 & *Apostolic Constitutions* 2:37:5).

9 The Baptist scholar A. T. Robertson, after writing "an article for a denominational paper concerning Diotrephes," noted: "The editor told me afterwards that twenty-five [church leaders] had ordered the paper stopped as a protest against the personal attack in the paper." But Dr. Robertson had simply explained that "Diotrephes was a typical church 'boss' who ruled the church to suit his own whims" (A. T.

Robertson, *Types of Preachers in the New Testament* [New York: George H. Doran Company, 1922], 221–222).

Apparently, his description hit too close to home, and his exposition of Scripture was viewed as a personal attack by those whose picture Scripture had painted too well. Unfortunately, the response of these sons of Diotrephes was not repentance but an attempt to shut down the source that exposed them.

[10] ὁ φιλοπρωτεύων αὐτῶν.

[11] φιλοπρωτεύω, William Arndt et al., *A Greek-English Lexicon of the New Testament and Other Early Christian Literature* [BDAG], (Chicago: University of Chicago Press, 2000).

[12] φιλοπρωτεύω, Johannes P. Louw and Eugene Albert Nida, *Greek-English Lexicon of the New Testament: Based on Semantic Domains* [LN], (New York: United Bible Societies, 1996).

[13] See the uses of φιλέω and φίλος in John 3:29; 5:20; 11:3, 11 (note Λάζαρος ὁ φίλος *ἡμῶν*—both Christ and the disciples share love for the sheep); 11:36; 15:13-15, 19; 16:27; 20:2; 21:15-17; 3 John 14.

[14] φιλάδελφος.

[15] BDAG, φίλος. Compare Aristotle's picturesque answer "[t]o the query, 'What is a friend?' ... 'A single soul dwelling in two bodies" (ἐρωτηθεὶς τί ἐστι φίλος, ἔφη, μία ψυχὴ δύο σώμασιν ἐνοικοῦσα. Diogenes Laertius, *Lives of Eminent Philosophers*, ed. R. D. Hicks [Kansas City Missouri: Harvard University Press, November 1, 2005], 462-463; 5.1.20) with Acts 4:29, "And the multitude of them that believed were of one heart and of one soul [Τοῦ δὲ πλήθους τῶν πιστευσάντων ἦν ἡ καρδία καὶ ἡ ψυχὴ μία]: neither said any *of them* that ought of the things which he possessed was his own; but they had all things common." Note also the New Covenant promise: "And I will give them one heart, and one way, that they may fear me for ever" (Jeremiah 32:39, καὶ δώσω αὐτοῖς ὁδὸν ἑτέραν καὶ καρδίαν ἑτέραν φοβηθῆναί με πάσας τὰς

ἡμέρας, LXX; וְנָתַתִּי לָהֶם לֵב אֶחָד וְדֶרֶךְ אֶחָד לְיִרְאָה אוֹתִי כָּל־הַיָּמִים); see also Ezekiel 11:19.

[16] κατ' ὄνομα.

[17] ἀσπάζομαι, BDAG; see 3 John 10.

[18] κατ' ὄνομα. John 10:3 and 3 John 14 contain the only two instances of κατά + ὄνομα in the New Testament; John's epistle clearly alludes to his gospel.

[19] Second Timothy 3:2, φίλαυτος.

[20] That is, his ψυχή: ὁ φιλῶν τὴν ψυχὴν αὐτοῦ ἀπολέσει αὐτήν, John 12:25a.

[21] Third John 9, φιλοπρωτεύω.

[22] Thus, one of the qualifications for the eldership is "not selfwilled," μὴ αὐθάδη. Etymologically a combination of αὐτός (he, she, it) and ἥδομαι, "to enjoy oneself, take one's pleasure" (Henry George Liddell, Robert Scott, Henry Stuart Jones, Roderick McKenzie, *A Greek-English Lexicon* [LSJ]. Oxford: Clarendon Press, 1996), the αὐθάδης is "self-pleasing, self-willed, arrogant" (Joseph Henry Thayer, *A Greek-English Lexicon of the New Testament: Being Grimm's Wilke's Clavis Novi Testamenti* [New York: Harper & Brothers, 1889], αὐθάδης; [Thayer]), and designates "to the Greek mind ... h[u]bris" (BDAG). He is "αὐτοάδης, or αὐτῷ ἁδῶν, as Aristotle informs us" (Richard Chenevix Trench [Trench], *Synonyms of the New Testament* [London: Macmillan, 1880], 349–353, § xciii. αὐθάδης, φίλαυτος). Compare the words that bear a common root with ἥδομαι in Mark 6:20; 12:37; Luke 8:14; Acts 2:41; 21:17; Romans 7:22; 2 Corinthians 11:19; 12:9, 15; 2 Timothy 3:4; Titus 1:7; 3:3; James 4:1, 3; 2 Peter 2:10, 13.

[23] αὐθάδεια, BDAG (a cognate of αὐθάδης).

[24] Note the association between the self-willed αὐθάδης and the one who remembers injuries (μνησικακέω, from μιμνῄσκω & κακός, "to

remember some injury with resentment, remember evil, bear malice, bear a grudge," BDAG) in Proverbs 21:24, LXX: θρασὺς καὶ αὐθάδης καὶ ἀλαζὼν λοιμὸς καλεῖται· ὃς δὲ μνησικακεῖ, παράνομος; "A bold and self-willed and insolent man is called a pest; and he that remembers injuries is a transgressor."

25 Thus, immediately following Titus 1:7's "not selfwilled" is "not soon angry": μὴ αὐθάδη, μὴ ὀργίλον. Furthermore, being "harsh" and "cruel" is part of the semantic domain of αὐθάδες (Franco Montanari, et. al., *Brill Dictionary of Ancient Greek* [BrDAG] [Boston: Brill, 2015]); compare Ῥουβὴν … σκληρὸς φέρεσθαι καὶ σκληρὸς αὐθάδης. ... Συμεὼν καὶ Λευὶ ... ἐπικατάρατος ὁ θυμὸς αὐτῶν, ὅτι αὐθάδης, καὶ ἡ μῆνις αὐτῶν, ὅτι ἐσκληρύνθη, "Ruben ... hard to be endured, *hard and* self-willed. ... Simeon and Levi[:] ... Cursed be their wrath, for it was self-centered, and their anger, for it was cruel" (Genesis 49:3, 7, LXX, Brenton & NETS).

26 Trench, § xciii, αὐθάδης, φίλαυτος.

27 After Peter's three-fold denial of Christ, the Lord Jesus restored His repentant and grieving apostle in John 21:15-17:

> *15 So when they had dined, Jesus saith to Simon Peter, Simon, son of Jonas, lovest thou me more than these? He saith unto him, Yea, Lord; thou knowest that I love thee. He saith unto him, Feed my lambs. 16 He saith to him again the second time, Simon, son of Jonas, lovest thou me? He saith unto him, Yea, Lord; thou knowest that I love thee. He saith unto him, Feed my sheep. 17 He saith unto him the third time, Simon, son of Jonas, lovest thou me? Peter was grieved because he said unto him the third time, Lovest thou me? And he said unto him, Lord, thou knowest all things; thou knowest that I love thee. Jesus saith unto him, Feed my sheep.*

> 15 Ὅτε οὖν ἠρίστησαν, λέγει τῷ Σίμωνι Πέτρῳ ὁ Ἰησοῦς, Σίμων Ἰωνᾶ, ἀγαπᾷς με πλεῖον τούτων; λέγει αὐτῷ, Ναὶ Κύριε· σὺ οἶδας ὅτι φιλῶ σε. λέγει αὐτῷ, Βόσκε τὰ ἀρνία μου. 16 λέγει αὐτῷ πάλιν δεύτερον, Σίμων Ἰωνᾶ, ἀγαπᾷς με; λέγει αὐτῷ, Ναὶ Κύριε· σὺ οἶδας ὅτι φιλῶ σε. λέγει αὐτῷ, Ποίμαινε τὰ πρόβατά μου. 17 λέγει αὐτῷ τὸ τρίτον, Σίμων

> Ἰωνᾶ, φιλεῖς με; ἐλυπήθη ὁ Πέτρος ὅτι εἶπεν αὐτῷ τὸ τρίτον, φιλεῖς με; καὶ εἶπεν αὐτῷ, Κύριε, σὺ πάντα οἶδας· σὺ γινώσκεις ὅτι φιλῶ σε. λέγει αὐτῷ ὁ Ἰησοῦς, Βόσκε τὰ πρόβατά μου.

Christ twice asked Peter about his love using ἀγαπάω, but the third time questioned Peter employing φιλέω. When Peter responds with φιλέω to each of the three inquiries, it seems best to view his response not as an affirmation of a lesser level of love but, as a reversal of his three-fold denial of allegiance to Christ—that is, as a semantic specification that his love involved allegiance. Peter had three times, out of fearful self-preservation, professed allegiance to the anti-Christ world system instead of to the Lord Jesus, but now he renewed his commitment to not being first a lover of lord Caesar, of being "Caesar's friend" (φίλος τοῦ Καίσαρος, John 19:12; 20:2) and a lover of this world (φιλέω, John 15:19) out of love for himself (John 12:25, φιλέω), but instead one whose loyal love and faithful allegiance was supremely for Christ: "I love thee" (φιλῶ σε, John 21:15-17). A friend (φίλος) is one with whom one shares close association and mutual interests—something not present in God's ἀγάπη for the world (John 3:16, ἀγαπάω). As Christ had shown His loyal love for His friends by laying down His life for them (John 15:13-15; cf. the uses of φιλέω / φίλος in John 11:3, 11, 36, where the Lord knew that raising Lazarus would be the final nail in His coffin, a miracle performed out of love that would lead to fatal hostility from the Jewish leadership), so Peter would show the truthfulness of his professed loyal love for, allegiance to, and association with Christ (John 21:15-17) through martyrdom (John 21:18-19), as had the martyred John the Baptist (ὁ ... φίλος τοῦ νυμφίου, John 3:29). Peter did not love (φιλέω) his life in this world and so lost his physical life, but he loved Christ preeminently, and so through martyrdom received life eternal (John 12:25).

True pastors, like Peter, manifest ultimate loyal love, allegiance, and affection for Christ and therefore also manifest true love for Christ's flock. But false pastors, like Diotrephes, love themselves and their own preeminence.

[28] Joel R. Beeke and Paul M. Smalley, *Reformed Systematic Theology:*

Man and Christ, vol. 2 (Wheaton, IL: Crossway, 2020), 1160–1162, citing VanderKemp, *The Christian Entirely the Property of Christ*, 1:265; Brakel, *The Christian's Reasonable Service*, 1:572-573 & David Laing, preface to *The Works of John Knox*, ed. David Laing, 6 vols. (Edinburgh: Thomas George Stevenson, 1864), 6:lii.

29 καὶ αὐτός ἐστιν ἡ κεφαλὴ τοῦ σώματος, τῆς ἐκκλησίας ... ἵνα γένηται ἐν πᾶσιν αὐτὸς πρωτεύων.

30 Compare the reference to Christ as πρωτεύω in Colossians 1:18—a NT *hapax legomenon*—with the *hapax* φιλοπρωτεύω in 3 John 9. Compare also πρωτοκλισία, "uppermost room," place of honor (Matthew 23:6; Mark 12:39; Luke 14:7-8; 20:46); πρωτοκαθεδρία (Mark 12:39; Luke 11:43; 20:46), chief seat, seat of honor; πρωτοστάτης, "ringleader" (Acts 24:5), προΐστημι, "ruleth" (Romans 12:8; 1 Thessalonians 5:12), προηγέομαι, "preferring" (Romans 12:10).

31 Of course, the Hebrew מָשִׁיחַ (Daniel 9:25) and the Greek Χριστός mean "Anointed One." It is true that all believers have been anointed by the Holy Spirit (χρῖσμα, 1 John 2:27), but Diotrephes arrogates more to himself than this when he claims to be the Lord's Anointed (cf. Jack Hyles, *Jack Hyles Speaks on Biblical Separation* [Hammond, IN: Hyles-Anderson Publishers, 1984] chapter 4, "A Christian's Attitude Toward Other Christians with Whom He Cannot Cooperate," & Roy L. Branson, Jr., *Dear Preacher, Please Quit!* [Bristol, TN: Landmark Publications, 1996], chapter 4, "The Untouchable Man"). Hyles taught: the "preacher ... [is] God's man ... I will never lift up my hand against God's anointed" (Jack Hyles, *From Vapor to Floods* (Hammond, IN: Hyles-Anderson Publishers, 1974, sermon 1, "I have sinned." Elec. acc. https://www.jackhyles.com/vapor.htm).

The Bible never calls those with the office of the bishop "anointed" in any sense other than what all God's people possess, nor are New Testament preachers called anything like "the Lord's Anointed," which is not surprising, since Old Testament anointings of priests and kings pointed forward in type to the exalted Lord Jesus Christ, not to pastors who are dust and ashes.

If one wishes to argue that "touch not mine anointed" (Psalm 105:15) can be applied to showing extreme deference to pastors, the fact that in Psalm 105:15 the anointed ones in view are not Israel's kings, but God's "people as a whole" (Beth Tanner & Rolf A. Jacobson, *The Book of Psalms*, ed. E. J. Young, R. K. Harrison, and Robert L. Hubbard Jr., The New International Commentary on the Old Testament [Grand Rapids, MI: Eerdmans, 2014], 790) in the patriarchal period, would at the bare minimum require showing all of God's people the same sort of extreme deference arrogated by a (non-contextual) application of this phrase to a pastor, rather than providing an exegetical basis for a head pastor dominating a church with an iron fist. If Psalm 105:15 is set aside and, instead, the narrative of David refusing to kill Saul because the king was God's anointed is pressed into service, the fact that all Old Testament priests were themselves God's anointed ones (Leviticus 4:5, 16; 6:22) would mean that oppression of the universal priesthood of New Testament believers (1 Peter 2:5, 9) would actually be touching Jehovah's Anointed—Saul raised his hand against God's Anointed when he slew the Lord's priests (1 Samuel 22:17-19). Perhaps instead of being twisted into a basis for excusing dictatorial pastors, "touch not mine anointed" should be made a rallying cry for congregational church government and the authority given to the royal priesthood of every believer in Christ. Or perhaps (even better) God's Word should simply be allowed to speak for itself and its plain meaning in context should not be set aside or distorted.

[32] Lockett notes:

> *There are several similarities that draw 1-3 John together. First, 1 and 2 John both speak to the same situation, where a secessionist group "went out from us" and denied "the coming of Jesus Christ in the flesh" (1 Jn 2:19, 22–23; 2 Jn 7). Second, John labels the secessionists as antichrists in 1 John (1 Jn 2:18, 22), as does the Elder in 2 John (2 Jn 7). The centrality of the love command is notably shared between 1 John (1 Jn 3:11, 23; 4:7, 21; 5:1–4) and 2 John (2 Jn 4–6), along with the desire to see his children walking in the truth (1 Jn 1:3–4; 2 Jn 4). Thus, there is a clear and strong connection between 1 and 2 John.*

There is an equally strong connection between 2 and 3 John. They share the same form; both follow the typical form of a Greco-Roman personal letter, including an introduction, main body, and conclusion. Both letters are written by the "Elder" (presbyteros; 2 Jn 1; 3 Jn 1) to those whom he loves in truth (2 Jn 1, to the "elect lady"; 3 Jn 1, to Gaius). Both letters express joy over "your children walking in truth" (2 Jn 4; 3 Jn 4), both implicitly warn of the antichrist (2 Jn 7; whom Diotrephes seems to embody, 3 Jn 9) and both letters conclude with a comment regarding wanting to talk face to face rather than to use paper and ink (2 Jn 12) or pen and ink (3 Jn 13).

In addition to this, there is one key term that draws all three letters together. The strongest connection in language shared between all three letters of John is the reoccurring term truth (alētheia). Not only does some form of alētheia appear in every chapter of 1 John (1 Jn 1:6, 8; 2:4, 21; 3:19; 4:6; 5:6), but the key term also stands in the opening and closing sections of the letter. After the prologue (1 Jn 1:1–4), the letter's opening set of contrasts in 1 John 1:5–2:2 articulates that those who fail to practice the truth (poioumen tēn alētheian; 1 Jn 1:6) will not have fellowship with God, and the one claiming to have no sin is deceived and does not have "the truth [hē alētheia]" (1 Jn 1:8). In 1 John 3:18 the author exhorts his readers to love "in action and in truth [alētheia]" and says that by such action they will know that they are of the truth (ek tēs alētheias; 1 Jn 3:19). Then, in 1 John 4–5, it is the "Spirit of truth [alētheias]" with whom John is concerned. Finally, 1 John concludes with the claim that "the Son of God has come," and therefore knowledge of "the true one," that is, Jesus Christ, and "the true God and eternal life" (1 Jn 5:20) is public. Thus, the theme and more importantly the term alētheia brackets the entire letter of 1 John.

The term alētheia in turn links 1 John to 2 and 3 John. In the opening verse of 2 John, the author qualifies his own love for the "elect lady and her children" as "in the truth [en alētheia]" and goes on to claim the same for "all who know the truth [tēn alētheian]." The term appears again in 2 John 2–4, where the author expresses joy over the fact that his readers have been walking the truth. Echoing 2 John 1, the term is used again in

> *the opening verse of 3 John: "The elder: To my dear friend Gaius, whom I love in truth [en alētheia]."*
>
> *Then, echoing 1 John 1:6, 8; 3 John 3 expresses joy at the fact that "you are walking in truth" (en alētheia peripateis). The term also appears in 3 John 4, 8, 12. (Darian R. Lockett, Letters for the Church: Reading James, 1-2 Peter, 1-3 John, and Jude as Canon [Downers Grove, IL: IVP Academic, 2021], 170–172)*

33 BDAG, ἀρνέομαι def #4. The verb ἀρνέομαι appears for the denial that the Lord Jesus is Christ and the denial of the Father and the Son (1 John 2:22-23), contrasted with confessing or acknowledging them (ὁμολογέω). One can either confess or deny God not only with true or false theological constructions but also with one's lifestyle (e. g., 1 Timothy 5:8; Titus 1:16).

34 Jack Hyles not only inculcated an extreme view of pastoral authority that would justify Diotrephes, but also denied that the lost must repent of their sin in order to be born again:

> *There are those who say we have to repent of our sins in order to be saved. No, we have to repent only of the thing that makes us unsaved, and that is unbelief[.] ... [F]alse doctrine ... says that in order for a person to be saved, he must make Jesus the Lord of his life. (Jack Hyles, Enemies of Soulwinning, chapters 4, 1, elec. acc. https://www.soulwinning.info/books/jack_hyles/enemies_of_soulwinning/misunderstood_repentance.htm)*

That is, Hyles claimed that the lost could "deny," that is, "refuse to pay attention to, disregard" (BDAG, ἀρνέομαι) that Jesus is the "Christ" (1 John 2:22); that is, the Lord, the Master, the King, and still be saved. Hyles viewed the doctrine that the lost must repent of their sin and submissively trust in Jesus as Lord and Christ as a false gospel, quoting Galatians 1:6-9. Hyles endorsed both a version of the doctrinal aberration on Jesus as the Lord Christ and a version of the practical aberration of Diotrephes condemned by the Apostle John in his inspired epistles.

35 Diotrephes' failure to abide in the truth is comparable to Judas' failure to similarly abide in John's Gospel, where Judas is the personified manifestation of the branch that does not continue and is burned up in hell (John 13; 15:6). Diotrephes' spirit of loving the preeminence that is due solely to Christ is also manifest in the spiritual antichrists that lead the current manifestation of the Roman empire predicted in Daniel and Revelation, the Roman Catholic whore of Babylon (Revelation 17) led by the self-professed "vicar of Christ" the Pope (*Catechism of the Catholic Church*, 2nd ed. [Washington, DC: United States Catholic Conference, 2000], 245–246, sec. 936), from whom will issue the singular future false prophet with whom the singular future Antichrist will join in Satan's final and ultimate display of idolatrous lusting after Christ's preeminence.

With the Latin word for *vicar* being the equivalent to the Greek preposition *anti* (cf. Leviticus 24:18, Latin Vulgate *vicarium*, Greek LXX ἀντί), claiming to be the "vicar of Christ," that is, "anti-Christ," appears to be a very unwise title for anyone to arrogate to himself, and an unwise position for anyone to place himself in, even if he technically disclaims such a blasphemous title.

36 Commenting on John 13:27, Matthew Henry notes:

> *After the sop, Satan entered into him: not to make him melancholy, nor drive him distracted, which was the effect of his possessing some; not to hurry him into the fire, nor into the water; happy had it been for him if that had been the worst of it, or if with the swine he had been choked in the sea; but Satan entered into him to possess him with a prevailing prejudice against Christ and his doctrine, and a contempt of him, as one whose life was of small value, to excite in him a covetous desire of the wages of unrighteousness and a resolution to stick at nothing for the obtaining of them. (Matthew Henry, Matthew Henry's Commentary on the Whole Bible: Complete and Unabridged in One Volume [Peabody: Hendrickson, 1994], 2009, note on John 13:18-30)*

[37] Mark 10:14, 41, ἀγανακτέω. Judas was similarly much displeased or indignant (Mark 14:4; Matthew 20:24) at the superlative self-sacrificial love of the woman who poured very costly ointment on Christ, for Judas wanted the money himself so that he could steal it (John 12:4-8)—pouring it on Christ was a "waste." Sadly, at least some of the other apostles were spiritually immature enough to be deceived by Judas' convincing words. The anti-Christ Jewish religious leaders were also much displeased or indignant at the manifestation of Christ's glory (Matthew 21:15; Luke 13:14).

[38] 1 Corinthians 10:7 & Exodus 32; Colossians 3:5.

[39] As expected and as discussed in more detail later in this study, sexual immorality permeates circles which practice the pro-Diotrephes doctrines taught by men such as Jack Hyles and Roy L. Branson, Jr., as leaders who convince their followers to view them as the "Lord's" untouchable "Anointed" ones abuse their positions of unbiblically extreme power to commit adultery and sodomy and molest children. See, e. g., Roy L. Branson Jr., *Dear Preacher, Please Quit!* (Bristol, TN: Landmark Publications, 1996) chapters 4, 10; Roy L. Branson, Jr., *Dear Abner: I Love You, Joab*, 2nd ed. (Bristol, TN: Landmark Publications, 1996), chapter 9; David Cloud, *The Hyles Effect: A Spreading Blight* (Port Huron, MI: Way of Life, 2020); Michael Stacey Shiflett, *Wolves Among Lambs: My Story of Sexual Abuse & Cover-Ups in the Church* (Dundalk, MD: SureWord, 2019); cf. Thomas Ross, "Quotations from Three Books by Roy L. Branson: *Dear Preacher, Please Quit! & Church Split & Dear Abner: I Love You, Joab*," elec. acc. https://faithsaves.net/roy-branson/; Thomas Ross, "Hyles-Anderson College & First Baptist of Hammond: Do They Now Please God?" elec. acc. https://kentbrandenburg.blogspot.com/2020/02/hyles-anderson-college-first-baptist-of.html/. Disgustingly, writers like Branson consistently blame women for seducing pastors—while Branson does not say it is acceptable for the pastors to commit adultery, the idea that pastors are manipulating their positions of Diotrephes-like preeminence and authority to slake their lusts is not warned against, for such dirty perverts are God's untouchable Anointed Ones.

[40] Bruce B. Barton and Grant R. Osborne, *1, 2 & 3 John*, Life Application Bible Commentary (Wheaton, IL: Tyndale House, 1998), 141.

[41] John F. MacArthur Jr., *John MacArthur Sermon Archive* (Panorama City, CA: Grace to You, 2014), "Love in the Fellowship, Part 2," 12/18/1977.

[42] ἀγαπητέ, μὴ μιμοῦ τὸ κακόν, ἀλλὰ τὸ ἀγαθόν. ὁ ἀγαθοποιῶν ἐκ τοῦ Θεοῦ ἐστίν· ὁ δὲ κακοποιῶν οὐχ ἑώρακε τὸν Θεόν.

[43] See, e. g., Thomas Ross, "Assurance of Salvation in 1 John: The Tests of Life." Elec. acc. https://faithsaves.net/assurance-john/.

[44] ὁ … ποιῶν τὴν ἀλήθειαν.

[45] ὑμεῖς φίλοι μου ἐστέ, ἐὰν ποιῆτε ὅσα ἐγὼ ἐντέλλομαι ὑμῖν.

[46] καὶ ἐκπορεύσονται, οἱ τὰ ἀγαθὰ ποιήσαντες, εἰς ἀνάστασιν ζωῆς· οἱ δὲ τὰ φαῦλα πράξαντες, εἰς ἀνάστασιν κρίσεως. Note the ongoing action portrayed with the present tense of ποιέω, both here and in the preceding passages referenced from John's Gospel.

[47] Ephesians 2:8-10; compare Matthew 7:17-18; Jeremiah 4:22. God's foreordination (προετοιμάζω) that those who are in Christ walk in good works (Ephesians 2:10) is as certain as His foreordination of all in Christ to eternal glory (Romans 9:23).

[48] Note the ongoing action portrayed with the present tense of ποιέω in 1 John 1:6; 2:17, 29; 3:8-10; Revelation 21:27; 22:14-15.

[49] Thus, note the present tenses in ὁ φιλοπρωτεύων, οὐκ ἐπιδέχεται, τὰ ἔργα ἃ ποιεῖ, λόγοις πονηροῖς φλυαρῶν, μὴ ἀρκούμενος, οὔτε αὐτὸς ἐπιδέχεται, τοὺς βουλομένους κωλύει, and ἐκ τῆς ἐκκλησίας ἐκβάλλει (3 John 9-10); contrast the aorists Ἔγραψα and ἔλθω, as well as the future ὑπομνήσω, when the ongoing actions of Diotrephes are not in view.

[50] ἐκ τοῦ Θεοῦ. Note the ἐκ + Θεοῦ constructions in John 1:13; 8:47; 1 John 3:9-10; 4:1-4, 6-7, 5:1, 4, 18-19.

[51] John 3:3; 11:40; Matthew 5:8; Acts 7:55; 2 Corinthians 3:18.

[52] For example, surely a regenerate man who is prematurely put into the pastoral office can fall into the dreadful sin of proud self-exaltation (1 Timothy 3:6). However, the "condemnation of the devil" is eternal hell fire, not just the chastisement God gives to His beloved children. First Timothy 3:6 contains an important warning not to place one "newly planted in the Christian community" (BDAG, νεόφυτος; cf. "my newly planted vine," τὴν ἄμπελόν μου τὴν νεόφυτον, Asenath 25:2) into the pastorate. If he turns out to be a false convert who has no root in himself, no genuine regeneration (Matthew 13:1-23), he can cause terrible trouble to a church and fall into the same eternal condemnation as the devil. But even a true convert who is too newly-planted in the faith can become proud and cause serious problems; the principle from 1 Timothy 3:6 certainly applies to such an immature saint.

[53] ἀγαπητέ, μὴ μιμοῦ τὸ κακόν, ἀλλὰ τὸ ἀγαθόν. The present imperative with μή indicates a general prohibition (Daniel B. Wallace, *Greek Grammar beyond the Basics: An Exegetical Syntax of the New Testament* [Grand Rapids, MI: Zondervan, 1996], 724–725).

[54] BDAG, μιμέομαι.

[55] Baptist churches traditionally commonly (and correctly) agreed to the "restriction of participation in congregational business meetings and insistence upon the silence of women in church meetings" (James Leo Garrett, Jr., *Baptist Church Discipline*, rev. ed. [Paris, AK: Baptist Standard Bearer, 2004], 28). Thus, for example, the *Summary of Church Discipline* published by the Charleston Baptist Association in 1774 confessed:

> *[Decisions are affected by] a majority of the male members[.] ... Female members may, when called upon, act as witnesses*

> *in a church and, when aggrieved, are to make known their case, either in person or by a brother, and must have a proper regard paid them. But they are excluded from all share of rule or government in the church (1 Corinthians 14:34-35; 1 Timothy 2:11-12).*

Not only 1 Corinthians 14 and 1 Timothy 2 affirm the correctness of this procedure, but also passages such as Isaiah 3:12: "*As for* my people, children *are* their oppressors, and women rule over them. O my people, they which lead thee cause *thee* to err, and destroy the way of thy paths." Women have a glorious spiritual equality in Christ (Galatians 3:28) but their blessed, good, and distinct God-ordained role does not involve ruling men.

[56] Joseph S. Baker, *Queries Considered, or An Investigation of Various Subjects Involved in the Exercise of Church Discipline* (1847), reprinted in Mark Dever, ed. *Polity: A Collection of Historic Baptist Documents: Biblical Arguments on How to Conduct Church Life* (Michigan: Sheridan Books, 2001), 292.

[57] W. J. McGlothlin, *Baptist Confessions of Faith* (Philadelphia: American Baptist Publication Society, 1911), 186, citing Article 42.

[58] Eleazar Savage, *Manual of Church Discipline* (New York: Sheldon & Co., 1863), reprinted in Mark Dever, ed. *Polity: A Collection of Historic Baptist Documents: Biblical Arguments on How to Conduct Church Life* (Michigan: Sheridan Books, 2001), 496-497.

[59] Edward Hiscox, *Standard Manual for Baptist Churches* [Philadelphia, PA: American Baptist Publication Society, 1890, 33-35.

[60] J. M. Pendleton, *Church Manual: Designed for the Use of Baptist Churches* (Philadelphia: Judson Press, 1846), Chapter 6, "The Discipline of the Church." Elec. acc. https://www.reformedreader.org/rbb/pendleton/churchmanual/bcmtitlepage.htm.

[61] Joseph S. Baker, *Queries Considered, or An Investigation of Various Subjects Involved in the Exercise of Church Discipline* (1847), reprinted in

---

Mark Dever, ed. *Polity: A Collection of Historic Baptist Documents: Biblical Arguments on How to Conduct Church Life* (Michigan: Sheridan Books, 2001), 272-276.

62 Edward T. Hiscox, *The New Directory For Baptist Churches* (Philadelphia: American Baptist Publication Society, 1902), 173-180, 188-190.

63 Gregory A. Willis, *Freedom, Authority, and Church Discipline in the Baptist South, 1785-1900* (Oxford: Oxford University Press, 1997), 23-24, 29, 33. Interestingly, even in the antebellum South "churches did not pattern their proceedings after the forms and rules of civil courts. State laws in the South, for example, prohibited slaves from testifying in civil courts against whites. In church courts, slave members could testify against whites ... [churches] could conceive of no basis for rejecting slave testimony" (*ibid,* 23-24).

64 Note that Matthew 18:16's σταθῇ πᾶν ῥῆμα, "every word may be established," refers to Deuteronomy 19:15's "shall the matter be established" (יָקוּם דָּבָר׃; σταθήσεται πᾶν ῥῆμα, LXX). The reference is not to verbal utterances alone, but to every word or thing (דָּבָר) that pertains to the case in question. Willis notes that historically, in "difficult cases" that related to church discipline, churches were very thorough:

> *[D]iscipline committees might busy themselves for months, meeting with witnesses and with the accused, citing interested parties to attend conference, and preparing a report for the church. ... In the report, the committee paraded the relevant evidence and testimony, including the demeanor of the accused and a resume of the course of the investigation. When churches concluded that the committee had neglected evidence or exercises insufficient diligence, they might reject the report and order the committee to continue its work.*
>
> *If the church accepted the committee's report, then it considered its recommendation. ...*

> *Churches generally adopted the recommendation of the committee but sometimes rejected it in favor of some other course of action. (Gregory A. Willis, Freedom, Authority, and Church Discipline in the Baptist South, 1785-1900 [Oxford: Oxford University Press, 1997], 21-22).*

65 Thus, note that it is not just one saint whom Diotrephes rejects, but "us" (3 John 9, cf. 3 John 12), casting a plurality of "brethren" out of the church (3 John 10).

66 Compare, e. g., Jack Hyles' teaching that a congregation cannot make any judgments about the actions of a pastor, because the pastor is outside their jurisdiction (Jack Hyles, *Jack Hyles on Justice* (Elec. acc. https://nashpublications.com/wp-content/uploads/2013/10/Great_Books/Hyles_PDF/Jack-Hyles-on-Justice-Dr.-Jack-Hyles.pdf), chapter 5, "Judging Another Master's Servant." A Diotrephes who is a dictator, a thief, or a pervert can easily use Hyles' false teaching to retain power.

67 Compare Saul's calling for Ahimelech the priest and all his father's house in order to cruelly murder them when they knew exactly nothing about Saul's pursuit of David. In his thirst to preserve his preeminence, Saul saw enemies everywhere. Innocence would not stand in his way:

> *Then the king sent to call Ahimelech the priest, the son of Ahitub, and all his father's house, the priests that were in Nob: and they came all of them to the king. And Saul said, Hear now, thou son of Ahitub. And he answered, Here I am, my lord. And Saul said unto him, Why have ye conspired against me, thou and the son of Jesse, in that thou hast given him bread, and a sword, and hast enquired of God for him, that he should rise against me, to lie in wait, as at this day? Then Ahimelech answered the king, and said, And who is so faithful among all thy servants as David, which is the king's son in law, and goeth at thy bidding, and is honourable in thine house? Did I then begin to enquire of God for him? be it far from me: let not the king impute any thing unto his servant, nor to all the house of my father: for thy servant knew nothing of all this, less or more. And the king said, Thou shalt surely die, Ahimelech, thou, and all thy father's house. (1 Samuel 22:11-16)*

To protect his preeminence, Saul would willingly shed the blood of Jehovah's priests or His prophets (1 Samuel 16:2, Samuel; Saul also strove to kill David, whom the Spirit moved to produce inspired prophecy). In order to save face and preserve his honor in relation to a foolish oath, Saul was also willing to kill his innocent and righteous son, Jonathan (1 Samuel 14:39, 44). Finally, Saul killed the king—himself, by suicide—to avoid discomfort or dishonor from the Philistines (1 Samuel 31:4, Hithpael of עָלַל, cf. Jeremiah 38:19; Judges 19:25). He not only killed others, but even killed himself in order to maintain what he could of preeminence. While Saul lived in a different dispensation from Pastor Diotrephes, the ungodly king's battle to retain supremacy when his sins disqualified him from the throne (1 Samuel 13:14) supplies numbers of valuable lessons for Pastor Diotrephes' ungodly methods of grasping preeminence. Saul should have stepped down, as Diotrephes should have voluntarily stepped aside in 3 John, but neither of them were willing to do so, bringing harm to the people of God and ruin to their individual souls. Contrast godly Jonathan's voluntary surrender of his royal garments to David in 1 Samuel 18:1-4 after David manifested that he was Jehovah's ordained ruler in 1 Samuel 17 with Saul's involuntarily stripping himself of his royal garments before David in 1 Samuel 19:24. Saul knew he should step down in favor of David (1 Samuel 24:20), but he still continued to fight against God and His purpose (1 Samuel 26), grasping for preeminence whatever the cost.

[68] Bruce K. Waltke, *The Book of Proverbs, Chapters 1–15*, The New International Commentary on the Old Testament (Grand Rapids, MI: Eerdmans, 2004), 332–333. See Psalm 64:5; 91:3; 119:110; 124:7; 142:3; Ecclesiastes 7:26; Jeremiah 5:26; 18:22; Hosea 9:8.

[69] הַוָּה.

[70] מִרְמָה.

[71] חָטָא.

[72] What Scripture describes with the language of traps and snares, the world often describes as perverts "grooming" their victims.

73 Michael Stacey Shiflett, *Wolves Among Lambs: My Story of Sexual Abuse & Cover-Ups in the Church* (Dundalk, MD: SureWord, 2019), 270-271.

74 1 Timothy 3:7; 6:9; 2 Timothy 2:26; compare the Pharisees' seeking to entrap (παγιδεύω) the Lord Jesus Christ, Matthew 22:15.

75 BDAG, παγίς.

76 Article 46 of the Baptist *Orthodox Creed*, "Of Liberty of Conscience," cited in Thomas Crosby, *The History of the English Baptists*, vol. 3 (Bellingham, WA: Logos Bible Software, 2011), 411. Passages cited in support include 1 Timothy 6:15; Acts 4:17; 10:36; James 4:12 & Romans 14:4.

77 1 Timothy 1:5, 19; 3:9; 2 Timothy 1:3; Hebrews 9:14; 13:18; 1 Peter 2:19; 3:16, 21.

78 That is, πεποίθαμεν γὰρ ὅτι καλὴν συνείδησιν ἔχομεν ("we trust we have a good conscience") because we are ἐν πᾶσι καλῶς θέλοντες ἀναστρέφεσθαι ("in all things willing to live honestly," Hebrews 13:18)—an excellent Biblical definition of a good conscience.

79 William Tyndale, *The Obedience of The Christian Man*, 21. Elec. acc. http://www.onthewing.org/user/Tyndale%20-%20Obedience%20of%20a%20 Christian%20Man%20-%20Modern.pdf. This edition modernizes Tyndale's language.

80 While "receive" translates προσλαμβάνω in Romans 14:1-15:7 but ἐπιδέχομαι in 3 John 9-10, they share significant semantic range, both appearing, e. g., in LN semantic domain 34.53, "to accept the presence of a person with friendliness — 'to welcome, to receive, to accept, to have as a guest.'"

81 The very strong word ἀπόλλυμι is employed.

82 ἐπιδέχομαι; the verb appears only in 3 John 9-10.

83 ἐπιδέχομαι, BDAG.

84 Note that φιλόξενος, the word rendered with a form of "hospitality" in 1 Timothy 3:2; Titus 1:8, combines *philos* and *xenos*, and so etymologically means "loving strangers" (Henry George Liddell et al., *A Greek-English Lexicon* [LSJ] [Oxford: Clarendon Press, 1996], φιλόξενος).

85 σὺ τί ἐξουθενεῖς τὸν ἀδελφόν σου; (Romans 14:10), BDAG, ἐξουθενέω, cf. ὁ ἐσθίων τὸν μὴ ἐσθίοντα μὴ ἐξουθενείτω (Romans 14:3 & see Luke 18:9; 23:11; Acts 4:11; 1 Corinthians 1:28; 6:4; 16:11; 2 Corinthians 10:10; Galatians 4:14; 1 Thessalonians 5:20). Note that setting at naught or despising one's brother (Romans 14:10, 3) takes place in the context of disrespect for his conscience (Romans 14:1-15:7).

86 The ascription of "thousands" to Saul was actually overly generous. In 1-2 Samuel, Saul himself never personally slays any of the enemies of God—he only fears to fight Goliath, seeks to slay David, seeks to slay Jonathan, hinders his men from effectiveness by foolishly requiring them to fast before battle, causes the Lord's priests to be slain, and finally slays the Lord's anointed by killing himself and causing his armorbearer to also commit suicide.

87 Roy L. Branson, *Church Split,* 2nd ed. (Bristol, TN: Landmark Publications, 1992), 33-46. Mr. Branson's books are classic examples of "Baptist" advocacy of a Diotrephes-style of pastoring. Shiflett correctly notes concerning pro-Diotrephes circles:

> *I saw ... young preachers try to emulate and worship some big-named preacher and it turned my stomach. Men became larger than life. They became drunk with power. They became god-like to their people ... [t]hey could do no wrong. ... It was the followers of these men who ultimately created the monsters they became. Preachers would say things like, "Let your people know that you have feet of clay, but never let*

> *them see your feet." You see, that would destroy the "mystique" they've created around themselves. The holy aura they've cultivated of being "God's man" would be jeopardized. ... Cult leaders are created by their cult-bait followers. ... They sit in the pew ... and say nothing. In doing so, they become part of the problem. Their cult leader becomes more and more supreme in the church, until the whole place is built on him and his personality. Their sin and hypocrisy goes unchecked. (Michael Stacey Shiflett, Wolves Among Lambs: My Story of Sexual Abuse & Cover-Ups in the Church [Dundalk, MD: SureWord, 2019], 220)*

Michal, Saul's daughter, wanted David to maintain a "mystique" of aloofness from God's people and despised David's genuine, humble, and spiritual joy in Jehovah (2 Samuel 6:16, 20; cf. 6:12-23). She found his true love for and self-effacing worship of the Lord, which led him to dance for joy with all his might at the prospect of the ark of his God coming into Jerusalem, something to despise and slander. She also considered his joining even the lowest of the people of Israel as common worshippers of their common Lord a compromise of his preeminence and a surrender of "mystique." But David, as a righteous ruler, refused to acquiesce to Michal's advice by becoming like an aloof heathen king. Rather, David insisted upon the rightness of his genuine spirituality before the Lord and reaffirmed that he would continue to lead in humility, rejecting aloofness:

> *And David said unto Michal, It was before the LORD, which chose me before thy father, and before all his house, to appoint me ruler over the people of the LORD, over Israel: therefore will I play before the LORD. And I will yet be more vile than thus, and will be base in mine own sight: and of the maidservants which thou hast spoken of, of them shall I be had in honour. (2 Samuel 6:21-22)*

God punished aloof Michal, bringing her line to an end (6:23), but graciously granted humble David the blessings of an everlasting covenant and seed that would culminate in the Messiah (2 Samuel 7), who became the ultimate example of self-abasing service (Philippians 2:5-11).

[88] Note ungodly Saul's projection of his own character on David as he plotted to murder that righteous man: "Saul ... thought ... he *is* not clean; surely he *is* not clean" (1 Samuel 20:26). Saul evidenced his own uncleanness in his ungodly speech (20:30) and murderous actions (20:32) shortly afterwards, while the text then falsifies Saul's assumption that David was unclean (21:5). Saul continued to project false and fantastical ungodly motives and actions to David (22:8, 13), using his imaginary imputations to justify very real and harsh responses (22:16-19).

[89] 1 Timothy 6:4, τυφόω; cf. endnote #109.

[90] BDAG, ὑπόνοια, cf. "suspicion, conjecture, guess" (LSJ); "to have an opinion based on scant evidence, often with the implication of regarding a false opinion as true — 'to imagine, to conjecture, to suspect, to falsely suspect, to be suspicious, suspicion'" (LN), used especially for "'conjecture,' 'unfounded opinion,' 'imagination,' 'illusion,' ... 'suspicion' ... In the list of vices in 1 Tm. 6:4f., which depicts the terrible effects of the pathological penchant of false teachers ... ὑπόνοιαι πονηραί, alongside βλασφημίαι, are wicked intrigues and common insinuations which ... they raise against their opponents in an attempt to discredit them in every possible way and to magnify themselves" (Gerhard Kittel, Geoffrey W. Bromiley & Gerhard Friedrich, eds., *Theological Dictionary of the New Testament* [TDNT]. Grand Rapids, MI: Eerdmans, 1964). Pastor Diotrephes fits the words of Sirach 3:24: "For many are deceived by their own vain opinion; and an evil suspicion hath overthrown their judgment" (πολλοὺς γὰρ ἐπλάνησεν ἡ ὑπόλημψις αὐτῶν, καὶ ὑπόνοια πονηρὰ ὠλίσθησεν διανοίας αὐτῶν). All uses of the related verb ὑπόνοεω in the LXX refer to a false supposition (Judith 14:14; Tobit 8:16; Sirach 23:21), a use which also appears in Acts 25:18. Acts 13:25 & 27:27 are somewhat different.

[91] Thus, in Hebrews 13:17, "obey" is from πείθω—emphasizing an obedience based on persuasion—not ὑπακούω, used for the obedience slaves offer masters, whether they understand the reason for the command or not (Colossians 3:22). While James 3:3 supports a

wideness in the semantic domain of πείθω, it does not undermine the fact that in Hebrews 13:17 the obedience required involves persuasion.

92 וַיֹּאמֶר חָטָאתִי עַתָּה כַּבְּדֵנִי נָא נֶגֶד זִקְנֵי־עַמִּי וְנֶגֶד יִשְׂרָאֵל. Compare the only other use of "honor" (כָּבֵד) with a suffix in the books of Samuel: "Wherefore the LORD God of Israel saith, I said indeed *that* thy house, and the house of thy father, should walk before me for ever: but now the LORD saith, Be it far from me; for them that honour me I will honour [כִּי־מְכַבְּדַי אֲכַבֵּד], and they that despise me shall be lightly esteemed" (1 Samuel 2:30). Jehovah says, "Honor me," while Diotrephes says, "Honor me!"

93 Bruce notes: "Twenty centuries of church history have witnessed many of [Diotrephes'] successors. The lust for power, from whatever form of inner insecurity it may spring, is always a curse, and preeminently so in the realm of religion" (F. F. Bruce, *The Epistles of John: Introduction, Exposition and Notes* [Nashville, TN: Kingsley Books, 2018], 153).

94 For an example of Diotrophes-style, slavish, blind obedience, consider rules mandated at Hyles-Anderson College:

> *1. ALWAYS THINK THE LEADER IS RIGHT. Never give your opinion when the leader feels strongly. ...*
>
> *4. DON'T CORRECT THE LEADER ANYTIME! The people are better off hearing a wrong answer than to see the leader put down by a follower. I look at it as a putdown when a leader is corrected. ...*
>
> *8. ALWAYS DO ANYTHING THE LEADER ASKS WHETHER IT IS RIGHT OR NOT. Why? a. I trust him to not ask me to do something immoral or sinful! b. If I do something I think will hurt someone, it is him who is responsible to God for it.*

These rules were "were required of Hyles-Anderson College students under Hyles' regime" and "handed out every year in work scholarship meetings," "repeated and emphasized each school year at Hyles

Anderson." (See David Cloud, "Another Warning About Unquestioning Loyalty to Church Leaders," elec. acc. https://www.wayoflife.org/database/another_warning_about_unquestioning_loyalty.html & David Cloud, "Unquestioning Loyalty to Pastoral Leadership the Mark of a Cult," elec. acc. https://www.wayoflife.org/database/unquestioningloyalty.html & "Ignoring the Sin of First Baptist of Hammond," elec. acc. https://www.wayoflife.org/reports/ignoring_sin_first_baptist_hammond.html). Similarly, Cloud notes:

> *During a Sunday sermon, Hyles held up a cup bearing the image of the skull and bones, which is a warning that the contents are poisonous. He said to Johnny Colsten, one of the men sitting behind him on the platform, 'I'd like for you, if you don't mind, to drink this,' and Colsten did not hesitate to drink. (David Cloud, The Hyles Effect: A Spreading Blight [Port Huron, MI: Way of Life Literature, 2012], 35)*

The Hyles-Anderson philosophy of never criticizing a leader—not the practice one finds in Scripture (Galatians 2:11-14)—explains why even when Jack Hyles taught something egregiously unbiblical, a plain statement that he was wrong and a public repudiation of his error does not follow. The very best that can take place is for the heresy to be downplayed or ignored while books teaching it are quietly allowed to pass out of circulation.

[95] Compare Saul's declaration, to people who were willing to assist his attempted murder of innocent David: "Blessed *be* ye of the LORD; for ye have compassion on me" (1 Samuel 23:21). Saul equated slavish loyalty to himself, which led the Ziphites to assist the evil king in his mad fight against David and against Jehovah's kingdom under David, with blessing from the self-made god his self-promoting imagination assumed would bless such submission, and which he misidentified as Jehovah. Saul gladly pronounced his blessing, couched in religious language, on those who helped him rebelliously retain preeminence.

[96] The sons of Diotrephes are "teaching things which they ought not, for filthy lucre's sake" (διδάσκοντες ἃ μὴ δεῖ, αἰσχροῦ κέρδους χάριν, Titus 1:11), disobeying: "not greedy of filthy lucre" (μὴ αἰσχροκερδῆ, 1

Timothy 3:3, μὴ αἰσχροκερδεῖς, 1 Timothy 3:8), "not given to filthy lucre" (μὴ αἰσχροκερδῆ, Titus 1:7), "not for filthy lucre, but of a ready mind" (1 Peter 5:2, μηδὲ αἰσχροκερδῶς, ἀλλὰ προθύμως); cf. 1 Samuel 8:3. While a covetous love of financial gain is certainly condemned in these passages, Diotrephes may also covet other types of non-monetary "gain" that he receives from the pastoral office. The godly pastor is not in his position for "any emoluments and profits attending [his position] ... or any perquisite belonging to the office" (Matthew Henry, *Matthew Henry's Commentary on the Whole Bible: Complete and Unabridged in One Volume* [Peabody: Hendrickson, 1994], 2432, note on 1 Peter 5:2)—a broader prohibition than mere money-grubbing. Many of Diotrephes' sons are in the pastorate for money, but many others covet at least as much the power, prestige, and opportunities provided to prey on others. They want the opportunity to fulfill their lusts which money can provide, but also want to fulfill their lusts if they hanker for honor, supremacy, or extra partners in bed, whom they view as their filthy (αἶσχος) gain.

In keeping with this fact, κέρδος, while frequently employed for money, more generally signifies "that which is gained or earned, a gain, profit ... something advantageous" (BDAG), "some advantage" (LSJ). "κέρδος in the sense of 'gain' is not restricted ... to monetary gain or profit. It may refer to any kind of benefit or advantage" (LN). This broader sense applies not only to the Greek κέρδος but also to the Latin *lucrum*, which is employed both for "material gains, profit" and for "non-material gains" (P. G. W. Glare, ed., *Oxford Latin Dictionary* [Oxford: Oxford University Press, 2012], entry *lucrum*), and the English *lucre*, which can refer broadly to "gain or profit derived from (something) ... acquisition of (something profitable)" (*Oxford English Dictionary*, "lucre (*n.*)," July 2023, https://doi.org/10.1093/OED/7158878269).

Diotrephes may well teach what he ought not, for filthy lucre's sake, when he exploits his pastoral office to build his bank account. But he is also teaching what he ought not, for filthy lucre's sake, when he preaches a hyper-pastoral authority doctrine not found in Scripture to build up his prestige, or to protect himself from criticism. He teaches what he ought not, for filthy lucre's sake, when he preaches that Matthew 18:15-17 is optional and he can cast people out on his own authority. He teaches what he ought not, for filthy lucre's sake, when he abuses his power to satisfy his lusts on adults, teenagers, or children, and then manipulates the Bible to manufacture reasons why they need to keep quiet, or why if they are not quiet, nobody should listen to them, but reject what they say out of hand and keep blindly following him, the Lord's Anointed.

97 2 Corinthians 13:14; John 3:16; 11:35-36; Romans 15:30.

98 σκληρός.

99 σκληρός, BDAG.

100 The "elder" son (Luke 15:25), like the "elders" who were Christ's Pharisaic opponents (Luke 9:22; 20:1; 22:52, 66), could say to God Ἰδού, τοσαῦτα ἔτη δουλεύω σοι, "Lo, these many years do I slavishly serve thee" (Luke 15:29) but he had no experiential knowledge of the love of the father, picture of God the Father.

101 Chantry, commenting on John 9, notes:

> *As the tension between the healed man and the synagogue leaders rose, the latter grew indignant that a mere member would question them [John 9:34]. "How dare you lecture us!" At the beginning the Pharisees were searching for grounds to accuse Jesus and the beneficiary of his work. In the end the issue was this man's daring to stand in opposition to them. A subtle shift had taken place. No longer was discipline used to oppose heresy and scandalous immorality. Discipline was now employed as a defense of the officers and their reputation. Now no sin was considered more grievous than that of criticizing the synagogue's leaders, no matter how valid that criticism might be. They had become paranoid, believing that nothing threatened the church more than a challenge to their authority, no matter how much that authority was being misused. (Walter J. Chantry, "Caution in Church Discipline," in Biblical Shepherding of God's Sheep: The Use and Abuse of*

Authority by Church Officers, ed. Steven Martin [Leominster: Day One, 2010], 152–153)

102 κυριεύω.

103 καταδουλόω.

104 φλυαρέω, a NT *hapax legomenon.*

105 BDAG & LSJ, φλυαρέω. Compare "talking a deal of nonsense, but uttering no word of truth," ἡ πολλὰ μὲν φλυαροῦσα, μηδὲν δὲ ἀληθὲς λέγουσα, Ireneus *Against Heresies* 1:14:7; cf. 1:15:5; "Besides, he is found in every way to talk nonsense, and to contradict himself," Ἔτι μὴν κατὰ πάντα τρόπον φλυαρῶν εὑρίσκεται, καὶ ἐναντία ἑαυτῷ λέγων, *Theophilus of Antioch, to Autolycus* 2:6; cf. 2:10, 30; "Pythagoras, too, is found venting similar nonsense, Τούτῳ ἀκόλουθα καὶ Πυθαγόρας εὑρίσκεται φλυαρῶν, 3:7; "Chrysippus, who talked a deal of nonsense," Χρύσιππος δὲ ὁ πολλὰ φλυαρήσας, 3:8; "Manetho, who among the Egyptians gave out a great deal of nonsense, and even impiously charged Moses and the Hebrews, Μαναιθὼς δὲ ὁ κατ' Αἰγυπτίους πολλὰ φλυαρήσας, ἔτι μὴν καὶ βλάσφημα εἰπὼν ὥστε Μωϋσέα καὶ τοὺς σὺν αὐτῷ Ἑβραίους, 3:21; "Thus they idly babble; but in this their perverseness I see nothing but unreasoning audacity and recklessness from the devil," Ταῦτα μὲν ἐκεῖνοι ληροῦντες φλυαροῦσιν· ἐγὼ δὲ οὐδὲν ἕτερον ἐν τῇ τοιαύτῃ αὐτῶν κακονοίᾳ βλέπω ἢ ἀλόγιστον τόλμαν καὶ διαβολικὴν ἀπόνοιαν, Athanasius, Arians 3:17; "But Arius ... talked very wildly," ὁ δὲ Ἄρειος ... πολλά τε φλυαρῶν, Athanasius, 2 Serapion 3; "I have babbled whatever came into my head," τί ποτ' ἐφλυάρησα τὰ ἐπελθόντα μοι, Epictetus, 2 Disc 21:11; "And if the husband foolishly prates," ἂν δὲ φλυαρῇ ὁ ἀνήρ, Epictetus, 3 Disc 7:16; cf. 3 Disc 13:23; 24:39; "he is talking folly, and speaking to no purpose," ὅτι ταῦτα φλυαρεῖ καὶ μάτην λέγει, Origen, *Against Celsus* 13:1.

106 LN, φλυαρέω.

107 BrDAG, φλυαρέω.

---

108 Contrast Solomon's humble prayer for wisdom, recognizing his insufficiency in himself for righteous judgment:

> *And now, O LORD my God, thou hast made thy servant king instead of David my father: and I am but a little child: I know not how to go out or come in. And thy servant is in the midst of thy people which thou hast chosen, a great people, that cannot be numbered nor counted for multitude. Give therefore thy servant an understanding heart to judge thy people, that I may discern between good and bad: for who is able to judge this thy so great a people? And the speech pleased the Lord, that Solomon had asked this thing. (1 Kings 3:7-10)*

109 Thus, the novice inappropriately placed in the pastorate is in grave danger of "being lifted up with pride" and "fall[ing] into the condemnation of the devil" (1 Timothy 3:6, μὴ νεόφυτον, ἵνα μὴ τυφωθεὶς εἰς κρίμα ἐμπέσῃ τοῦ διαβόλου). The verb τυφόω bears the primary sense of "becloud, delude" and is related to τύφω, "to give off smoke." From "becloud, delude," τυφόω developed the figurative senses of "be puffed up, conceited ... be blinded, become foolish ... be mentally ill." Pastor Diotrephes' judgment is inaccurate because he is "delude[d]" like one "filled with insane arrogance" (BDAG & LSJ, τυφόω, τῦφος & τύφω; cf. BrDAG). Compare 2 Kings 14:10 with 1 Timothy 3:6: "Thou hast indeed smitten Edom, and thine heart hath lifted thee up [וּנְשָׂאֲךָ לִבֶּךָ]: glory of this, and tarry at home: for why shouldest thou meddle to thy hurt, that thou shouldest fall [וְנָפַלְתָּה], even thou, and Judah with thee?" (2 Kings 14:10; cf. 2 Chronicles 25:19). Amaziah was indeed lifted up with pride, and as a result exercised poor judgment that not only had negative personal consequences but was deadly to vast multitudes in his kingdom. So a pastor who is lifted up with pride and falls into the devil's condemnation hurts not only himself, but many others also.

110 τυφόω.

111 "νοσέω ... *to be sick*; metaphorically, of any ailment of the mind" (Thayer), "to be sick, in body or soul" (TDNT).

[112] διαστρέφω; see Matthew 17:17; Luke 9:41; 23:2; Acts 13:8, 10; 20:30; Philippians 2:15.

[113] διαστρέφω; Numbers 32:7; Ezekiel 13:22, LXX.

[114] ματαιολόγος.

[115] ματαιολογία.

[116] ἡ δὲ ἔνθεος διδασκαλία καὶ ἡ κατὰ Χριστὸν πίστις τὴν μὲν τούτων ματαιολογίαν ὡς ἀθεότητα διαβάλλει (Athanasius, *On The Incarnation of the Word* 3:1; Athanasius of Alexandria, "On the Incarnation of the Word," in *St. Athanasius: Select Works and Letters*, ed. Philip Schaff and Henry Wace, trans. Archibald T. Robertson, vol. 4, A Select Library of the Nicene and Post-Nicene Fathers of the Christian Church, Second Series [New York: Christian Literature Company, 1892], 37 & Athanasius of Alexandria, "On the Incarnation: Greek Text," ed. John Behr, Popular Patristics Series [St. Vladimir's Seminary Press, 2011], 54–56).

[117] ἀστήρικτος.

[118] ταράσσω.

[119] BDAG, ταράσσω.

[120] στηρίζω; see Luke 22:32; Acts 14:22; Romans 1:11; 16:25; 1 Thessalonians 3:2, 13; 2 Thessalonians 2:17; James 5:8; 1 Peter 5:10; 2 Peter 1:12; Revelation 3:2 & ἐπιστηρίζω, Acts 15:32, 41; 18:23.

[121] στηριγμός.

[122] BDAG, στηριγμός.

[123] In Scripture, blindly following a human leader does not work out well. The elders in Samaria unconditionally followed Ahab and Jezebel, condemning and executing Naboth and his family after a sham trial

because they were told to do it (1 Kings 21:1-15). They acted as the ungodly king and queen wished, and it seemed to work out well for both the monarch's family and the elders for a while. However, once Jehu took power, the elders of Samaria unconditionally followed him, at Jehu's command slaying Ahab's seventy sons the way they had killed Naboth (2 Kings 10:1-9). However, shifting their blind loyalty was insufficient—Jehu killed all of Ahab's elders anyway (2 Kings 10:11).

124 Joseph Henry Thayer, *A Greek-English Lexicon of the New Testament: Being Grimm's Wilke's Clavis Novi Testamenti* [Thayer] (New York: Harper & Brothers, 1889), φλυαρέω.

125 Cleon L. Rogers Jr. and Cleon L. Rogers III, *The New Linguistic and Exegetical Key to the Greek New Testament*, Accordance electronic ed. (Grand Rapids: Zondervan, 1998), paragraph 41903, on 3 John 10.

126 φρεναπάτης, a "soul-deceiver" (LSJ), "mind-deceiver" (Thayer), a "deceiver of souls" (BrDAG). The word is a "derivative of φρεναπατάω 'to lead astray' ... one who misleads people concerning the truth — 'person who misleads, deceiver'" (LN). Φρεναπάτης is derived from φρήν, the "heart, mind, or soul ... intellect ... good sense, reason" (BrDAG) and ἀπάτη, "trick, fraud, betrayal, illusion ... deception" (BrDAG). The cognate verb φρεναπατάω (Galatians 6:3) means "mislead concerning the truth, deceive" (BDAG), "to cause someone to have misleading or erroneous views concerning the truth" (LN).

127 ἐργάτης δόλιος.

128 Shiflett, coming from a background that was too soft on Diotrephes and seeing the dangers in it, comments:

> *[Some professedly] Baptist pastors, evangelists and leaders operate in a manner much like the mafia. Their tactics are so underhanded that it can leave their church members broken and scarred for life. Their actions reflect a genuine belief that they are God's "Untouchables." Their favorite passage of Scripture is Psalm 105:15, "Saying, Touch not mine anointed, and do my prophets no harm." They teach it to the children, and they quote it from the pulpit. Often.*

Many of these guys pull out that verse like a dirty cop flashing his badge when he's breaking the law. That verse is their license to do what they want, say what they want, treat people any way they want, and there is nothing you can do or say about it. ... These ministry kingpins surround themselves with subordinates who jump when they say to jump.

They always have a few fixers in their circle who will do their dirty work for them. They manipulate and coordinate the utter destruction of other people while pretending to know nothing about it. They insulate themselves so they can maintain a certain plausible deniability. They work behind the scenes planning, scheming, undermining, and doing whatever is necessary to protect their turf and their kingdom.

The backroom discussions, while without the cigar smoke and machine guns, are no less corrupt and destructive. ... They organize their schedules so they can attend whatever will provide them the greatest amount of exposure. ... Every decision they make is made on the basis of how it will help them move further up the food chain. They will butter up one preacher friend and then take the same knife and slit the throat of another.

These IFB "Untouchables" will not tolerate anyone who challenges their decisions, their actions, and their unbiblical preaching. They will not tolerate anyone questioning their ministry philosophy and wisdom. They will fight, maim, and cripple in defense of their friends, if it is to their advantage. But they will remain silent and detached when a young preacher or pastor is getting his guts ripped out, especially if there is nothing in it for them.

I learned long ago that for these "Untouchables," the bottom line is money and power. If it doesn't get you one or both of those things, it's not important. ... [T]hese men make up a small minority of IFB preachers [but] ... they dominate [in certain circles.] ... It is high time that the men of God who are honest and genuine and aware of what is going on help to lead our people away from the cult leaders[.] ... The only way to stop these "Untouchables" is to stop supporting their meetings, buying their how-to books and ministry manuals. We need to stop justifying their crimes and misdemeanors against the church of the living God. We must stop bowing at their altars and tiptoeing around their blatant disregard for Christ's example. Their power was given to them by their blind and silent followers.

The smaller churches and hundreds of unknown pastors need to turn to the Lord and His word for guidance; not the big, "successful" ministries. The politics have to end. The unquestioned loyalty for men who will stand in their pulpits and mislead their people must end. Accountability, transparency, and integrity must be restored in those places where it is lacking. ... The people of God deserve men of principle as their leaders. ... The church[es] of the living God must repent and turn back to biblical principles if we want to see revival. We must get away from man-worship, and get back to pleasing the Lord in all we do. ...

With God's help, we must keep our eyes on the infallibile Jesus and not on fallible men. They will let you down, but He never will. (Michael Stacey Shiflett, Wolves Among Lambs: My Story of Sexual Abuse & Cover-Ups in the Church [Dundalk, MD: SureWord, 2019], 228-232)

[129] To please Ahab, Jezebel secretly commanded the nobles in Naboth's city to hire two false witnesses to condemn righteous Naboth; the nobles were supposed to hire the false witnesses, and then make sure that whatever these two testified was assumed to be true. The nobles were simply to follow Jezebel without any understanding, justification, or challenge allowed, and then the two false witnesses were similarly to be simply believed without any challenge allowed or fair trial for Naboth. After Naboth's murder, Jezebel could easily pretend ignorance of the whole situation, and Ahab could do it so much the more, as he could claim ignorance of Jezebel's actions, those of the nobles, and those of the false witnesses. On account of the cut-outs, there would be no need for Ahab or Jezebel to answer uncomfortable questions about the "trial" and condemnation of Naboth. But did God hold them accountable, despite their cutouts? Elijah said to Ahab: "Thus saith the LORD, Hast thou

killed, and also taken possession? ... Thus saith the LORD, In the place where dogs licked the blood of Naboth shall dogs lick thy blood, even thine" (1 Kings 21:19).

130 Matthew 26:4; Mark 14:1 δόλος; cf. also Acts 13:10; Romans 3:13 and, by contrast, John 1:47; 1 Thessalonians 2:3; 1 Peter 2:1-2, 22; 3:10; Revelation 14:5.

131 BDAG, δόλος.

132 Diotrephes "serve[s] not our Lord Jesus Christ, but [his] own belly" (Romans 16:18; cf. Philippians 3:19, "whose god is their belly"). Christ is not uppermost, but Diotrephes' own self-serving desires are so.

133 διὰ τῆς χρηστολογίας καὶ εὐλογίας ἐξαπατῶσι τὰς καρδίας τῶν ἀκάκων. Note the Granville-Sharp construction in τῆς χρηστολογίας καὶ εὐλογίας; both nouns describe the same sort of speech.

134 BDAG, χρηστολογία.

135 BDAG, εὐλογία. Compare the εὐλογία of the Assyrians as they sought mastery over Judah in order to lead God's people into captivity (2 Kings 18:31, LXX).

136 "You see, my friend, the method which these men employ to deceive themselves, while they abuse the Scriptures by endeavouring to support their own system out of them." Ὁρᾷς, ἀγαπητέ, τὴν μέθοδον, ᾗ οἱ χρώμενοι φρεναπατοῦσιν ἑαυτούς, ἐπηρεάζοντες τὰς Γραφάς, τὸ πλάσμα αὐτῶν ἐξ αὐτῶν συνιστάνειν πειρώμενοι (Irenaeus, *Against Heresies* 9:1; in Irenaeus of Lyons, *The Writings of Irenæus*, ed. Alexander Roberts and James Donaldson, trans. Alexander Roberts and W. H. Rambaut, vol. 1, Ante-Nicene Christian Library [Edinburgh: T. & T. Clark, 1868–1869], 38 & J. P. Migne, *Patrologia Graeca* vol. 6 [J. P. Migne: 1857]).

137 πιθανολογία, BDAG.

[138] Absalom "stole the hearts of the men of Israel" by flattery and truth-twisting when men came to King David for judgment: "See, thy matters *are* good and right; but *there is* no man *deputed* of the king to hear thee. ... Oh that I were made judge in the land, that every man which hath any suit or cause might come unto me, and I would do him justice!" (2 Samuel 15:1-6). In a certain sense, Absalom was stating a fact when he said that David had not deputed anyone to hear cases—king David often heard such cases personally, rather than deputing them to others. Absalom's subtle deception and flattery sounded very convincing if one only heard his side of the matter. Such speech still steals many a heart today. Compare also Ziba's false accusation of Mephibosheth, too readily believed by David (2 Samuel 16; 19:24-30).

[139] While the "proud" man who supposes that "gain is godliness" (πορισμὸν εἶναι τὴν εὐσέβειαν) can certainly be in pursuit of money (Titus 1:11, cf. Titus 1:7; 1 Timothy 3:3, 8), the semantic domain of "gain" (πορισμός, 1 Timothy 6:5) includes more than the strictly monetary. Godliness with contentment is true "gain" (1 Timothy 6:6), true "advantage" and a true "benefit" (LN, πορισμός). Outside the New Testament, πορισμός is used for "for gaining [πορισμός] and getting, and for good success of his hands ... desire of gain [ὄρεξις πορισμῶν]" (Wisdom 13:19, 14:2, LXX); for providing support for a family (Epictetus, 3 Disc 22:70), for the business interests of farmers (Aristeas 111), and to "gain" a pardon for a crime (Josephus, *War* 2:603 / 2.21.3). The semantic domain of πορισμός includes not just an increase of money, but also "providing oneself an advantage ... means to gain" (BrDAG). The related verb πορίζω means "to cause a thing to get on well, to carry forward, to convey, to acquire ... to bring about or procure for oneself, to gain" (Thayer).

[140] ἀπεστερημένων τῆς ἀληθείας.

[141] ἀποστερέω, BDAG.

[142] ἀποστερέω, BrDAG.

143 ἀποστερέω, LN. Note that the form in 1 Timothy 6:5 is passive. However, the passage suggests that the false teacher would also be willing to engage in such actions himself.

144 For example, Robert Sumner records:

> *[N]ote the exalted opinion Hyles has of himself and of his ministry. ... A typical claim about his importance can be seen in his sermon, "Led by the Holy Spirit to be Tempted of the Devil." ... [He] asked the people why God made him [Hyles] endure such torture. The answer[:]*
>
> *God knew back yonder years ago that Dr. Jack Hyles was going to pastor this church and God knew that probably 10,000 preachers across this nation would call me their pastor, and God knew that somebody needed to grab the old steering wheel of Fundamentalism—at least to help to do it—to try to steer it ... God knew that somebody in this age would have to grab the steering wheel and hold it firm while others are turning, and others are changing, and others are pussy-footing, and God said, "I've got to make him strong enough to take care of it someday. I'll put him through the fire and make him strong," but the victory was never in doubt.*
>
> *Actually, this estimate of his worth is one of his milder descriptions. Sometimes he carries on a shouting match with his congregation, a la Jesse Jackson visiting an inner-city grammar school. He shouts, "Which is the greatest soul-winning church?" and the crowd screams, "First Baptist Church." He comes back, "Who is the best-known preacher that stands for soul winning?" and a loud chorus responds, "Brother Hyles!" ... Then he shouts, "What preacher stands for standards?" and the people scream back, "Brother Hyles." He ended this particular exchange, "WE ARE THE GREATEST!" (Robert L. Sumner, "The Saddest Story We Ever Published!" The Biblical Evangelist 23:5 (May 1, 1989)*

145 Sumner notes:

> *[I]n [his] "Merit vs. Demerit" sermon ... Hyles ... called what he was teaching "stumbling insurance" and said flatly, "God's degree of patience when you stumble will be totally dependent on how fast you were running." In fact, his first point was, "God's degree of patience with you when you stumble is determined by how fast you were running." His second point was, "Your chance on a second chance will depend on what you did with your first chance." His conclusion was, "You'd better be worth enough to God, [have] enough merits built up, so when you stumble the demerits will not overbalance the merits." (Robert L. Sumner, "The Hyles Reply!" The Biblical Evangelist 23:8, August 1, 1989 & Robert L. Sumner, "One of the Blights of Bigness!" The Biblical Evangelist 22:10, October 1, 1988)*

[146] Compare, e. g., Roy L. Branson:

> *This is the most important chapter in this book because it contains the most important statement[,] [which is:] ...* ***IT IS MORE IMPORTANT FOR THE PREACHER TO SURVIVE THAN THE CHURCH!*** *... [T]he reader [may] thro[w] up his hands in horror at such an unorthodox statement ... contrary to all we hear and have been taught. ... If the choice must be made between the survival of a local church and the survival of a divinely called man of God, it is imperative that the man of God be salvaged. ...* ***That is the Bible model. ... God's work depends upon God's man*** *... [I]f a church must close its doors, the people can find another. They have lost little. ... A good preacher will do God's work with or without a certain group of local Christians. ...* ***God saw the congregation as expendable; the man was not.*** *... The proverb goes, "If you can't do something with the church, clean it out so the next man can." ... The pastor should do whatever is necessary to salvage his ministry[.] (Roy L. Branson, Jr. Church Split, 2nd ed. [Bristol, TN: Landmark Publications, 1992], Chapter 20. Bold print, and capitalization have been retained from the source.)*

Passages such as "the good shepherd giveth his life for the sheep" (John 10:11) are not cited anywhere in Branson's corrupt book.

[147] Matthew Henry, *Matthew Henry's Commentary on the Whole Bible: Complete and Unabridged in One Volume* (Peabody: Hendrickson, 1994),

681, comment on Job 12:12-25.

148 διαμαρτύρομαι ἐνώπιον τοῦ Θεοῦ καὶ Κυρίου Ἰησοῦ Χριστοῦ καὶ τῶν ἐκλεκτῶν ἀγγέλων, ἵνα ταῦτα φυλάξῃς χωρὶς προκρίματος, μηδὲν ποιῶν κατὰ πρόσκλισιν. Note the single article on τοῦ Θεοῦ καὶ Κυρίου Ἰησοῦ Χριστοῦ, distinguished by a separate article from τῶν ἐκλεκτῶν ἀγγέλων. Paul's solemn charge for impartiality is made in the presence of the God and Lord Jesus Christ (cf. 3:16, Θεὸς ἐφανερώθη ἐν σαρκί, "God was manifest in the flesh"), the great Head of the church, and also before all the elect angels.

149 Roy L. Branson, Jr. *Church Split*, 2nd ed. (Bristol, TN: Landmark Publications, 1992), chapters 5, 6, 9. Branson viewed absolute subordination as so important that he supplied capital letters, bold print, and an exclamation point for it. The associate pastor must "**ALWAYS exal[t] the pastor, deferring to him in all things!**" (chapter 6). Branson supplies no sound exegesis of Scripture for his affirmation.

150 BDAG, πρόκριμα.

151 LSJ, προκρίνω.

152 LN, πρόκριμα.

153 Thayer, πρόκριμα.

154 TDNT, πρόκριμα.

155 BDAG, πρόσκλισις.

156 LN, πρόσκλισις.

157 Thayer, πρόσκλισις.

158 PGL, πρόσκλισις.

159 Compare the tragic alteration seen in:

> *Unto the angel of the church of* ***Ephesus*** *write,* Τῷ ἀγγέλῳ τῆς **Ἐφεσίνης** ἐκκλησίας γράψον *(Revelation 2:1)*
> *And unto the angel of the church in* ***Smyrna*** *write,* Καὶ τῷ ἀγγέλῳ τῆς ἐκκλησίας **Σμυρναίων** γράψον *(Revelation 2:8)*
> *And to the angel of the church in* ***Pergamos*** *write,* Καὶ τῷ ἀγγέλῳ τῆς ἐν **Περγάμῳ** ἐκκλησίας γράψον *(Revelation 2:12)*
> *And unto the angel of the church in* ***Thyatira*** *write,* Καὶ τῷ ἀγγέλῳ τῆς ἐν **Θυατείροις** ἐκκλησίας γράψον *(Revelation 2:18)*
> *And unto the angel of the church in* ***Sardis*** *write,* Καὶ τῷ ἀγγέλῳ τῆς ἐν **Σάρδεσιν** ἐκκλησίας γράψον *(Revelation 3:1)*
> *And to the angel of the church in* ***Philadelphia*** *write,* Καὶ τῷ ἀγγέλῳ τῆς ἐν **Φιλαδελφείᾳ** ἐκκλησίας γράψον *(Revelation 3:7)*
> *And unto the angel of the church of the* ***Laodiceans*** *write,* Καὶ τῷ ἀγγέλῳ τῆς ἐκκλησίας **Λαοδικέων** γράψον *(Revelation 3:14)*

Notice that, uniquely to the seven churches, the seventh church is called the church "of the Laodiceans," rather than being a church in a location such as Ephesus or Smyrna or Philadelphia. The last congregation is not addressed as Christ's church in the city of Laodicea (Λαοδίκεια) but as the Laodiceans' (Λαοδικεύς) church; Christ is outside this last congregation, knocking to get back in (Revelation 3:20). While those words are not necessarily conclusive of themselves (cf. Colossians 4:16), the alteration of language for this church alone of the seven, along with the content of Christ's message to the Laodiceans' church, confirms its significance. A church where Christ is not preeminent, but Pastor Diotrephes has replaced the Lord, is in grave danger of transitioning from being Christ's church in a particular city to being Pastor Diotrephes' church in that place.

160 ὑπομιμνῄσκω.

161 ὑπομιμνῄσκω.

162 BDAG, ὑπομιμνῄσκω.

[163] 3 John 14, εὐθέως, BDAG; KJV "shortly." John's intention was to come quickly (3 John 14), at which point he would not only build up the brethren (3 John 14) but also expose Diotrephes (3 John 10).

[164] E. g., Roy L. Branson, Jr., *Dear Preacher, Please Quit!* (Bristol, TN: Landmark Publications, 1996), 31-38, where Branson recounts how he supported covering up the sin of an unrepentant pastoral adulterer. Some churches impacted by Diotrephes, but not so blind that they cannot see that Branson's advice will turn the pastorate into a den of iniquity, agree that pastoral adultery should be exposed, but are willing to overlook and cover up other equally disqualifying sins.

Of course, David's refusal to harm "the Lord's Anointed" referred to not assassinating King Saul. It could reasonably be extended to not assassinating others who were literally anointed, like the high priest. It has exactly nothing to do with covering up filthy adultery or other disqualifying sins in pastors.

[165] Branson claims that 1 Timothy 5:20's requirement of public rebuke before all refers only to "the other preachers on a local church staff ... a conclusion [that] can be reached only by mental gymnastics" (Robert L Sumner, *Fights I Didn't Start: And Some I Did* [Raleigh, NC: Biblical Evangelism, 2009], 64-65), and one that is very convenient for a Pastor Diotrephes who wishes to keep his sins covered.

[166] A. T. Robertson, *Types of Preachers in the New Testament* (New York: George H. Doran Company, 1922), 228.

[167] Gregory A. Willis, *Freedom, Authority, and Church Discipline in the Baptist South, 1785-1900* (Oxford: Oxford University Press, 1997), 42-43.

[168] δόλος, BDAG.

[169] It is also very possible that Demetrius himself was carrying 3 John to Gaius. That possibility does not exclude the likelihood that Demetrius was someone who had suffered the wrath of Diotrephes, either by, as the member of a different church, not being received by

Diotrephes, or as a member of the church of Diotrephes, not being received and then being cast out.

170 Earl F. Palmer and Lloyd J. Ogilvie, *1, 2 & 3 John / Revelation*, vol. 35, The Preacher's Commentary Series (Nashville, TN: Thomas Nelson Inc, 1982), 86. Igor Lorencin, who wrote his doctoral dissertation on 3 John ("Hospitality versus Patronage: An Investigation of Social Dynamics in the Third Epistle of John" [Ph.D., Andrews University, 2007]), argues:

> *To aid Gaius in his hospitable works, the Elder strongly recommended a partner, Demetrius, who might have been one of those who had already been thrown out of the church by Diotrephes[.] ... The Elder invited Gaius to join forces with the isolated Demetrius and continue with his good works. ... If Demetrius was an expelled member of the church of 3 John, then his recommendation points to the fact that even though hospitality was directed primarily toward itinerants coming from outside, it also needed to be practiced toward members inside the local church. (Igor Lorencin, "Hospitality Versus Patronage: An Investigation of Social Dynamics in the Third Epistle of John," Andrews University Seminary Studies 46:2, 173-74)*

171 Henry A. Ironside, *Addresses on the Epistles of John* (Neptune, NJ: Loizeaux Brothers, 1931), 233–235.

172 Note the emphasis from the expressed pronoun: ἡμεῖς ... μαρτυροῦμε.

173 Δημητρίῳ μεμαρτύρηται ὑπὸ πάντων, καὶ ὑπ' αὐτῆς τῆς ἀληθείας.

174 Note the perfect tense of the verb μεμαρτύρηται.

175 John 3:21; 16:13; 17:17; 1 John 5:6.

176 *Apostolic Constitutions* 7.46, in Alexander Roberts, James Donaldson, and A. Cleveland Coxe, eds., "Constitutions of the Holy Apostles," in *Fathers of the Third and Fourth Centuries: Lactantius, Venantius, Asterius, Victorinus, Dionysius, Apostolic Teaching and*

Constitutions, Homily, and Liturgies, trans. James Donaldson, vol. 7, The Ante-Nicene Fathers (Buffalo, NY: Christian Literature Company, 1886), 478.

[177] Henry A. Sawtelle, *Commentary on the Epistles of John*, ed. Alvah Hovey, An American Commentary on the New Testament (Philadelphia: American Baptist Publication Society, 1888), 84.

[178] The patristic writer Ambrosiaster affirms that the Gaius who received 3 John is the same one mentioned in Romans 16:23, likely a significant leader in the Roman church (Ambrosiaster, *Commentaries on Romans and 1-2 Corinthians*, ed. Thomas C. Oden and Gerald L. Bray, trans. Gerald L. Bray, Ancient Christian Texts [Downers Grove, IL: IVP Academic: An Imprint of InterVarsity Press, 2009], 117, on Romans 16:23).

[179] The Received Text's 2nd person plural οἴδατε, "ye know," is correct, while the 2nd person singular οἶδας in the Nestle-Aland *Textus Rejectus* follows a small minority of MSS.

[180] Gilbert Tennent, *The Danger of an Unconverted Ministry, Considered in a Sermon on Mark VI.34. Preached at Nottingham, in Pennsylvania, March 8. Anno 1739-40*, Early American Imprints, 1639-1800; No. 4610 (Philadelphia: Benjamin Franklin, in Market-Street, 1740), 3.

[181] See, e. g., Thomas Ross, "Will I Be Saved if I Ask Jesus to Come into my Heart or Repeat the Sinners Prayer?" elec. acc. https://faithsaves.net/sinners-prayer/ & "The "Sinner's Prayer"–is it Taught in Romans 10:9-10 or Romans 10:13?" elec. acc. https://faithsaves.net/romans-10-sinners-prayer/.

[182] See, e. g., R. L. Hymers & Christopher Cagan, *Today's Apostasy: How Decisionism is Destroying our Churches*, 2nd ed. (Oklahoma City, OK: Hearthstone, 2001), elec. acc. https://faithsaves.net/soteriology/.

[183] See, e. g., Thomas Ross, "Assurance of Salvation in 1 John: The Tests of Life," elec. acc. https://faithsaves.net/assurance-john/.

[184] Curtis Hutson, anti-repentance editor of the *Sword of the Lord* and defender of Jack Hyles, testified that he would re-repeat the sinner's prayer every time he doubted his salvation:

> *I trusted Jesus when I was eleven years old; but I lacked assurance of salvation, not knowing upon what to base my assurance. One day I would think I was saved, and the next, I would wonder if maybe I was wrong about it and perhaps was lost; until finally I came out of the darkness of doubt into the broad daylight of certainty. ... When I doubted I was trusting Him, I didn't argue about it; I just prayed again and told the Lord if I had never trusted Him, I was then trusting Him. When the Devil would say, "How do you know you are trusting Him?" I would pray out loud, "Dear Lord, if I have never trusted You, I am trusting You now." Immediately all doubt would leave. (Curtis Hutson, "As Many As Received Him," elec. acc. https://cavaliersonly.com/christian_articles_and_messages/as_many_as_received_him_by_curtis_hutson)*

Scripture never states that one is initially born again on account of saying the sinner's prayer, nor does Scripture teach that someone receives assurance of salvation because he says the sinner's prayer over and over again. It does not appear that Hutson was rebaptized every time he resaid the sinner's prayer to reconfirm his far from well-grounded assurance. Nor does he say how long the doubt would be gone after he bid it leave through his sinner's prayer sacrament, as the fact that he had to keep repeating the religious ritual showed that the doubts kept coming back.

[185] E. g., see how confusing justification by repentant faith alone with asking Jesus into one's heart deceived a Baptist preacher and many in his congregation in Ovid Need, Jr., "The Other Jesus: The Gospel Perverted By Asking Jesus into Your Heart," elec. acc. https://faithsaves.net/asking-jesus-into-your-heart/.

[186] E. g., see David Cloud, *The Hyles Effect: A Spreading Blight* (Port Huron, MI: Way of Life Literature, 2012), 38-78 & David Cloud, "The Jack

Hyles Philosophy," elec. acc. https://www.wayoflife.org/reports/jack_hyles_philosophy.html.

[187] E. g., if—God forbid—a spiritual leader in your congregation engages in an abominable act with a minor, pro-Diotrephes pastors would advise you to cover up the sin so that your church does not get a bad reputation in the eyes of the community. Righteous men would advise you, instead, to do the hard and right thing—place the offender under church discipline, rebuke him publicly, and turn him over to the civil power (Romans 13:4). You will have a worse reputation in your community in the short term, but you will be upright in the eyes of Jehovah—which is what is by far the most important. Furthermore, if you fail to do right, when your cover-up eventually fails (Proverbs 28:13), you will have a much worse reputation in the community than if you had come clean right away. You will also probably have more victims and shattered lives. You will also certainly have God's terrifying judgment (Matthew 18:6).

[188] BDAG, δοκιμάζω.

[189] Matthew 16:22-23; Acts 15:39; Galatians 2:11-13; Revelation 22:8-9.

[190] Matthew 26:6-13; John 12:4-6. Judas initiated the condemnation of the godly woman in this pericope, but his criticism was then taken up by the other apostles.

[191] The recommendations of classic Baptist church manuals concerning procedures for excommunication, while not infallible, are in very large measure a careful, Spirit-led application of Biblical principles. For example, while the Bible contains no explicit statement that an accused person must receive his charge in writing, Scripture indicates that a notice for divorce must be made in writing (Deuteronomy 24:1-4), modeling a principle of placing weighty and serious changes, such as separating a person from Christ's bride the church, in writing. Similarly, Scripture contains no explicit statement that in church-trials an accused person must be able to cross-examine his accuser, but it does set a pattern of an accused person being to

answer his accusers face to face (Deuteronomy 19:17-18; Acts 23:35; 25:5, 16) and of unjust conclusions when such a procedure is not followed, but accusers are too hastily believed (2 Samuel 16:3-4; 19:25-27).

[192] Proverbs 19:1-2.

[193] Charles Bridges, *An Exposition of the Book of Proverbs* (New York: Robert Carter & Brothers, 1865), 257–259, comment on Proverbs 19:2. Bridges cites Proverbs 4:26; Joshua 9:14-15; 1 Samuel 13:12-14; 2 Samuel 16:1-4; 2 Chronicles 18:1-4; 19:2; Proverbs 28:20, 22; Exodus 14:13; Isaiah 30:7 & Isaiah 28:16 in this quotation.

[194] John Owen, *An Exposition of the Epistle to the Hebrews*, ed. W. H. Goold, vol. 24, Works of John Owen (Edinburgh: Johnstone and Hunter, 1854), 464–465.

[195] James M. Renihan, "The Limits of Pastoral Authority," in *Biblical Shepherding of God's Sheep: The Use and Abuse of Authority by Church Officers*, ed. Steven Martin, Ministry Mission (Leominster: Day One, 2010), 225.

[196] James M. Renihan, "The Limits of Pastoral Authority," in *Biblical Shepherding of God's Sheep: The Use and Abuse of Authority by Church Officers*, ed. Steven Martin, Ministry Mission (Leominster: Day One, 2010), 225.

[197] 1689 London Baptist Confession of Faith, Article 16, "Of Good Works," cited from W. J. McGlothlin, *Baptist Confessions of Faith* (Philadelphia: American Baptist Publication Society, 1911), 249–250; the Confession cites Micah 6:8; Hebrews 13:21; Matthew 15:9 & Isaiah 29:13 as proof texts.

[198] For example, Jack Hyles wrote that only the "head pastor is to judge in the church," with sole jurisdiction—it is his "area" alone. Everyone else is not only to follow outwardly without question, but not even think with discernment. Rather, everyone must blindly follow without even thinking: "Not only are you not to take any action about

things outside your own area, but you are not to make mental judgments outside your own area" (Jack Hyles, *Jack Hyles on Justice*, Chapter 2, "Areas of Judging"). Comparably, Roy Branson claims:

> *Divinely called men are called prophets, priests, preachers, pastors, bishops, elders, ministers, [etc.] ... [T]he man who is truly called of God is equipped with Divine insight to deal with any situation that arises in the affairs of an individual, a church, a community or a nation. ... [G]ood, Godly people will often give good, Godly and sound advice ... However, such people are far more likely to give faulty advice than the preacher. ... Therefore, the pastor with his special knowledge, peculiar leadership of the Spirit ... in every instance, is most qualified to give help in all of these areas. ...*
>
> *[T]he pastor is the best one to help people in their problems. He is the expert. He, alone! ... **The preacher also has a Divine insight into the needs of the church.** ... We will find no place in Scripture where the people of God were taught other than that which the pastors (priests, elders, bishops, preachers, etc.) determined. ... [N]ot even the church voting in body, should be allowed to determine the teaching program administered to the church. ... [T]he responsibility for the spiritual program of the church, in its entirety ... [rests] solely on the shoulders of the pastor. ... [T]he preacher, and the preacher alone, will give an account to God for what goes on in his church. ... [I]t was His Sovereign will that preachers actually hold the reins of political power ... everything that happened to Israel is an example for us today. ... [This is still] God's Sovereign will for a nation. ... **God gives the Divinely called preacher the insight to see into the needs of the nation.** (Roy L. Branson, Jr., Dear Preacher, Please Quit! [Bristol, TN: Landmark Publications, 1996], 65-74)*

Branson manipulates 2 Timothy 3:16 to claim that because Scripture can make the "man of God ... throughly furnished unto all good works," the head pastor—who, apparently, is the only one who can be thoroughly furnished unto all good works from Scripture, despite 2 Timothy 3:15 indicating differently—has supernatural Divine insight into every area of life above every other man, not only for his own congregation, but even for the entire country in which he resides. Furthermore, the entire church body is allegedly not accountable for what happens in their congregation—the pastor alone will give account to God for it. The fact that God warned that He would severely judge people other than the pastor for sin in their church in Revelation 2-3, or that God killed people other than the pastor when the Lord's Supper was being corrupted in 1 Corinthians 11, is ignored.

199 The pastor must be "blameless" (ἀνεπίληπτος) in that he "afford[s] nothing which an adversary could take hold of, on which he might ground a charge" (Richard Chenevix Trench, *Synonyms of the New Testament* [London: Macmillan and Co., 1880], 381–382, § ciii. ἄμωμος, ἄμεμπτος, ἀνέγκλητος, ἀνεπίληπτος). He is "not exposed to attack" (BrDAG, ἀνεπίληπτος), "unassailable" (LSJ). The adjective is derived from επιλαμβάνω with a negative prefix; the overseer has nothing one can "pounce on [that is] compromising, catch" at in him (BDAG, ἐπιλαμβάνομαι). Someone who is in this sense blameless should not fear false accusations. Someone who is not in this sense blameless is not qualified, in God's eyes, to pastor—whether any mere man makes an accusation against him or not.

200 There is no just κατηγορία against the ἀκατάγνωστος (1 Timothy 5:19; Titus 2:8).

201 ναθεωρέω, BDAG.

202 μιμέομαι, BDAG.

203 1 Corinthians 4:16; 11:1; Philippians 3:17; 1 Thessalonians 1:6; 2 Thessalonians 3:9; 1 Timothy 4:12; Titus 2:7 & 1 Peter 5:3, employing μιμητής, συμμιμητής & τύπος.

204 Scripture, however, nowhere teaches a hard distinction between an (alleged) "ruling elder" and an (alleged) "teaching elder," as found in Presbyterianism.

205 See, e. g., David Cloud, *The Hyles Effect: A Spreading Blight* (Port Huron, MI: Way of Life Literature, 2012), 35-59. Leaders greatly

impacted by Hyles include Jack Trieber, leader of Golden State Baptist College; Curtis Hutson, president of The Sword of the Lord; and Bob Gray Sr., of Texas Baptist College, all of whom received honorary doctorates from Hyles-Anderson.

206 "There are those who say we have to repent of our sins in order to be saved. No, we have to repent only of the thing that makes us unsaved, and that is unbelief" (Jack Hyles, *Enemies of Soulwinning*, chapter 4, "Misunderstood Repentance"). Contrast the Biblical exposition at Thomas Ross, "Repentance Defended Against Antinomian Heresy—A Brief Defense of the Indubitable Biblical Fact that Repentance is a Change of Mind that Always Results in a Change of Action," elec. acc. https://faithsaves.net/repentance/. For a presentation where the Biblical position and the position of Jack Hyles and the "New IFB" movement of Hyles' disciple Steven Anderson receive equal time, see the Thomas Ross / Tommy McMurtry discussion of the questions:

> *1.) Does the Old Testament teach that the lost must turn from their sins (repent) to be saved?*
> *2.) Does the New Testament teach that the lost must turn from their sins (repent) to be saved?*
> *3.) Does one become a disciple at the moment of the new birth, or at some point afterwards?*
> *4.) How does regeneration change someone?*
> *5.) Can people be born again without calling on the Lord / saying the "sinner's prayer"?*
> *6.) Did Christ suffer in hell after His death on the cross?*
> *7.) How do our beliefs on the issues above impact how we seek to fulfill the Great Commission?*

This colloquy is available at https://faithsaves.net/mcmurtry-ross-repent/.

207 For example, on one day—May 3, 1998—Jack Hyles claimed that 15,000 were "saved" through the outreach of his congregation. However, "very, very few of [those] ... that were counted as saved that day had any abiding interest in Jesus Christ," and none of them were added to the church's membership (David Cloud, "Pentecost vs.

Hylescost," elec. acc. https://www.wayoflife.org/database/hylescost.html.

[208] See, e. g., David Cloud, *The Hyles Effect: A Spreading Blight* (Port Huron, MI: Way of Life Literature, 2012), 81-89.

[209] For example, Hyles taught that Christ was eternally human, rather than becoming human at the incarnation: "Jesus was always the God-human in His personality. ... Jesus ... [did] not ... just become the God-man in Bethlehem ... but He has always been what He is today. ... His humanity was always, just as His deity was always!" (Jack Hyles, *Exploring Prayer With Jack Hyles* Chapter 6, elec. acc. https://www.jackhyles.com/exploringprayer.htm). However, Scripture testifies that "Jesus Christ is come in the flesh" (Ἰησοῦν Χριστὸν ἐν σαρκὶ ἐληλυθότα) while he who "confesseth not that Jesus Christ is come in the flesh is not of God: and this is that *spirit* of antichrist" (μὴ ὁμολογεῖ τὸν Ἰησοῦν Χριστὸν ἐν σαρκὶ ἐληλυθότα ἐκ τοῦ Θεοῦ οὐκ ἔστι· καὶ τοῦτό ἐστι τὸ τοῦ ἀντιχρίστου). The perfect tense ἐληλυθότα indicates Christ became flesh at a point in time, with results that continue; Christ has come in the flesh, and so He now is come in true human flesh. The claim that the Lord Jesus was always human rejects the teaching of 1 John 4:2-3 and is explicitly a doctrine of Antichrist (as Diotrephes himself is an example of an antichrist in the Johannine epistles).

Hyles also taught that people cannot be saved unless they encounter the King James Version:

> *The words of God are the genes of regeneration. ... Now if the very words of God must be pure, and if in fact the King James Bible contains the preserved words of God, then any other words are not the words of God. This means that the Revised Version is not precious seed because it is not incorruptible. This means that the Good News for Modern Man is not precious seed, because it is not incorruptible. This means that the Living Bible is not precious seed because it is not incorruptible. This means that the Reader's Digest Bible is not precious seed, because it is not incorruptible. This means that the New King James Bible is not precious seed because it is not incorruptible.*

> *This means that the New Scofield Bible is not precious seed, because it is not incorruptible. This means that the New International Version (NIV) is not precious seed, and it is not incorruptible. This means that the American Standard Version is not precious seed because it is not incorruptible. ... The genes of the new birth must be incorruptible ... we must have the incorruptible seed in order to be ... regenerated, or born again. ... Suppose corruptible seed is used. Can a person then be born again from it? [I]f corruptible seed is used, one cannot be born again. I have a conviction as deep as my soul that every English-speaking person who has ever been born again was born of incorruptible seed; that is, the King James Bible. Does that mean that if someone goes soul winning and takes a false Bible that the person who receives Christ is not saved? I believe with all of my soul that the incorruptible seed must have been used somewhere in that person's life. If all a person has ever read is the Revised Standard Version, he cannot be born again, because corruptible seed is used, and 1 Peter 1:23 is very plain to tell us that a person cannot be born again of corruptible seed, but of incorruptible seed, and it explains that that incorruptible seed is the Word of God, and it explains that it liveth and abideth forever. (Jack Hyles, Enemies of Soulwinning, chapter 5, "False Bibles: Enemies of Soulwinning.")*

Hyles corrupted the gospel when he taught that someone will necessarily be eternally damned if he reads verses such as "For God so loved the world that He gave His only begotten Son, that whoever believes in Him should not perish but have everlasting life" (John 3:16, NKJV); a sinner can allegedly only be saved if he reads instead: "For God so loved the world, that he gave his only begotten Son, that whosoever believeth in him should not perish, but have everlasting life" (John 3:16, KJV). Of course, 1 Peter 1:23 does not say a word about needing to read the English KJV in order to be born again. It is one thing to argue that modern English substitutes to the KJV are inferior because they are almost all translated from an inferior original language text, and their translation is not as accurate, and quite another thing—a heresy—to say that people can only be saved if they are exposed to the English KJV and will be eternally damned and cannot trust in Christ if they read passages like John 3:16 from versions like the NKJV that are (in those passages) equally faithful translations of the infallible original language text.

[210] Roy L. Branson, Jr., *Church Split,* 2nd ed. (Bristol, TN: Landmark Publications, 1992); *Dear Abner: I Love You, Joab*, 2nd ed. (Bristol, TN: Landmark Publications, 1996); *Dear Preacher, Please Quit!* (Bristol, TN: Landmark Publications, 1996).

[211] Robert Sumner correctly concludes:

> *How can I sum up this book? Weird? Unscriptural? Bizzare? Uninformed? All these ... and more! I think its circulation—with the unbiblical philosophies [Branson] espouses—will do untold damage to the cause of Christ. ... [F]ollowing the thinking outlined in Dear Abner will corrupt the church, filling it with low and loose standards that can only ruin, not build up. ... Dear Abner, I Love You, Joab ... contains some of the strangest—and [most] unbiblical—teachings we've ever read ... anywhere! (Robert L Sumner, Fights I Didn't Start: And Some I Did [Raleigh, NC: Biblical Evangelism, 2009], 47, 118-119)*

[212] Robert L Sumner, *Fights I Didn't Start: And Some I Did* (Raleigh, NC: Biblical Evangelism, 2009), 119.

[213] *Dear Preacher, Please Quit!* (Bristol, TN: Landmark Publications, 1996), iv. It must be noted that this author was unable to verify that Branson's claims about endorsements from the men cited above. Branson cited no sources, and a direct inquiry to him about his sources in this matter failed to produce verification. Since an examination of Branson's writings evidences a level of composition that cannot be called scholarship, his claims about these endorsements must remain uncertain. One is hesitant to ascribe to godly men the endorsement of such corruption as fills Branson's books without clear and compelling evidence.

[214] *The Sword of the Lord* 55:11 (May 26, 1989), 12A.

[215] See, e. g., Ruckman's statement that he had read both Branson's *Dear Preacher, Please Quit!* and *Church Split* in Peter S. Ruckman,

"'Humanism' and 'Love' Are Major Problems Among Baptists," *Bible Believers Bulletin* (August 1993). While Ruckman testified that he had read Branson's books, their influence in Ruckmanite circles is uncertain.

[216] Robert L Sumner, *Fights I Didn't Start: And Some I Did* (Raleigh, NC: Biblical Evangelism, 2009), 46, 119. One initially wonders how books filled with such revolting and obviously unbiblical garbage as are Branson's can be widely endorsed by pastors—but then remembers how easy it is for fallen human flesh to like ear-tickling counsel that one is (pretty much) always right. Pastors are not immune from proudly finding such flattery appealing. The wide impact of Branson's books illustrate how much proud blindness dominates the unregenerate human heart and remains even in the regenerate man, and should lead every Christian to redouble his own pursuit of humility and watchfulness against vainglory.

[217] Roy L. Branson Jr., *Dear Preacher, Please Quit!* (Bristol, TN: Landmark Publications, 1996), 194-195. That Branson believes one can explain the gospel in twenty seconds does not, of course, mean that he usually spent only twenty seconds when he spoke to lost sinners one-on-one.

[218] Roy L. Branson Jr., *Dear Preacher, Please Quit!* (Bristol, TN: Landmark Publications, 1996), iii.

[219] Roy L. Branson, Jr., *Dear Abner: I Love You, Joab*, 2nd ed. (Bristol, TN: Landmark Publications, 1996), 338-341.

[220] Roy L. Branson, Jr., *Dear Abner: I Love You, Joab*, 2nd ed. (Bristol, TN: Landmark Publications, 1996), 333.

[221] Roy L. Branson, Jr., *Church Split.,* 2nd ed. (Bristol, TN: Landmark Publications, 1992), 103, 118, 148, 188-190.

[222] See, e. g., Ernest C. Reisinger, "The Carnal Christian," elec. acc. https://www.reformedreader.org/rbb/reisinger/tcc.htm.

[223] 1/4 x 1/10 = 2.5/100. Of course, this is not a firm and certain number, but a generalization derived from an author who regularly makes extravagant statements. It would be reasonable to conclude, however, that Hyles or Branson-type churches have a fearfully large percentage of unregenerate members.

[224] Thomas Ascol, "Southern Baptists at the Crossroads: Returning to the Old Paths," *The Founders Journal: Southern Baptists at the Crossroads: Returning to the Old Paths, Winter/Spring*, no. 19/20 (1995): 6.

[225] H. Leon McBeth, *The Baptist Heritage* (Nashville, TN: Broadman & Holman Publishers, 1987), 699.

[226] "Preachers ought to read ... *Dear Preacher, Please Quit* [by] Roy Branson ... [his] book is well worth reading" (R. L. Hymers & Christopher Cagan, *Preaching to A Dying Nation* [Los Angeles: Fundamental Baptist Tabernacle, 1999], 56; cf. R. L. Hymers & Christopher Cagan, *Today's Apostasy: How Decisionism is Destroying Our Churches*, 2nd. ed. [Oklahoma City: Hearthstone, 2001], 45, 59).

[227] R. L. Hymers, Jr. "Lessons From Dr. Roy Branson," (8/2/2020, Baptist Tabernacle of Los Angeles) & "More Lessons From Dr. Roy Branson," (8/9/2020, Baptist Tabernacle of Los Angeles), https://www.rlhymersjr.com/Online_Sermons/2020/080220PM_LessonsFromDrRoyBranson.html & https://www.rlhymersjr.com/Online_Sermons/2020/080920PM_MoreLessonsFromDrRoyBranson.html. See also R. L. Hymers, "Has America Been Given Up By God?" (2/21/2021, Baptist Tabernacle of Los Angeles, elec. acc. https://www.rlhymersjr.com/Online_Sermons/2021/022121PM_HasAmericaBeenGivenUpByGod.html) where Branson is again profusely and supportively quoted, while, amazingly, Dr. Hymers also warns: "One of the worst things in America is the sin of the leading evangelical preachers – men like Jimmy Swaggart, Jerry Falwell, Jr., Jack Hyles and Ravi Zacharias." Hymers recognizes the sin of Jack Hyles but somehow maintains a profound disconnect between the sin of Hyles and the pro-Diotrephes philosophy of pastoring espoused by Branson and Hyles.

Unsurprisingly, Hymers' congregation, where he was promoting the philosophy of Branson, experienced "every few years ... another church split" ("Lessons From Dr. Roy Branson," *ibid*). Of course, they did not ascribe the fault to Branson's pro-Diotrephes philosophy. See also Hymers' extensive citation of Branson and commendation of Branson's book *Church Split* at http://www.drrlhymersjranswershiscritics.com/.

[228] See, e.g., Michael Stacey Shiflett, *Wolves Among Lambs: My Story of Sexual Abuse & Cover-Ups in the Church* (Dundalk, MD: SureWord, 2019), 52-63, where a sodomite Pastor Diotrephes was able to "groom" a trusting young assistant pastor, preparing him to commit abominable homosexual acts with lesser steps that were obviously wrong, but were designed to break down the young man's conscience. The assistant let it all go, because of a soft-on-Diotrephes pastoral philosophy:

> *I was always afraid to cross the line of rebuking or correcting my pastor. ... [S]omehow I always felt like it was my fault. I was too sheltered. I was reading too much into it. I was guilty of thinking he was doing something wrong, when there was no way he could be doing something wrong. He was the pastor. He was God's man. ... I chided myself for being so critical of him.*

Therefore the grooming went on, desensitizing the young man until the sodomite pastor was ready to cross the final line. This youth was not the first—this pervert Pastor Diotrephes "had used his position of power to manipulate, intimidate, abuse ... violate ... groo[m], seduc[e], and moles[t]" for years (*ibid.,* 107). However, he was never placed under church discipline (Matthew 18:15-17), rebuked before all (1 Timothy 5:19-21), or turned over for prosecution (Romans 13:4). Instead, because of a pro-Diotrephes pastoral philosophy, he was allowed to move from church to church, to become the principal of a Christian school, and to continue to abuse and molest while pastoring, until he died and faced the God who destroyed Sodom with fire and brimstone. Meanwhile, a whistleblower preacher who did not want a sodomite pastoring and sodomizing learned that "by standing up to a sexual predator and an admitted homosexual deviant, I essentially burned my bridges ... I had essentially committed ministerial suicide" (*ibid.,* 111-112, cf. 105-114).

Any Baptist pastor or church member who runs in such pro-Diotrephes circles should burn bridges with it immediately and fellowship instead with truly Bible-believing and practicing congregations that reject Diotrephes.

[229] See, e. g., David Cloud, *The Hyles Effect: A Spreading Blight* (Port Huron, MI: Way of Life Literature, 2012), 60-78, where many sources and extensive documentation is provided.

[230] Roy L. Branson, Jr., *Dear Abner: I Love You, Joab*, 2nd ed. (Bristol, TN: Landmark Publications, 1996), 39. Branson provides his defense of Hyles on pgs. 13-79. Compare the devastating critique of Branson's argument in Robert L. Sumner, *Fights I Didn't Start: And Some I Did* (Raleigh, NC: Biblical Evangelism, 2009), 46-99.

[231] Branson seems to have trouble spelling "anointed" correctly.

[232] Roy L. Branson, Jr., *Dear Preacher, Please Quit!* (Bristol, TN: Landmark Publications, 1996), 31-37. Branson continued to boldly defend covering up adultery in his later books, specifically stating and rejecting that "what [he] advise[s] ... has resulted in wholesale adulterous affairs by preachers in our day." On the contrary (according to Branson), those who want adulterers out of the ministry are not concerned about the purity of Christ's church, but "are far more likely to have hidden immorality in their own lives," which (although hidden) Branson apparently can diagnose and draw conclusions about (Roy L. Branson, Jr., *Dear Abner: I Love You, Joab*, 2nd ed. [Bristol, TN: Landmark Publications, 1996], 123-124, 131-132).

[233] Roy L. Branson, Jr., *Dear Abner: I Love You, Joab*, 2nd ed. (Bristol, TN: Landmark Publications, 1996), 113-139, chapter 5, "The 'Fallen' Man." Branson's justifications for filthy preachers are almost surreal, but they are the logical conclusions of his pro-Diotrephes, antichrist view of pastoral authority.

Branson is himself a divorced and remarried preacher (Robert L. Sumner, *Fights I Didn't Start: And Some I Did* [Raleigh, NC: Biblical Evangelism, 2009], 119) and offers radical defenses of keeping divorced and remarried men in the ministry, as well as making simply bizarre affirmations such as: "God does not recognize marriage between unbelievers" (Roy L. Branson, Jr., *Church Split.,* 2nd ed. [Bristol, TN: Landmark Publications, 1992], 183).

234 Roy L. Branson, Jr., *Dear Abner: I Love You, Joab*, 2nd ed. (Bristol, TN: Landmark Publications, 1996), 202. Of course, Branson places the lion's share of the blame on those corrupted by the pastor, not on the Untouchable Man, abusing his position of power, for the commission of sexual sin. The problem is not pro-Diotrephes idolatry—no—nor that many such idolatrously preeminent pastors set out to seduce women (that is never stated). Rather, "Many women set out to seduce preachers. ... Modern women are bold, immodest, [and] seductive" (*ibid*, 202-203).

Shiflett also describes the problem of pastoral immorality in very stark terms (e. g., Michael Stacey Shiflett, *Wolves Among Lambs: My Story of Sexual Abuse & Cover-Ups in the Church* [Dundalk, MD: SureWord, 2019], 248, 253, 257, 271). While Branson and Shiflett may be correct for the extent of the problem in pro-Diotrephes circles where man is preeminent over Christ, because of his background within more Diotrephes-sympathetic circles Shiflett overgeneralizes the problem. David Cloud's conclusion is more accurate:

> *The Hyles circle ... has been as shockingly rife with immorality as the Roman Catholic priesthood. ... Hyles encouraged preachers to continue in the pastorate after they committed adultery, pedophilia, and even homosexuality. He helped men move from one part of the country to the other to escape their sordid reputations and continue in the ministry. ... I thank the Lord that this is not true of many of the IFB "circles," such as Bob Jones University and Tennessee Temple and Maranatha Baptist Bible College in Wisconsin and many others. Regardless of any failings they had, Dr. Jones and Dr. Roberson and Dr. Cederholm, to mention a few, were honorable men who set a godly example which has tended to good moral fruit in the*

> *lives and ministries of their graduates. There are BJU and Temple and Maranatha grads who have had moral blowouts, but those are the rare exception, and adultery and such is not a plague in these circles. (David Cloud, The Hyles Effect: A Spreading Blight [Port Huron, MI: Way of Life Literature, 2012], 76. Note that institutions such as Bob Jones University and Maranatha Baptist Bible College separated from Jack Hyles and are not under Hyles' pernicious influence.)*

Most—the large majority—of independent Baptist churches are not led by pervert Pastors Diotrephes. The Lord Jesus had one Judas among the twelve apostles, not eight or nine or ten or eleven Judases. However, the modern Judases like to congregate together and come up with justifications for their actions; in networks of churches that are soft on Diotrephes, a fearfully higher percentage of his perverted sons may be found. Practicing personal and ecclesiastical separation from Diotrephes, marking and avoiding him (Romans 16:17) and those sympathetic to him, is necessary to both please the Lord and to protect one's own little boy and girl.

[235] E. g., Robert L. Sumner, *Fights I Didn't Start: And Some I Did* (Raleigh, NC: Biblical Evangelism, 2009), 59.

[236] David Cloud, *The Hyles Effect: A Spreading Blight* (Port Huron, MI: Way of Life Literature, 2012), 47, 61, 66.

[237] Roy L. Branson, Jr., *Dear Abner: I Love You, Joab*, 2nd ed. (Bristol, TN: Landmark Publications, 1996), 34.

[238] Roy L. Branson, Jr., *Dear Abner: I Love You, Joab*, 2nd ed. (Bristol, TN: Landmark Publications, 1996), 34.

[239] Contrast Branson's revolting claim that the women with whom pervert Pastors Diotrephes commit adultery are "thirsting to be ruined" with the Biblically accurate assessment by Shiflett: "A powerful, persuasive man seduced, groomed, and broke down a woman until she was in so far she could not see a way out" (Michael Stacey Shiflett, *Wolves Among Lambs: My Story of Sexual Abuse & Cover-Ups in the Church* [Dundalk, MD: SureWord, 2019], 270-271). In such a situation, has the

woman or the teenager also committed a grievous transgression? Yes—but the pervert Pastor Diotrephes has by far the greater sin. However, Hyles-Branson pro-Diotrephes writers cannot acknowledge this obvious fact, because it would (allegedly) be to touch the Lord's Anointed.

240 Robert L. Sumner, *Fights I Didn't Start: And Some I Did* (Raleigh, NC: Biblical Evangelism, 2009), 119.

241 Robert L. Sumner, *Fights I Didn't Start: And Some I Did* (Raleigh, NC: Biblical Evangelism, 2009), 119-122.

242 Robert Sumner, "History of Jack Hyles Exposé," chapter 8, elec. acc. https://www.biblicalevangelist.org/jack_hyles_story.php.

243 See, e. g., the studies on ecclesiology at https://faithsaves.net/ecclesiology/.

244 For example, one can read W. J. McGlothlin's *Baptist Confessions of Faith* (Philadelphia: American Baptist Publication Society, 1911) cover to cover and not find one word in favor of Hyles' distinctive doctrinal aberrations.

245 Note that the verb translated in Revelation 2:20 with a form of "to seduce" is πλανάω, which frequently refers to misleading and deception (e. g., Revelation 12:9; 13:14; 18:23; 19:20; 20:3, 8, 10). Wicked people almost always employ deception when they seduce and entice others to commit fornication.

246 E. g., R. L. Hymers claims:

> *Dr. Branson's ... great book Church Split ... [is endorsed by the following men]: Dr. W. A. Criswell said, "If you miss any other book this year, do not miss Church Split. It is one that every pastor needs to read." Dr. Paige Patterson said, "Dr. Roy Branson's book Church Split speaks of an epidemic sweeping our land[.] ... Whether you agree with every sentence or not, you will benefit profoundly from this amazing book. ("Is God Judging America? A Review of 'The Hard Things of God' by Dr.*

Roy Branson, Jr. (Baptist Tabernacle of Los Angeles, 3/21/2021, elec. acc. https://www.rlhymersjr.com/Online_Sermons/2021/032121PM_IsGodJudgingAmerica.html)

This writer has been unable to discover primary sources for these Criswell and Patterson quotations. Branson's books themselves contain unsourced and unverifiable quotations of endorsement by a variety of Christian leaders, including Criswell.

[247] See, e. g., Robert Downen, Lise Olsen & John Tedesco, "20 years, 700 victims: Southern Baptist Sexual Abuse Spreads as Leaders Resist Reforms." *Houston Chronicle* 2/10/2019. Elec. acc. https://www.houstonchronicle.com/news/investigations/article/Southern-Baptist-sexual-abuse-spreads-as-leaders-13588038.php. One should note that the *Chronicle* article is in significant ways a hit piece, as at least some of the examples of what the paper alleges were Southern Baptist leaders resisting reform and covering for abusers were actually the SBC not doing what is actually impossible for the Convention. The Convention cannot impose mandatory ministerial requirements on local congregations without forsaking Biblical congregational polity. Baptist (and Biblical) church polity does not allow a national organization to force autonomous churches to make decisions about their leaders, even to stop something as grossly unbiblical as pervert Pastors Diotrephes, and immorality in hierarchical religious denominations in Christendom demonstrates that a national organization taking control away from local churches does not stop the infiltration of wolves and perverts. Nor is the SBC set up to replace local police forces, engage in criminal investigations, and maintain national criminal databases. When SBC leaders recognize these facts, they are hardly "resisting reform," as the *Houston Chronicle* slanderously affirms. Nevertheless, while the article is biased against the Baptists, it still documents far too many cases of people harmed by lustful sons of Diotrephes.

[248] See, e. g., Thomas Ross, "Southern Baptist Evangelism and Unregenerate Evangelicals," elec. acc.

https://kentbrandenburg.blogspot.com/2016/01/southern-baptist-evangelism-and.html.

249 Michael Stacey Shiflett, *Wolves Among Lambs: My Story of Sexual Abuse & Cover-Ups in the Church*. (Dundalk, MD: SureWord, 2019), 344.

250 הָיָה נַעַר וְרַךְ־לֵבָב וְלֹא הִתְחַזַּק לִפְנֵיהֶם׃.

251 While the focus of churches in the New Testament dispensation (as seen in Acts) is on making disciples and multiplying churches, not social reform, God's laws against abominations like sodomy, rape, incest, and adultery are good laws, and it would be right for modern governments to execute those found guilty of these sins, as they were put to death in the ancient Jewish republic established in the Torah. Individual believers must show love and turn the other cheek (Matthew 5:44), knowing that those guilty of these sins can be saved from hell (1 Corinthians 6:9-11), but the civil government's responsibility is to punish evildoers (Romans 13:4). The State would do well to enforce the punishments of the Second Table of the Ten Commandments while recognizing that the civil penalties for violations of the First Table pertained specifically to the Hebrew theocratic republic. While in this dispensation Scripture mandates complete religious liberty, it would be right for the civil government to enforce, after a fair trial, the death penalty mandated in Israel for filthy men who do things like rape children (cf. Deuteronomy 22:25-27).

252 From the Bible alone one can know that when the husband's seed is spilled on the ground, instead of received by the wife, pregnancy will not result (Genesis 38:8-10).

253 וְאִישׁ כִּי־יִשְׁכַּב אֶת־אִשָּׁה שִׁכְבַת־זֶרַע, "A man who will lie with a woman with emission of seed." The "lying with" someone language of Scripture that results in pregnancy is associated with intimate association with another naked individual (2 Samuel 11:2-4), kisses (Song 1:2), contact with the breasts and the opening of the feet (Song 1:13; 7:8; Ezekiel 16:25; 23:3).

[254] Genesis 9:21-23; Deuteronomy 27:20. These texts curse uncovering the nakedness of one's "father" (certainly a basis for having parents always appear only in modest clothing before their children), but Scripture also uses "father" in a looser sense of other types of authority figures (e. g., Judges 17:10; Isaiah 22:21; 2 Kings 2:12; 5:13).

[255] A very young child who cannot tell the difference between his right hand and his left (Jonah 4:11) commits no sin if an adult vilely abuses him or her, but a preteen and especially a teenager sins when he or she is seduced, without resistance, by a pervert who commits statutory rape. The adult commits by far the greater sin, but the teenager who does not Biblically resist such advances has also sinned, and it does not help the teen to present him or her as *only* a victim. Such a person is indeed a victim, but by failing to resist and immediately report the immorality or attempted immorality, the teenager has also sinned.

[256] The "stronger than she" and "forced her, and lay with her" of 2 Samuel 13:14 shows Tamar was fighting. Scripture's designation of rape with phrases like "to force" (Judges 20:5; 2 Samuel 13:14, 22; Proverbs 7:21) shows that God wants victims to fight back against attempted rapists.

A pervert Diotrephes could kill his victims not only by actual murder, nor only by traumatizing them to the point that they commit suicide, but also by transmitting to them incurable and deadly sexual diseases.

[257] Of course, teaching children God's Word on the topic of sinful sexual relations is for both the glory of God and for their good. A child should be taught that he should scream and run away if an authority figure attempts to abuse him to commit a great sin, but a child who is exposed to such a wicked person and is initially so shocked that he forgets to immediately scream or run should be comforted, not harshly chastised.

[258] Bruce K. Waltke, *The Book of Proverbs, Chapters 1–15*, The New

International Commentary on the Old Testament (Grand Rapids, MI: Eerdmans, 2004), 376.

259 In 1 Thessalonians 5:22 (ἀπὸ παντὸς εἴδους πονηροῦ ἀπέχεσθε) Paul does indeed command that believers abstain from all "appearance" of evil, not merely every "form" (NKJV) or kind of evil. First, the primary meaning of εἶδος is "the shape and structure of something as it appears to someone, form, outward appearance" (BDAG), "that which strikes the eye, which is exposed to view … the external appearance, form, figure, shape" (Thayer). Every other use of εἶδος in the New Testament supports "appearance," not "form" in the sense of "kind" (Luke 3:22; 9:29; John 5:37; 2 Corinthians 5:7). The overwhelming majority of examples of εἶδος in the LXX, both in the canonical and the apocryphal books, support "appearance" (Genesis 29:17; 39:6; 41:2-4, 18-19; Exodus 24:10, 17; 26:30; 28:33; Leviticus 13:43; Numbers 8:4; 9:15-16; 11:7; 12:8; Deuteronomy 21:11; Judges 8:18; 1 Samuel 16:18; 25:3; 2 Samuel 11:2; 13:1; Esther 2:2-3, 7; Proverbs 7:10; Song 5:15; Job 33:16; 41:10; Isaiah 52:14; 53:2-3; Jeremiah 11:16; Lamentations 4:8; Ezekiel 1:16, 26; 1 Esdras 4:18; Judith 8:7; 11:23 Wisdom 15:4-5; Sirach 43:1; Susanna 1:7) while only a small minority fit with "form" (Jeremiah 15:3; Sirach 23:16; 25:2). The Vulgate's translation *species* also supports "appearance" over "form." While εἶδος can mean "form" at times, "appearance" is the superior rendering in 1 Thessalonians 5:22.

260 The literal meaning of 1 Corinthians 7:1's καλὸν ἀνθρώπῳ γυναικὸς μὴ ἅπτεσθαι should be maintained; Paul does not employ a mere euphemism for sexual intercourse. The verse not only prohibits fornication, but "[t]he expression also may carry in it an intimation that Christians must avoid all occasions of this sin, and flee all fleshly lusts, and incentives to them; must neither look on nor touch a woman, so as to provoke lustful inclinations" (Matthew Henry, *Matthew Henry's Commentary on the Whole Bible: Complete and Unabridged in One Volume* [Peabody: Hendrickson, 1994], 2255, comment on 1 Corinthians 7:1). First, the Apostle would not merely say that it was "good" not to touch a woman were he referring to fornication, for in the previous chapter he had said fornicators will go to hell (1 Corinthians 6:9-11). It is not merely "good" not to fornicate, nor merely "expedient" not to fornicate.

It is necessary. Alternatively, Paul is not likely to contradict all of Scripture that marital intercourse is a positive blessing ordained by God even before the Fall (Genesis 1:28; Song of Solomon). These problems are resolved by viewing 1 Corinthians 7:1 as a statement that it is good for men to abstain not just from fornication, but from (at least) any kind of potentially arousing touch, and, better, from touching completely, outside of one's family circle (Mark 1:31 & 5:41 might provide specific warrant for a handshake exception, although a little girl, not a physically mature woman, is in view). However, 1 Corinthians 7:1's statement is "good" but not "absolutely necessary" or "sinful if ever violated" because it is not a sin for a man to touch a woman to prevent her (for example) from falling off from a cliff. Second, while this phrase can be used euphemistically (Genesis 20:6; Proverbs 6:29; cf. Josephus, *Antiquities* 1:163; Plato, *Laws* 8:840; Aristotle, *Politics* 7:14:12), in Ruth 2:9 it seems much more likely that Boaz commanded his menservants to actually not touch Ruth than that Boaz would need to command them not to rape her (Ruth 2:9). Rape was a serious crime in Israel, nor would Ruth have derived much comfort from a bare assurance that Boaz told his servants not to commit rape. At a minimum, "have I not charged the young men that they shall not touch thee?" (הֲלוֹא צִוִּיתִי אֶת־הַנְּעָרִים לְבִלְתִּי נָגְעֵךְ, ἰδοὺ ἐνετειλάμην τοῖς παιδαρίοις τοῦ μὴ ἅψασθαί σου) must mean "Have not I commanded the young men not to inappropriately touch thee?" not merely "Have not I commanded the young men not to rape you, but they can touch you inappropriately whenever they want, because 'touch' is just a euphemism." In Proverbs 6:29b it is also likely that "touch" is an intensification of Proverbs 6:29a rather than simply exact parallelism (cf. Proverbs 6:16), forbidding not only the act of adultery but all inappropriate simple and literal touching of another man's wife.

It is necessary not to commit fornication. It is good, outside of special circumstances, for a man to simply not touch a woman at all.

261 Can one truly pray "lead us not into temptation" (Matthew 6:13) while insisting that he constantly carry in his pocket a phone that contains the equivalent of millions of pornographic magazines, accessible in seconds and in complete privacy, by refusing to place filters on his electronic devices? Is such a refusal not madness?

[262] Michael Stacey Shiflett, *Wolves Among Lambs: My Story of Sexual Abuse & Cover-Ups in the Church* (Dundalk, MD: SureWord, 2019), 331-374.

[263] In Genesis 3, at some point before Adam physically partook of the forbidden fruit, that sin had already become inevitable because of both the first man's tragic failure to flee from Satan and his failure to protect Eve from falling for Satan's deception.

[264] Of course, knowing and loving Christ will lead one to install safeguards so that Christ is not displeased by one's falling into sin.

[265] Proverbs is not just a book of "street smarts." It is Divine Wisdom revealed by the Father through the Son by the Spirit (cf. Proverbs 30:4; 1:23) in infallible Scripture, a book revealed by the Triune Jehovah to bless His believing, covenant people, a book set within the context of the true worship of the true God, based upon the earlier revelation Jehovah made to Israel in the Torah and other already inspired books of the canon, and pointing forward to the greater blessings to come in the times of the Messiah. In Proverbs 30:1-6, Agur gives a "prophecy," a Messianic prediction (Numbers 24:3, 15; 2 Samuel 23:1). Agur speaks to "Ithiel," whose name means "with me is God" (BDB). The personal application of the Messiah's name "Immanuel," "God with us" (Isaiah 7:14; Matthew 1:23), is to call Him "Ithiel," "God with me." The Messiah is also "Ucal," the "Mighty One." Agur humbly confessed his sinfulness and need of wisdom (Proverbs 30:2-3) and that he could only become wise through knowledge of God's Personal Wisdom, the Messiah, the Son of God (Proverbs 30:4), and His written Wisdom, Scripture (Proverbs 30:5-6; cf. Proverbs 8:22-31). The New Testament confirms that Jesus Christ is God's Personal and eternal Wisdom (1 Corinthians 1:24; Luke 11:49; Colossians 2:1-3; John 1:1). Compare Jason S. DeRouchie, "Redemptive-Historical, Christocentric Approach," in *Five Views of Christ in the Old Testament: Genre, Authorial Intent, and the Nature of Scripture*, ed. Brian J. Tabb, Andrew M. King, and Stanley N. Gundry, Counterpoints: Bible and Theology (Grand Rapids, MI: Zondervan Academic, 2022), 199-204.

---

266 Because of the imputation of Adam's sin and the transmission of the sin nature, children are born "simple" (פֶּתִי); they are unconverted and need to be born again, but they are moldable. If they embrace God's Wisdom, Christ, they become "wise" (חָכָם) and receive eternal life. If they refuse Christ they are in fearful danger of moving from being moldable "simple" sinners into being hardened and unmoldable fools, sluggards, and scorners.

267 See W. Brian Shelton, *Quest for the Historical Apostles: Tracing Their Lives and Legacies* (Grand Rapids, MI: Baker Academic, 2018).

268 E. g., Matthew 14:28; 16:22; John 18:10.

269 Discussing the danger of creating false memories, Loftus recounts:

> *[A] ... counselor helped Beth Rutherford to remember during therapy that her father, a clergyman, had regularly raped her between the ages of seven and fourteen and that her mother sometimes helped him by holding her down. Under her therapist's guidance, Rutherford developed memories of her father twice impregnating her and forcing her to abort the fetus herself with a coat hanger. The father had to resign from his post as a clergyman when the allegations were made public. Later medical examination of the daughter revealed, however, that she was still a virgin at age twenty-two and had never been pregnant. The daughter sued the therapist and received a $1 million settlement[.] (Elizabeth F. Loftus, "Creating False Memories," in Scott O. Lilienfeld, John Ruscio, and Steven Jay Lynn, Navigating the Mindfield: A Guide to Separating Science from Pseudoscience in Mental Health. [Amherst, NY: Prometheus Books, 2008], 273-274)*

Scripture indicates that man's heart—what is inside of him, which includes his thinking faculty—is deceptive (Jeremiah 17:9; Isaiah 10:7). This fact receives strong scientific corroboration:

> *[O]ur memories, although reasonably accurate much of the time, are quite malleable in many cases ... we can be fooled*

> *into recalling things differently from how they actually occurred ... we may even recall nonexistent events. ... Well-intentioned therapists who believe that a client was sexually abused in childhood may repeatedly prompt [their] client to recall early memories of abuse by using ... suggestive techniques ... [causing] at least some of these clients ... to "remember" imaginary traumatic events ... and even accuse family members of having abused them. ... [M]any individuals can be led to construct complex, vivid and detailed false memories via a rather simple procedure. ... [Utilizing one technique,] [f]ully 78.2 percent of the sample reported at least one [impossible and false] memory. ... [In another study,] 55 percent of the [group] reported [a false] memory ... [and, in another study when children had false memories implanted,] [a]ll kindergarten participants believed that their memories corresponded to real events. ... Without corroboration, there is little that can be done to help even the most experienced evaluator to differentiate true memories from ones that were suggestively planted. (Scott O. Lilienfeld, John Ruscio, and Steven Jay Lynn, Navigating the Mindfield: A Guide to Separating Science from Pseudoscience in Mental Health. [Amherst, NY: Prometheus Books, 2008], 271, 280, 282, 288, 293)*

Before receiving an accusation against an elder—or against anyone else—it is absolutely essential to have the corroboration of multiple witnesses (1 Timothy 5:19).

[270] First Timothy 5:19 does not provide a higher standard for an accusation against a pastor than for any other person—no accusation against anyone is to be received unless there are multiple witnesses to it, and all accused persons are presumed innocent until proven guilty. However, Paul's reiteration of that standard for an elder emphasizes its importance. While Scripture never spells out the reasons for this emphasis with the elder, it is reasonable to speculate that Satan will especially seek to accuse pastors because of their crucial leadership role and because a false accusation against a member can damage a church, but a false accusation against a pastor has a greater danger of not just damaging, but of destroying a church. The necessity of multiple witnesses in the context of a presumption of innocence is

emphasized for pastors—impartial, unbiased, righteous judgment must be exercised for all, and thus certainly for them.

271 In 1 Timothy 5:21 διαμαρτύρομαι ἐνώπιον τοῦ Θεοῦ καὶ Κυρίου Ἰησοῦ Χριστοῦ καὶ τῶν ἐκλεκτῶν ἀγγέλων fits the Granville-Sharp rule—neither θεός nor κύριος is impersonal, plural, or a proper name, while τοῦ Θεοῦ καὶ Κυρίου Ἰησοῦ Χριστοῦ is united with a single article, in contrast with the separate article for τῶν ἐκλεκτῶν ἀγγέλων. One should not be surprised that Paul identifies Jesus Christ as God and Lord in 1 Timothy 5:21 when in 1 Timothy 3:16 the Apostle had identified the Lord Jesus as "God manifest in the flesh," Θεὸς ἐφανερώθη ἐν σαρκί.

272 See, e. g., David Cloud, *The Hyles Effect: A Spreading Blight* (Port Huron, MI: Way of Life Literature, 2012), 38-55; the standard Jack Hyles set forth made it impossible for a congregation to recognize and deal with pastoral sin.

273 Compare "And Jonathan smote the garrison of the Philistines that *was* in Geba ... And all Israel heard say *that* Saul had smitten a garrison of the Philistines" (1 Samuel 13:3-4). Saul had not actually done anything to advance God's kingdom and smite the Lord's enemies.

274 3 John 9-11; 1 John 4:1-6.

275 BDAG, δοκιμάζω; see 1 John 4:1.

276 1 Corinthians 14:29; οἱ ἄλλοι διακρινέτωσαν is an imperative, not a suggestion. The whole church must "evaluate by paying careful attention to" and "judge," having "the ability to distinguish and evaluate" with the Word of God (BDAG, διακρίνω & διάκρισις; cf. 1 Corithians 12:10 & Hebrews 5:14).

277 1 Corinthians 10:15; κρίνατε ὑμεῖς ὅ φημι contains an imperative, not a suggestion.

278 Contrast Jeremiah 17:9.

[279] For an extreme example, see Roy L. Branson, Jr., *Dear Preacher, Please Quit!* (Bristol, TN: Landmark Publications, 1996), chapter 7.

[280] In many situations it is wise to trust that a godly pastor has correctly judged a situation; but in church discipline, Scripture specifically commands careful verification of every word and thing (πᾶν ῥῆμα, Matthew 18:16).

[281] Compare the mandate at Hyles-Anderson College during (at least part of) the pastorate of Hyles: "DON'T CORRECT THE LEADER ANYTIME! The people are better off hearing a wrong answer than to see the leader put down by a follower. … [It is] a putdown when a leader is corrected" (David Cloud, *The Hyles Effect: A Spreading Blight* [Port Huron, MI: Way of Life, 2020], 36).

[282] The Apostle John wrote His apostolic message directly to the church (3 John 9), but Diotrephes forbade such righteous communication with the whole congregation.

[283] φλυαρέω, "to indulge in utterance that makes no sense, talk nonsense" (BDAG), 3 John 10.

[284] Note that what is forbidden in Jude 9 is bringing a κρίσις βλασφημίας, a judgment based on slander and defamation (cf. BDAG). Churches and individual Christians are positively commanded to "judge righteous judgment" (John 7:24, δικαίαν κρίσιν κρίνατε); but slander and defamation is always wrong. If it is wrong to slander and defame a wicked person, or even Satan, how much the more is it wrong to defame the righteous and innocent?

[285] Jack Hyles' absurd claim that "[t]he sin discussed in 1 Timothy 5:19 is not the sin of the accused but the sin of the one doing the accusing" (Jack Hyles, *Jack Hyles on Justice*, Chapter 11, "Justice and Witnesses") is an egregious example of support for Diotrephes, but others sons of Diotrephes may make similar and more plausible arguments that do not quite as egregiously torture Scripture.

Hyles also claims that to "receive" an accusation in 1 Timothy 5:19 does not mean to "believe" it and receive its truth (*ibid*). However, his claim is based on home-spun stories, while he does not engage the fact that the word translated "receive," παραδέχομαι, means "to acknowledge something to be correct, accept" (BDAG), "to come to believe something to be true and to respond accordingly" (LN).

[286] First Timothy 5:19 reads: κατὰ πρεσβυτέρου κατηγορίαν μὴ παραδέχου, ἐκτὸς εἰ μὴ ἐπὶ δύο ἢ τριῶν μαρτύρων. This verse does not by any means condemn going to an assistant pastor in one's church for help or confidentially asking a trusted and godly friend for advice in what looks like a difficult and unbiblical situation with a pastor. (An obvious and radical difference exists between ungodly slander and evil-speaking and confidentially seeking advice in order to do right by God and by a pastor.) First, κατηγορία, "accusation," refers to an "accusation" that is "nearly always [a] legal technical term[,] [meaning] *bring charges* in court" (BDAG, κατηγορία & κατηγορέω). The noun "accusation" is used for a formal and public charge, frequently in a court, against a person. It does not refer to something like confidentially asking an assistant pastor or a trusted friend for advice. The NT employs κατηγορία (Luke 6:7; John 18:29; 1 Timothy 5:19; Titus 1:6) for matters such as the Pharisees seeking for a reason to accuse Christ in a Roman court and have Him killed. No NT use relates to asking a godly third person's confidential advice about how to honor God and do right in a difficult situation with a pastor. Similarly, none of the 21 instances of the verb "accuse" (κατηγορέω) has anything whatsoever to do with seeking confidential advice (Matthew 12:10; 27:12; Mark 3:2; 15:3; Luke 11:54; 23:2, 10, 14; John 5:45; 8:6; Acts 22:30; 24:2, 8, 13, 19; 25:5, 11, 16; 28:19; Romans 2:15; Revelation 12:10). Nor does the noun "accuser" (κατήγορος, John 8:10; Acts 23:30, 35; 24:8; 25:16, 18; Revelation 12:10) refer to seeking for private, confidential advice with the intention of doing right. No usage of the word in the New Testament provides any support whatever for the idea that asking for private counsel from a godly third party about a bad situation with a pastor is condemned in 1 Timothy 5:19.

Since 1 Timothy 5:19 refers to Old Testament passages concerning accusations in public trials (Numbers 35:30; Deuteronomy 17:6; 19:15-19), the conclusion from an examination of all uses of the relevant Greek words in the New Testament is also overwhelmingly supported by context. (Compare also Paul's other two allusions to "two or three witnesses" language in 2 Corinthians 13:1 & Hebrews 10:28.)

When Timothy received Paul's letter and read 1 Timothy 5:19, he would not have thought that someone getting confidential counsel from one or a small number of godly friends in order to make sure he was thinking Biblically (Proverbs 11:14; 15:22; 24:6) was what the Holy Ghost was forbidding in 1 Timothy 5:19.

Consider also that *katagore / katagoreo / kategoros* is etymologically associated with the *agora* (ἀγορά), the "market place ... scene of public events" (BDAG). Seeking confidential counsel is not how one does *kat-agoreo*. The "accusation" of 1 Timothy 5:19 refers to something done in public. Furthermore, 1 Timothy 5:19 refers to not receiving an "accusation" "against" an elder (κατὰ πρεσβυτέρου κατηγορίαν). Someone who harbors no hatred for, prays for, and wishes to think the best about, and wants the best for his pastor if at all possible, but has concerns because of what seem like clear violations of Scripture, is not "against" (*kata,* κατά) the pastor the way wicked men were who made "accusations" "against" Christ or "against" the Apostle Paul in courtrooms. Not confidentially seeking for Biblical guidance, but publicly making an unverifiable or slanderous "accusation," is what 1 Timothy 5:19 condemns.

A pastor who knows how to study Scripture will not claim that 1 Timothy 5:19 is violated if one of his church members, having seriously attempted to resolve problems with him one-on-one, proceeds to confidentially ask an assistant pastor or assistant pastors in the church or a godly person outside the church for advice so that he can do right by God and by the pastor with whom he has a concern. Someone who claims that such a course of action is a violation of 1 Timothy 5:19 is handling the word of God deceitfully (2 Corinthians 4:2). Such a claim could indicate either a serious lack of understanding of hermeneutics, or a lack of proper, careful Bible study, or the presence of a Diotrephes.

One who would cast out a church member for seeking such confidential advice is a Pastor Diotrephes.

[287] Jack Hyles argued that only if "two [living, distinct, human] witnesses come to you ... you must then investigate ... we are not to read [much less receive as true] accusations against individuals in magazines or newspapers" or other written sources, regardless of their documentation (Jack Hyles, *Jack Hyles on Justice*, Chapter 15, "The Most Common Method of Injustice").

[288] Of course, the situation is different if (for example) the accuser is a computer genius who knows how to create fake electronic evidence and has done so, or if one's email has been penetrated by a hacker, etc.

[289] Genesis 21:30; 31:46-48; Exodus 22:13; Joshua 22:28, 34; Job 16:8; Acts 14:17; Titus 1:12-13; James 5:3.

[290] Diotrephes is a γόης (2 Timothy 3:13, "seducer," KJV), a "swindler, cheat ... imposter" (BDAG), "one who habitually fools or deceives people through pretense — 'impostor, hypocrite'" (LN).

[291] παροτρύνω, "stir up strong emotion against, arouse, incite" (BDAG).

[292] See, e. g., https://faithsaves.net/catholic/.

[293] Note that χειροτονέω, used of congregational voting in texts such as Acts 14:23 & 2 Corinthians 8:19, bore the primary meaning of "stretch out the hand, for the purpose of giving one's vote in the assembly ... elect, properly by show of hands" (LSJ) in classical Greek. This sense is retained in the Koine Greek of the New Testament. Compare χειροτονία, "voting by show of hands" (LSJ; cf. Isaiah 58:9, LXX). Calvin notes:

> *[P]resbyters were appointed through the churches ... by votes—"presbyters elected by show of hands in every church," [Luke] says [Acts 14:23]. Therefore ... the whole group, as was the custom of the Greeks in elections, declared*

> *whom it wished to have by raising hands. In like manner, the Roman historians frequently say that the consul who convened the assemblies "created" new magistrates for no other reason than that he received the votes and acted as moderator of the people in the election. ... [B]ishops [were appointed] by vote of the people. (John Calvin, Institutes of the Christian Religion, ed. John T. McNeill, trans. Ford Lewis Battles, vol. 1 & 2, The Library of Christian Classics [Louisville, KY: Westminster John Knox Press, 2011], 1066, sec. IV:3:15)*

294 Compare the apostles' lack of recognition of Judas in John 13:27-30, concerning which Henry comments:

> *[I]t did not enter into [the apostles'] heads that Judas was such a [traitor], or would prove so. Note, It is an excusable dulness in the disciples of Christ not to be quick-sighted in their censures. Most are ready enough to say, when they hear harsh things spoken in general, Now such a one is meant, and now such a one; but Christ's disciples were so well taught to love one another that they could not easily learn to suspect one another; charity thinks no evil. (Matthew Henry, Matthew Henry's Commentary on the Whole Bible: Complete and Unabridged in One Volume [Peabody: Hendrickson, 1994], 2009, note on John 13:18-30)*

There are severe negative consequences for misidentifying a righteous man as Diotrephes, and for misidentifying Diotrephes as righteous. It is certainly best to avoid either error. But if one must err, it is better, like the eleven godly apostles, to be too slow to identify a modern Judas as a traitor than to mistakenly brand a godly man as a Judas.

295 Situations may arise where the Biblical imperative to protect life and punish serious criminals requires bypassing Matthew 18:15-17. When righteous civil laws are broken, the government is the minister of God to execute wrath against evildoers (Romans 13). New Testament regulations on church discipline do not mean that someone who commits murder should only be approached privately, then by two or three, and finally called upon to come before the entire congregation, giving him time to escape civil punishment for his bloody deed. A child molester should be both taken into custody by

the police and placed under church discipline. If—God forbid—a pastor turns out to be a sexual pervert like Jack Schapp, son-in-law of Jack Hyles, who needed to be arrested and imprisoned by the civil government for his wickedness, there is no need to first approach him privately so that he can escape arrest. Lock him up!

[296] σπουδάζοντες—an ongoing action, "to be especially conscientious in discharging an obligation, *be zealous/eager, take pains, make every effort, be conscientious*" (BDAG).

[297] Matthew 18:15-17 mandates that one goes to the person alone to seek restoration and unity. When the Christian "go[es] and tell[s] him his fault," there are no other persons present—the meeting is "between thee and him alone" (18:15). The passage does not say that one cannot first confidentially ask a godly counselor or a few godly counsellors for prayer or for advice about what to say or how to make the meeting go well. However, since the point of the text is to maintain privacy, the spirit of the passage is violated if one first talks about the sin in question to crowds of other individuals before going in private to the person who sinned.

[298] E. g., Roy L. Branson, Jr., *Church Split*, 2nd ed. (Bristol, TN: Landmark Publications, 1992), chapters 1-2; Roy L. Branson, Jr., *Dear Preacher, Please Quit!* (Bristol, TN: Landmark Publications, 1996), chapter 4.

[299] Note that even the worst liars do not always lie. Even Satan sometimes says things that are true (Acts 16:17). Diotrephes is a liar, but that does not mean that he always lies.

[300] While it may well be wise for the two or three others to be pastors for numbers of reasons, Christ did not specifically mandate in Matthew 18:15-17 that the others brought in be pastors, deacons, or any other person in a position of church leadership. Asking the other pastors to be the two or three is likely to be wise, as they should be men that evidence the godliness and wisdom mandated in 1 Timothy 3 and Titus 1, but it is not specifically required in every instance. It is neither the

explicit statement nor the necessary consequence of any text of Scripture.

[301] If incriminating portions of messages mysteriously disappear, replaced with edited and white-washed forms on the church website, something inappropriate is going on, unless, of course, the pastor recognized that what he said was not right and removed it because he admitted error. (However, since the Bible supports the public admission of serious public error, in such a situation portions of sermons should not be mysteriously disappearing.)

[302] It is sadly possible that one Pastor Diotrephes can, at least for a time, deceive numbers of righteous pastors. Judas deceived the eleven righteous apostles and led them to unjustly condemn the righteous (John 12:1-7; Matthew 26:8); Absalom deceived many people innocent of his plots (2 Samuel 15:11); false Judaizers deceived Barnabas and Peter (Galatians 2:11-13); and Satan deceived Peter and other leaders (Matthew 16:22-23; Galatians 2:11).

[303] Compare David Cloud, "The Women Who Knew Jack Hyles," elec. acc. https://www.wayoflife.org/reports/the_women_who_knew_jack_hyles.php.

[304] Compare 1 Corinthians 16:3; 2 Corinthians 3:1.

[305] Steven Martin notes:

> *Sad to say, the sheep themselves contribute their own sins to the creation of authoritarian ministries. Having talked with and ministered to several wounded sheep, it has struck me how seldom they have seen their own culpability. They are quick to foist all blame upon their harsh former taskmasters. But petty dictators cannot reign without the consent of their bowing and scraping subjects who, when they are not fawning all over their leaders, are assuming the role of doormats for the leader to wipe his feet on. There are at least three sins which laymen contribute to the sinful pathology of authoritarian churches.*

(a) Idolatry

Sinful flesh is not content with the unseen reality of the one true God. It wants to fashion an idol in place of the invisible God who is spirit. There is always the temptation to act like the Jews of King Saul's time who wanted a human leader whom they could see, rather than the unseen God himself (1 Sam. 8:1–18). But God shares his glory with no man, not even "called men" who are promoted to demigod status by their adoring flock. Such flocks too often find for themselves a man who likes to lord it over the flock. Thus a sinfully symbiotic relationship is complete with an abusive authority figure coupled to idol-worshiping minions (e.g. Jer. 5:30–31). People who populate such churches boast of their preacher but speak little of Jesus Christ! People of such churches are more afraid of their pastor finding out that they sinned than the fact that Jesus Christ already knows that they sinned! Such people are more centered on the authoritarian leader than they are on their Savior and Lord. A mere man, an idol, has replaced the glorious Lord Jesus Christ as king of their hearts.

(b) Fear of man

Too many sheep are more gripped by the desire to please a man or more fearful of displeasing a man than they are of pleasing or displeasing Almighty God (see Prov. 29:25; John 5:41–44). They spend their time dancing around their idol, expending all their energy catering to his every whim and seeking to avoid his wrath. Men-pleasers have little stomach for potential conflict or simple disagreement. They would never dare question their exalted leader, no matter how respectfully. They would never ask for the biblical basis for a decision made by the leadership, even when that decision seems to fly in the face of clear biblical teaching. Such men-pleasers crave the smile of a man's countenance more than the smile of God, and they will not speak the truth in love (Eph. 5:15). Pastors, do your people fear you more than they fear Jesus Christ? Laymen, do you fear your pastor more than you fear God?

(c) Unbelief

> *Too many believers do not believe that God still guides his people today through the means of prayerful meditation upon the Word of God and the illuminating ministry of the Holy Spirit. It is easier for the flesh to suspend the use of spiritual faculties and biblical means of guidance for the shortcut of asking the leader to determine God's will and make the decisions all the time. It is not surprising that Christians who put men of clay on pedestals (and who then cravenly serve these idol-leaders and who do not believe that God still guides through his Word) should fall prey to abusive leaders. It is only the grace of God that it does not happen more frequently than it does. (Even good leaders know the temptation to become surrogate "gods" or infallible "oracles" for their people. Faithful men learn to stoutly resist the frequent temptation placed before them by individuals to infallibly answer their questions of guidance and decision-making.) Perhaps authoritarian shepherds are God's chastening rods upon the backs of idol-worshiping, men-pleasing, unbelieving sheep who will not have God to be their God and who substitute a mere creature in his place (see Isa. 2:22 and Ps. 33:13–19). (Steven Martin, ed., Biblical Shepherding of God's Sheep: The Use and Abuse of Authority by Church Officers [Leominster: Day One, 2010], 171–173)*

[306] In the case of the scandalous, public, undeniable, and flagrant sin in 1 Corinthians 5, it is possible that the steps of Matthew 18:15-17 can be bypassed. But if you are guilty of scandalous, public, and undeniable sin, it hardly needs to be said that you are the problem, not the church that wishes to preserve its purity for the glory of Jesus Christ. If you disagree, you should examine yourself to see if you are truly born again (2 Corinthians 13:5). You are either not truly regenerate or, at best, you are incredibly spiritually weak (2 Corinthians 13:5).

[307] The inspired prohibition "to speak evil of no man" (μηδένα βλασφημεῖν) in Titus 3:2 forbids you from speaking "in a disrespectful way that demeans, denigrates, maligns"; you cannot "slander, revile, [or] defame" (BDAG, βλασφημέω). Titus 3:2 does not prohibit you from respectfully sharing truth about Diotrephes to the appropriate parties,

even if the truth shows that Diotrephes has done wrong, is sinning, and is not qualified to be in his position of overseer.

308 E. g., "Doesn't Matthew 18:15-17 say that I am supposed to receive a trial before the church?" "Why is it that I am not being allowed to freely speak in my defense, or cross-examine my accuser? Doesn't Matthew 18:16 say that 'every word' of this accusation needs to be carefully proven and established?" "Why is it that this panel is not being allowed to read the actual statements that form the alleged basis of my guilt in context?" "Matthew 18:15-17 is referencing the procedure for civil trials in Israel, quoting Deuteronomy. In civil trials in Israel were the judges supposed to just believe whatever accusation someone came up with, or was proof required?"

309 συναπάγω, Galatians 2:13; 2 Peter 3:17.

310 τῇ τῶν ἀθέσμων πλάνῃ συναπαχθέντες.

311 στηριγμός.

312 While in Biblical anthropology the semantic domain of the words *heart* and *mind* overlap significantly, it is noteworthy that Scripture indicates that false teachers "by good words and fair speeches deceive the hearts of the simple" (Romans 16:18), not their minds—a consistent pattern (James 1:26; Deuteronomy 11:16; Job 31:9; Isaiah 44:20; Obadiah 3). Pastor Diotrephes will deceive others through manipulating their emotions rather than by calling them, with a "sound mind" (2 Timothy 1:7) and sober moderation, to unbiased searching of Scripture and of factual data that pertain to God's real world.

313 Edward Hiscox, *Standard Manual for Baptist Churches* (Philadelphia, PA: American Baptist Publication Society, 1890), 37

314 Psalm 106:36; Jeremiah 50:24. In Isaiah 28:13 carelessness about Scripture results in those who view it as merely childish gibberish (וְהָיָה לָהֶם דְּבַר־יְהוָה צַו לָצָו צַו לָצָו קַו לָקָו קַו לָקָו זְעֵיר שָׁם זְעֵיר שָׁם, *w^{e}hāyâ lahem d^{e}ḇar-Y^{e}hôwāh ṣaw lāṣāw ṣaw lāṣāw qaw lāqāw qaw lāqāw z^{e}ʿēr šām z^{e}ʿēr šām*, But the word of the LORD was unto them precept upon precept, precept upon

precept; line upon line, line upon line; here a little, *and* there a little) being broken, snared, and taken.

315 If someone is properly placed under church discipline for being a thief, the video footage or the police report will validate his guilt; if someone is properly placed under church discipline for immorality, various sorts of verified proof will be available; but if someone is cast out by Diotrephes, Pastor Diotrephes may insist that others simply believe that what he did was just, without being able to provide any proof that can withstand scrutiny.

316 παραδιατριβή, 1 Timothy 6:5, TR; the Nestle-Aland text changes the Received Text's reading to διαπαρατριβή.

317 παραδιατριβή, BDAG.

318 Barnes notes:

> *The word which is [in 1 Timothy 6:5] used in the Received Text—παραδιατρίβη—occurs nowhere else in the New Testament. It properly means mis-employment; then idle occupation. ... The verb from which this is derived means to rub in pieces, to wear away; and hence the word here used refers to what was a mere wearing away of time. The idea is that of employments that merely consumed time without any advantage ... the allusion is to inquiries or discussions that were of no practical value, but were a mere consumption of time. (Albert Barnes, Notes on the New Testament: I Thessalonians to Philemon, ed. Robert Frew [London: Blackie & Son, 1884–1885], 195, comment on 1 Timothy 6:5)*

319 Compare Marvin Richardson Vincent, *Word Studies in the New Testament*, vol. 4 (New York: Charles Scribner's Sons, 1887), 274–275, comment on 1 Timothy 6:5.

320 As 3 John 10 describes Diotrephes' casting out of the saints with ἐκβάλλω, so compare:

καὶ ἀναστάντες **ἐξέβαλον** αὐτὸν ἔξω τῆς πόλεως, καὶ ἤγαγον αὐτὸν ἕως τῆς ὀφρύος τοῦ ὄρους ἐφ' οὗ ἡ πόλις αὐτῶν ᾠκοδόμητο, εἰς τὸ κατακρημνίσαι αὐτόν. *(Luke 4:29)*
καὶ λαβόντες αὐτὸν **ἐξέβαλον** ἔξω τοῦ ἀμπελῶνος καὶ ἀπέκτειναν. *(Matthew 21:39)*
καὶ λαβόντες αὐτὸν ἀπέκτειναν, καὶ **ἐξέβαλον** ἔξω τοῦ ἀμπελῶνος. *(Mark 12:8)*
καὶ προσέθετο πέμψαι τρίτον· οἱ δὲ καὶ τοῦτον τραυματίσαντες **ἐξέβαλον**. … καὶ **ἐκβαλόντες** αὐτὸν ἔξω τοῦ ἀμπελῶνος, ἀπέκτειναν. τί οὖν ποιήσει αὐτοῖς ὁ κύριος τοῦ ἀμπελῶνος; *(Luke 20:12, 15)*

μακάριοί ἐστε, ὅταν μισήσωσιν ὑμᾶς οἱ ἄνθρωποι, καὶ ὅταν ἀφορίσωσιν ὑμᾶς, καὶ ὀνειδίσωσι, καὶ **ἐκβάλωσι** τὸ ὄνομα ὑμῶν ὡς πονηρόν, ἕνεκα τοῦ υἱοῦ τοῦ ἀνθρώπου. *(Luke 6:22)*
καὶ **ἐκβαλόντες** ἔξω τῆς πόλεως, ἐλιθοβόλουν· καὶ οἱ μάρτυρες ἀπέθεντο τὰ ἱμάτια αὐτῶν παρὰ τοὺς πόδας νεανίου καλουμένου Σαύλου. *(Acts 7:58)*
οἱ δὲ Ἰουδαῖοι παρώτρυναν τὰς σεβομένας γυναῖκας καὶ τὰς εὐσχήμονας καὶ τοὺς πρώτους τῆς πόλεως, καὶ ἐπήγειραν διωγμὸν ἐπὶ τὸν Παῦλον καὶ τὸν Βαρνάβαν, καὶ **ἐξέβαλον** αὐτοὺς ἀπὸ τῶν ὁρίων αὐτῶν. *(Acts 13:50)*

[321] ἐκβάλλω.

[322] ἐκβάλλω.

[323] Matthew 8:12, employing ἐκβάλλω, which is also used for the lost being cast out into the lake of fire in Matthew 22:13; 25:30 & Luke 13:28; Christ also casts out Satan (John 12:31).

[324] The Lord Jesus, Author of the whole Scripture as God's ultimate Prophet, both inspired the imprecatory psalms and sang them Himself during His earthly ministry. Every person, therefore, either has Christ pray the matchlessly gracious prayer of John 17 for him or the imprecations of Psalm 109 against him—whichever one he chooses is what he will get. If he repents and believes, he gets John 17; if he refuses, he gets Psalm 109.

[325] ἀσπάσασθε Ἀπελλῆν τὸν δόκιμον ἐν Χριστῷ.

[326] δόκιμος, BDAG.

[327] The promises are given to the δόκιμος, the one who overcomes when tested: Μακάριος ἀνὴρ ὃς ὑπομένει πειρασμόν· ὅτι δόκιμος γενόμενος λήψεται τὸν στέφανον τῆς ζωῆς, ὃν ἐπηγγείλατο ὁ Κύριος τοῖς ἀγαπῶσιν αὐτόν.

[328] In the context of 1-3 John, it is very possible that Diotrephes is viewed as an antichrist who has committed the sin unto death and is not, therefore, one for whom continuing prayer is mandated (1 John 5:16-17).

[329] Southern Baptists acknowledge:

> *[O]ur churches have generally abandoned scriptural church discipline. We practice a thin discipline—church staff who sin are given paid leave, Christian counseling, a generous severance package, and are declared cured. We then commend them to another church where they repeat the same crimes." (Gregory A. Wills, "Who Are the True Baptists? The Conservative Resurgence and the Influence of Moderate Views of Baptist Identity," Southern Baptist Journal of Theology 9:1 [2005]: 32)*

They ask: "What is to be done about the present abandonment of church discipline, especially in its negative aspects?" (James Leo Garrett Jr., "Church Discipline: Lost, but Recoverable," *The Founders Journal: Systematic Theology and Preaching, Spring*, 4 [1991]: 26). Their historians recognize: "One hundred fifty years ago ... Baptists and most other evangelicals practiced a thorough church discipline. Over the next fifty years most evangelicals abandoned the practice. For at least three generations now, evangelical churches in the West have neglected it" (Gregory A. Wills, "Was Dagg Right?," *9Marks Journal* 6:5 [2009]: 18).

[330] James Leo Garrett, Jr., *Baptist Church Discipline*, rev. ed. [Paris, AK: Baptist Standard Bearer, 2004], 1. The words *evangelical* and *fundamentalist* are employed in a variety of ways. In this composition, a *fundamentalist* is someone who practices Biblical and ecclesiastical separation and seeks to earnestly contend for the faith (Jude 3), while an *evangelical* either ignores or is wobbly at best on ecclesiastical and personal separation, while defending only certain portions of the faith deemed "essentials." Compare Kevin T. Bauder et al., *Four Views on the Spectrum of Evangelicalism*, Zondervan Counterpoints Collection (Grand Rapids, MI: Zondervan, 2011) and Thomas Ross, "Four Views On the Spectrum of Evangelicalism: A Book Review," elec. acc. https://kentbrandenburg.com/2023/05/05/four-views-on-the-spectrum-of-evangelicalism-a-book-review/.

[331] Don Baker, *Beyond Forgiveness: The Healing Touch of Church Discipline* (Portland, OR: Multanomah Press, 1984), 16, 22-24, 48-54, 79, 89. The adulterer was already allowed to do things like teach the largest Sunday School class in the congregation on an even shorter time frame than the one-year gap between his turning in his ordination papers and his re-ordination.

Baker's book is endorsed by anti-Lordship salvation leader Earl Radmacher (pgs. 9-10), former president of Western Conservative Baptist Seminary, under whose leadership the school dropped the name "Baptist" to just become "Western Seminary" and merged into the broader evangelical world. Sadly, the book never suggests that the adulterous pastor needed to examine himself to see whether he was truly converted (2 Corinthians 13:5) on account of the perpetual sin in which he was living (1 Corinthians 6:9-11). Nor are texts such as Proverbs 6:32-33 ever cited in the book: "*But* whoso committeth adultery with a woman lacketh understanding: he *that* doeth it destroyeth his own soul. A wound and dishonour shall he get; and his reproach shall not be wiped away."

Furthermore, in Baker's book the church did not vote on what happened to the adulterer—the leadership just decided and told the congregation. Furthermore, the book claims that the whole congregation does not need to decide to excommunicate, but a "representative body" can be substituted and make a "binding" decision (pg. 42). Such affirmations are a repudiation of Baptist polity. It was also noteworthy that "most of the immoral relationships had developed in counseling sessions" (pg. 91).

332 Don Baker, *Beyond Forgiveness: The Healing Touch of Church Discipline* (Portland, OR: Multanomah Press, 1984), 66.

333 φλυαρέω, 3 John 10.

334 φλύαρος, 1 Timothy 5:13.

335 Edward Hiscox, *Standard Manual for Baptist Churches* (Philadelphia, PA: American Baptist Publication Society, 1890), 37.

336 φιλόξενος.

337 φιλοφρόνως ἐξένισεν.

338 φιλάγαθος.

339 Matthew 18:18-19 (ἀμὴν λέγω ὑμῖν, ἐὰν δήσητε ἐπὶ τῆς γῆς, ἔσται δεδεμένα ἐν τῷ οὐρανῷ· καὶ ὅσα ἐὰν λύσητε ἐπὶ τῆς γῆς, ἔσται λελυμένα ἐν τῷ οὐρανῷ. πάλιν λέγω ὑμῖν, ὅτι ἐὰν δύο ὑμῶν συμφωνήσωσιν ἐπὶ τῆς γῆς περὶ παντὸς πράγματος οὗ ἐὰν αἰτήσωνται, γενήσεται αὐτοῖς παρὰ τοῦ πατρός μου τοῦ ἐν οὐρανοῖς.) indirectly applies to valid church discipline, and the passage should be considered when necessity arises to practice that solemn duty (Matthew 18:15-20).

However, it is not persons, but teachings, that are "bound" and "loosed"; the passage speaks of "whatsoever" (ὅσα, neuter) not "whosoever" (ὅσους, masculine) is bound. Furthermore, the church does not bind and loose as does a master who commands with his own independent authority, but binds and looses as a steward (cf. Isaiah 22:22); her directives are authoritative only when they are what her risen Master directs. The church authoritatively binds men to obey all Scripture and looses them from all that is not required in the New

Testament dispensation, such as the sacrificial system of the Old Testament, and what the church authoritatively teaches from Scripture on earth is what God has already bound and loosed in heaven, from whence He gave the Word that the church proclaims. When church members disobey what Christ has bound in heaven and their pastors proclaim on earth from Scripture, the church has authority to follow Christ's directives concerning excommunication of the unrepentant (Matthew 18:15-20).

Pastor Diotrephes may twist Matthew 18:18-19 so that it (allegedly) means that if he is successful in manipulating a panel or the congregation to vote to cast someone out, that decision is necessarily authoritative in heaven, even if the casting out was egregiously unjust and unbiblical. Diotrephes' conclusion both requires a Roman Catholic *ex opere operato* view of church ordinances instead of a Biblical Baptist one and involves a distortion of what the passage itself plainly teaches in its immediate and canonical contexts.

[340] Wyman Lewis Richardson, *On Earth as It Is in Heaven: Reclaiming Regenerate Church Membership* (Cape Coral, FL: Founders Press, 2011), 18. Hiscox's book was not only widely used in the English-speaking world, but was also taken by foreign evangelists to other lands, where it has been been translated into multiple languages (see, e. g., William Cathcart, ed., *The Baptist Encyclopædia* [Philadelphia: Louis H. Everts, 1881], 528-529).

[341] Edward Hiscox, *Standard Manual for Baptist Churches* (Philadelphia, PA: American Baptist Publication Society, 1890), 28-41.

[342] This assumes that the congregation from which the sheep was cast out was one that had professed Biblical beliefs and practices and with which your church used to be in ecclesiastical fellowship. There is no need to contact a former minister when someone leaves a cult that preaches a false gospel or in some other way is evidently a corrupt false religion. Hopefully your church never was in ecclesiastical fellowship with such, so there will be no need to disfellowship.

343 Carroll provides a number of helpful instances of the classical use of ἐκκλησία [transliterating the word as *ecclesia*], documenting that the word, in classical Greek, signified "an organized assembly of citizens, regularly summoned, as opposed to other meetings":

> *Thucydides 2:22: – "Pericles, seeing them angry at the present state of things ... did not call them to an assembly (ecclesia) or any other meeting."*
> *Demosthenes 378, 24: – "When after this the assembly (ecclesia) adjourned, they came together and planned[.] ... For the future still being uncertain, meetings and speeches of all sorts took place in the marketplace. They were afraid that an assembly (ecclesia) would be summoned suddenly, etc." Compare the distinction here between a lawfully assembled business body and a mere gathering together of the people in unofficial capacity, with the town-clerk's statement in Acts 19:35, 40.*
>
> *[Note also] some instances of the particular ecclesia of the several Greek states–*
>
> *Thucydides 1,87: – "Having said such things, he himself, since he was ephor, put the question to vote in the assembly (ecclesia) of the Spartans."*
> *Thucydides 1,139: – "And the Athenians having made a house (or called an assembly, ecclesia) freely exchanged their sentiments."*
> *Aristophanes Act 169: – "But I forbid you calling an assembly (ecclesia) for the Thracians about pay."*
> *Thucydides 6,8: – "And the Athenians having convened an assembly (ecclesia) ... voted, etc."*
> *Thucydides 6,2: – "And the Syracusans having buried their dead, summoned an assembly (ecclesia)."*
>
> *This historical reading concerning the business assemblies of the several petty but independent, self-governing Greek states, with their lawful conference, their free speech, their decision by vote, whether of Spartans, Thracians, Syracusans or Athenians, sounds much like the proceedings of particular*

> *and independent Baptist churches today (Ecclesia, B. H. Carroll, pgs. 35-36).*

While the parallels are not perfect, what Aristotle discusses concerning tyranny in a classical Greek *ekklesia* still has some relevance to tyranny in Christ's New Testament *ekklesia* or church. Compare τύραννος, Acts 19:9, and in the LXX, the uses of τυραννίς and τύραννος for heathen rulers (Esther 1:8; 9:3; cf. also in the LXX Proverbs 8:16, 28:15; Job 2:11; 42:17; Habakkuk 1:10; outside of the canon, see 1 Maccabees 1:4; 2 Maccabees 4:25; 5:8; 7:27; 3 Maccabees 3:8; 6:24; 4 Maccabees 1:11; 5:1, 4, 14, 27, 38-6:1; 6:21, 23; 7:2; 8:2-4, 13, 15, 29-9:1; 9:3, 7, 10, 15, 24, 29-30, 32; 10:10, 15-16; 11:2, 12-13, 21, 24, 27; 12:2, 11; 15:1-2; 16:14; 17:2, 9, 14, 17, 21, 23; 18:5, 20, 22; Wisdom 6:9, 21; 8:15; 10:14; 12:14; 14:17, 21; 16:4; Sirach 11:5; 47:21).

[344] Aristotle, *The Works of Aristotle*, ed. W. D. Ross, trans. Benjamin Jowett, E. S. Forster, and Frederic G. Kenyon, vol. 10 (Oxford: The Clarendon Press, 1921), xvi; *Politics* 1313a.30-1314a.30.

[345] Ignatius here misuses 1 Samuel 15:22 in an astonishing way, making a verse about submission to God and His Word into one about blind submission to one's Catholic superior.

[346] Ignatius of Loyola, *Ignatius of Loyola: Letters and Instructions*, ed. John W. Padberg, et al (St. Louis, MO: Institute of Jesuit Sources, 1996), 412-421, "To the Members of the Society in Portugal, Rome, March 26, 1553."

[347] W. J. McGlothlin, *Baptist Confessions of Faith* (Philadelphia: American Baptist Publication Society, 1911), 258–259, citing chapter 21 of the 2nd London Baptist Confession of 1689.

[348] Names and locations in this study are fictional. The events recorded are not fictional. The point of the records is to illustrate how both the righteous pastor and Pastor Diotrephes work, and how Christ's people should act in such situations. The point is not for readers to speculate on what events may or may not underlie the case studies given. Biblical churches should warn plainly and by name

about wolves in sheep's clothing when that action is warranted. This written study is not a substitute for obedience to 1 Timothy 5:20.

[349] Brother Sheep may not have been able to articulate it at the time, but the idea that the Son was "separated" from the Father is Trinitarian heresy if it has respect to the Son's Divine Person, for the Father, Son, and Spirit are one essence (*homoousios*) with one undivided nature, and the Son cannot be separated from the Father in the ontological Trinity. If the (alleged) separation pertains to Christ's human nature, the affirmation is the Christological heresy of Nestorianism, for Christ's two natures are inseparably united within His one Person, as correctly affirmed by the Council of Chalcedon.

There is no basis for the contention that the Son was "separated" from the Father in Matthew 27:46's "My God, my God, why hast thou forsaken me?" (Θεέ μου, Θεέ μου, ἱνατί με ἐγκατέλιπες;), quoting Psalm 22:1a (אֵלִ֣י אֵ֭לִי לָמָ֣ה עֲזַבְתָּ֑נִי). Certainly the Lord endured ineffable suffering on the cross for the sin of mankind:

> *Christ in truth bore unspeakable distress, sorrows, horror, and hellish torment on the cross in order that he might redeem us from them. ... [He endured both] physical suffering and death ... [and] suffer[ed] in his rational soul ... unspeakable distress and hellish torments in the work of salvation. ... Yet we do not suggest that God was ever inimical or angry toward him. How could he be angry toward his beloved Son, 'in whom his heart [was well pleased] [cf. Matt. 3:17]? How could Christ by his intercession appease the Father toward others, if he were himself hateful to God? ... [H]e bore the weight of divine severity, since he was 'stricken and afflicted' [cf. Isa. 53:5] by God's hand, and experienced all the signs of a wrathful and avenging God ... He drank the cup of suffering to the last drop and tasted death in all its bitterness in order to completely deliver us from the fear of death and death itself. Thus he destroyed him who had the power of death and by a single offering perfected for all time those who are sanctified (Heb. 10:14). (Herman Bavinck, John Bolt, and John Vriend, Reformed Dogmatics: Sin and Salvation in Christ, vol. 3 [Grand Rapids, MI: Baker Academic, 2006], 416–417)*

However, even while Christ endured the bitter cup of substitutionary suffering, He still called the Father "my God" (Matthew 27:46; Psalm 22:1), trusted in Him (Psalm 22:8), and looked forward to His coming resurrection, as prophesied later in Psalm 22 (vv. 8-10, 19-31). Furthermore, the verb עָזַב in Psalm 22:1 does not require Christ was "separated" from the Father any more than "my heart faileth me" (וְלִבִּי עֲזָבָנִי׃, Psalm 40:12) means that David's human heart was separated from his body (and one must also remember that the psalter employs the often figurative language of vibrant and affective spirituality, not the technical theological terminology found, for example, in certain portions of the Pauline epistles).

> *God is the God of Christ as he is man; he prepared a body for him, an human nature; anointed it with the oil of gladness; supported it under all its sorrows and sufferings, and at last exalted it at his own right hand: and Christ behaved towards him as his covenant-God; prayed to him, believed in him, loved him, and was obedient to him as such; and here expresses his faith of interest in him, when he hid his face from him, on account of which he expostulates with him thus, why hast thou forsaken me? which is to be understood, not as if the hypostatical or personal union of the divine and human natures were dissolved, or that the one was now separated from the other: for the fulness of the Godhead still dwelt bodily in him; nor that he ceased to be the object of the Father's love; for so he was in the midst of all his sufferings, yea, his Father loved him because he laid down his life for the sheep; nor that the principle of joy and comfort was lost in him, only the act and sense of it; he was now deprived of the gracious presence of God, of the manifestations of his love to his human soul, and had a sense of divine wrath, not for his own sins, but for the sins of his people, and was for a while destitute of help and comfort; all which were necessary in order to make satisfaction for sin: for as he had the sins of his people imputed to him, he must bear the whole punishment of them, which is two-fold the punishment of loss and the punishment of sense; the former lies in a deprivation of the divine presence, and the latter in a sense of divine wrath, and both Christ sustained as the surety of his people. (John Gill, An*

Exposition of the Old Testament, vol. 3, [London: Mathews and Leigh, 1810], 616)

Brother Sheep, without necessarily articulating all of the above, simply thought that it was strange and unbiblical to speak of the Son as separated from His Father. He thought it was not good to change the good gospel literature BBC already had into inferior gospel literature that misled an already confused world by teaching that two Persons in the Trinity were separated the one from the other. However, because of how easily offended Pastor D. was when questioned, Brother Sheep never asked him about it.

350 See, e. g., Thomas Ross, "An Exegesis and Application of Romans 10:9-14 for Soulwinning Churches and Christians, in Relation to the Question of the 'Sinner's Prayer,'" elec. acc. https://faithsaves.net/romans-10-sinners-prayer/ & Paul Harrison Chitwood, *The Sinners Prayer: A Historical and Theological Analysis* (Ph. D. Dissertation, Southern Baptist Theological Seminary, 2001), elec. acc. https://faithsaves.net/the-sinners-prayer/.

351 The sinfulness of minced oaths is both taught in Scripture and widely recognized. God is still referred to when He is called "the Blessed" (Mark 14:61) or "the Highest" (Psalm 18:13), or God's kingdom called the kingdom "of heaven" (Matthew 3:2), and one must not take His name in vain underneath such alternative expressions. In the words of a modern evangelical:

> *Profanity is the attempt of a feeble mind to express itself forcibly ... sometimes Christians fall into this trap. Oh, we would never use the curse words of profanity, but we do second-handed cursing. We have little euphemistic statements, you know, like gol*y, and g*e whiz, and g*sh d*rn, and d*rned, and h*ck, and all of these things. These are all just simply ways of second-handed cursing. Webster's New International Dictionary says g*e is a form of Jesus used in minced oaths; g*lly—a euphemism for God used in minced oaths; g*sh—a substitute for God used in minced oaths; d*rn, d*rned, and d*rnation—colloquial euphemisms for damn, damned, and damnation. Perhaps a person who says "g*sh*

> *d*rn" would be amazed at what he's saying by means of second-handed cursing. "Thou shalt not take the name of the LORD thy God in vain; for [God] will not hold him guiltless that taketh his name in vain" (Exodus 20:7). It shows a lack of understanding. It shows a lack of ability for a person to express himself in the way that he ought to express himself. (Adrian Rogers, "The Third Commandment," in Adrian Rogers Sermon Archive [Signal Hill, CA: Rogers Family Trust, 2017], Ex 20:7. "*" has been supplied to avoid reproducing the minced oaths.)*

Thomas Boston explains:

> *God requires men's speech in their ordinary converse to be plain and simple, as yea and nay, without unhallowed additions ... [James 5:12 and other passages] exclude[e] out of speech in common conversation, all that which is akin to oaths, where there is no sufficient call thereunto. And so it condemns not only all express swearing by God or the creatures, but ... [a]ll minced oaths, where the form of swearing is not used, but suppressed. ...*
>
> *(1.) Though one could not be convinced that these things are evil, yet he cannot miss the conviction that they are evil-like. And you can never think that it is duty to God or your neighbour to speak so. On this very ground ye ought to forbear them, 1 Thess. 5:22. "Abstain from all appearance of evil." Jude, 23. "Hating even the garments spotted by the flesh." Whoso will not shun appearances of evil, will easily venture on real evils.*
>
> *(2.) I appeal to your consciences, whether these be the language of the most tender and serious sort of Christians, or of profane men and rough untender professors; and whether or not the more tender any one is in [his] walk, [his] speech is purged from these. Let that then have weight with you, spoken by the apostle, Phil. 4:9. "Those things which ye have both learned and received, and heard and seen in me, do."*
>
> *(3.) They are offensive to the serious godly; they grate on their ears, as the language of hell. It is grievous to them to hear men who are baptized in the name of Christ, speaking half the*

language of Canaan, and half that of Ashdod. And on this score they are dangerous, Matth. 18:6, 7. ...

(4.) At best they are idle words, and therefore sinful. What good purpose do they serve for? Are they of any use for God's honour, your own good, or the good of those with whom ye converse? Consider therefore that declaration, Matth. 12:36. "I say unto you, That every idle word that men shall speak, they shall give account thereof in the day of judgment. ... But some may be ready to say, They are but little sins. ... Every sin deserves God's wrath; and there is none so little, but they will ruin you for ever, if they be not washed away by the Redeemer's blood, as one little leak will sink the ship. ...

If they are but little, how wilt thou do a great thing for God, that wilt not please him in such a small matter? Alas! if they be little, they are not few. Many grains make a mountain, and many drops an ocean. If one be drowned, it is all one to him, whether it be in a little water or in the ocean. (Thomas Boston, The Whole Works of Thomas Boston: A Soliloquy on the Art of Man-Fishing, ed. Samuel M'Millan, vol. 5 [Aberdeen: George and Robert King, 1849], 137–139)

The Confessions of Faith and the Books of Discipline of the Church of Scotland rightly ask "concerning a minister ... Hath [the] minister a Gospel walk and conversation before the people? ... Is he a swearer of small or minced oaths?" (Church of Scotland, *The Confessions of Faith and the Books of Discipline of the Church of Scotland* [London: Baldwin and Cradock, 1831], 166).

[352] Later on, in a meeting with Pastor D. and an assistant pastor when this matter of minced oaths came up, Brother Sheep heard the assistant pastor say the minced oath many times. This was very surprising to Brother Sheep and very uncharacteristic of the assistant pastor. Brother Sheep later asked the assistant pastor about it, and the assistant said that he "felt a twinge" every time he said it. It seems highly likely that, in order to justify his own actions, Pastor D. had commanded the assistant pastor to start using the minced oath that Pastor D. had repeated over and over again from God's pulpit, and the assistant pastor had agreed, violating his conscience and enduring its

"twinges" to please Pastor D. This probably helped prepare the assistant pastor to support Pastor D. in greater violations of conscience yet to come.

353 Brother Sheep had scored higher than the average high school senior on a college entrance exam when he was only in the seventh grade, and, after entering college at age fifteen, had completed both first-year calculus and multivariable or vector calculus at a college level, as well as science classes utilizing calculus, before his eighteenth birthday. Pastor D. did not know these facts because (as he had repeatedly explained, and confirmed in writing) he was not interested in anything Brother Sheep had to say—he did not take such information from subordinates. Pastor D. did not know Brother Sheep.

Brother Sheep never pointed these facts out—he let Pastor D.'s new condemnation of him for ignorance of basic mathematics stand without a response. Brother Sheep had no desire to boast about himself, and he was perfectly willing to be viewed as a simpleton so Pastor D. could save face.

354 Brother Sheep, wanting to respect Pastor D.'s pastoral office, dutifully repeated to Sister Sheep Pastor D.'s claims about her being in sin, causing Sister Sheep deep concern. However, later when they both went back to their Bibles, it became clear that Pastor D.'s accusations were wildly inaccurate and did not even come close to proving his harsh judgment about Sister Sheep.

355 Physical maladies in the brain may contribute to a person believing delusions. See, e. g., Charles C. Dike, "Pathological Lying: Symptom or Disease? *Psychiatric Times* (June 2008) 67-73.

356 When Brother Sheep later read several of Roy L. Branson's egregiously unbiblical books, Brother Sheep began to understand why it was hard for Pastor D. to admit that an unregenerate man should not be left in the pastoral office.

357 Because of how egregiously biased it was to have Pastor D. be both the accuser and also the moderator, a man in the congregation

who was not allowed to vote to acquit or condemn was proclaimed the "umpire" to give a veneer of unbiased action. After the show-trial was over, the "umpire" wrote to Brother Sheep: "I didn't think that the panel paid sufficient attention to your defense ... there should have been discussion of your defense." In Pastor D.'s communications to blacken Brother Sheep's reputation to pastors and churches in other places, Pastor D. concealed the fact that he was himself both prosecutor and moderator and lied, stating that this non-voting "umpire" was really the meeting moderator. Furthermore, the actual judgment of this "umpire" that Brother Sheep's defense should have received consideration, instead of being ignored and not discussed, was also hidden. Finally, since Pastor D. was perfectly well aware that Brother Sheep was not guilty of what he had been accused of on the actual discipline document, other slanders were invented and claimed to be the reasons why Brother Sheep was cast out, although these other accusations were not what he was even on trial for and nothing like Matthew 18 was followed for them.

[358] Later, after studying Scripture more carefully and personally feeling more of Pastor D's harsh wrath, Brother Sheep realized he had sinned by following without understanding and receiving unverified accusations against this other family based on Pastor D's words alone. He asked if the congregation could be told that he had done wrong by going along with this violation of Matthew 18:15-17, but he was repentant. Pastor Diotrephes rejected Brother Sheep's request.

[359] While the author received the testimony of a plurality of witnesses in favor of the accuracy of the events narrated below, for this account it was not possible for this author to hear the other side of the story to the extent that he would have wished (Proverbs 18:17). While he thinks the details in this story represent reality, he believes the narrative is vague enough to prevent the specific identification of the parties involved. Any reader who thinks he knows who is referred to in this narrative should *not* use it as evidence to think poorly (or highly) of any other real, identifiable person, both because 1.) The reader's assumptions about who this narrative describes could be wrong. 2.) Even if somehow a reader could prove beyond a reasonable doubt that he has correctly identified the persons involved, this author is here

stating that he was not able to hear a defense from the party negatively portrayed, so the account could be biased or inaccurate. The author was able to obtain and assess evidence of clearly greater solidity for the classic and pervert Diotrephes narratives than for this one concerning a thieving Diotrephes.

Therefore, this narrative of a thieving Diotrephes, while likely accurate, should be viewed as simply paradigmatic of what could have and probably has happened at some point in history, or as a fictional but instructive example of dealing with a pseudo-pastor who is a thief. Readers should consider the serious commands of 1 Timothy 5:19-21 and refrain from using this account to condemn godly pastors. Evidence that a particular person is actually a thieving Diotrephes must come from facts derived independently of this book.

[360] 1 Timothy 3:3, 8; Titus 1:7, 11; 1 Peter 5:2.

[361] "*Hogget* ... [signifies in Britain] a yearling sheep ... [and in New Zealand] a lamb between weaning and its first shearing" (Catherine Soanes and Angus Stevenson, eds., *Concise Oxford English Dictionary* [Oxford: Oxford University Press, 2004]).

[362] See Michael Stacey Shiflett, *Wolves Among Lambs: My Story of Sexual Abuse & Cover-Ups in the Church* (Dundalk, MD: SureWord, 2019), 24-114. Shiflett's narrative has been abbreviated and retold here with his permission.

[363] This author fully recognizes that it is much easier to evaluate what someone else should have done in a given situation than, when a scared and immature youth, to do those things in the heat of the moment. Suggestions about what Brother Hogget should have done better are made not to condemn him—for he deserves support and compassion—but for the better protection of other saints, so that situations like the one Brother Hogget was forced to endure arise in the future as infrequently as possible, are dealt with properly, and are stopped as soon as possible.

[364] In times when everyone has an electronic device, it is possible that a picture or recording in the hotel room could have provided the proof that this pervert Diotrephes was guilty, which could then have been shared immediately. In a time before the universality of such electronic devices, immediate proof of Diotrephes' perversion would have been harder to instantly verify. Of course, when a youth is in utter shock at finding himself in such an evil situation, quick thinking is very hard to come by, regardless of the presence or absence of an appropriate electronic device.

www.ingramcontent.com/pod-product-compliance
Lightning Source LLC
LaVergne TN
LVHW100505110826
845146LV00002B/520